PENGUIN BOOKS

The Thurber Carnival

James Thurber was born in 1894 at Columbus, Ohio, where, as he once said, so many awful things happened to him. After university (Ohio State) he worked at the American Embassy in Paris from 1918 to 1920, and then turned to journalism. From 1927 onwards he was on the staff of the *New Yorker*, and first published much of his work in it.

Thurber's art was easy to recognize but hard to define. He created a world in which mournfully sagacious hounds loom over frightened little men who are trying desperately to master life's problems. His drawings and prose alike were marked by economy, wry humour, and an inimitable blend of precision and fantasy. Perhaps his most justly famous character was Walter Mitty, whose *Secret Life* gloriously makes up for the shy young man's failures in competitive real life. Thurberites – and they are many – hardly need reminding that the classic Thurberisms are preserved in *Thurber's Dogs*, *The Thurber Album*, *Thurber Country*, and many more like-minded collections.

In later life James Thurber became increasingly blind. He died in New York in 1961. In an *Observer* appreciation, Paul Jennings wrote that 'he somehow gave us a sense of revelation . . . He created a *genre* and was a giant in it.'

The Thurber Carnival

WRITTEN AND ILLUSTRATED BY

JAMES THURBER

PENGUIN BOOKS

in association with Hamish Hamilton

Penguin Books Ltd, Harmondsworth,
Middlesex, England
Penguin Books, 625 Madison Avenue,
New York, New York 10022, U.S.A.
Penguin Books Australia Ltd, Ringwood,
Victoria, Australia
Penguin Books Canada Ltd, 2801 John Street,
Markham, Ontario, Canada L3R 1B4
Penguin Books (N.Z.) Ltd, 182–190 Wairau Road,
Auckland 10, New Zealand

First published 1945
An abridged edition was published in Penguin Books 1953
Reprinted 1953, 1954, 1956, 1957, 1959, 1962
Unabridged edition published in Penguin Books 1965
Reprinted 1971, 1972, 1973, 1975, 1976, 1977, 1978, 1979, 1981

Set, printed and bound in Great Britain by
Cox & Wyman Ltd, Reading
Set in Monotype Times

For

HAROLD ROSS
with increasing admiration,
wonder, and affection

Contents

4

From The Middle-Aged Man on the Flying Trapeze:

5

My Life and Hard Times:

6

From Fables for Our Time and Illustrated Poems:

7

From The Owl in the Attic:

8

9

Foreword

FOR their helpful advice and criticism I want to thank Helen Thurber, Gus Lobrano, Kenneth MacLean, and John McGiffert. I am indebted to *The New Yorker* for permission to include many of the pieces and drawings which originally appeared in that magazine.

Most of the books represented here were published in America under the supervision of the late Gene Saxton, and this anthology was his idea. I salute the memory of a good friend and a wise and kindly counsellor.

My Fifty Years
with James Thurber

I have not actually known Thurber for fifty years, since he was only forty-eight on his last birthday, but the publishers of this volume felt that 'fifty' would sound more effective than 'forty-eight' in the title of an introduction to so large a book, a point which I was too tired to argue about.

James Thurber was born on a night of wild portent and high wind in the year 1894, at 147 Parsons Avenue, Columbus, Ohio. The house, which is still standing, bears no tablet or plaque of any description, and is never pointed out to visitors. Once Thurber's mother, walking past the place with an old lady from Fostoria, Ohio, said to her, 'My son James was born in that house', to which the old lady, who was extremely deaf, replied, 'Why, on the Tuesday morning train, unless my sister is worse.' Mrs Thurber let it go at that.

The infant Thurber was brought into the world by an old practical nurse named Margery Albright, who had delivered the babies of neighbour women before the Civil War. He was, of course, much too young at the time to have been affected by the quaint and homely circumstances of his birth, to which he once alluded, a little awkwardly, I think, as 'the Currier and Ives, or old steel engraving, touch, attendant upon my entry into this vale of tears'. Not a great deal is known about his earliest years, beyond the fact that he could walk when he was only two years old, and was able to speak whole sentences by the time he was four.

Thurber's boyhood (1900–13) was pretty well devoid of significance. I see no reason why it should take up much of our time. There is no clearly traceable figure or pattern in this phase of his life. If he knew where he was going, it is not apparent from this distance. He fell down a great deal during this period, because of a trick he had of walking into himself. His gold-rimmed glasses forever needed straightening, which gave him the appearance of a person who hears somebody calling but can't make out where

15

the sound is coming from. Because of his badly focused lenses, he saw, not two of everything, but one and a half. Thus, a four-wheeled wagon would not have eight wheels for him, but six. How he succeeded in preventing these two extra wheels from getting into his work, I have no way of knowing.

Thurber's life baffles and irritates the biographer because of its lack of design. One has the disturbing feeling that the man contrived to be some place without actually having gone there. His drawings, for example, sometimes seem to have reached completion by some other route than the common one of intent.

The writing, is, I think, different. In his prose pieces he appears always to have started from the beginning and to have reached the end by way of the middle. It is impossible to read any of the stories from the last line to the first without experiencing a definite sensation of going backward. This seems to me to prove that the stories were written and did not, like the drawings, just suddenly materialize.

Thurber's very first bit of writing was a so-called poem entitled 'My Aunt Mrs John T. Savage's Garden at 185 South Fifth Street, Columbus, Ohio'. It is of no value or importance except insofar as it demonstrates the man's appalling memory for names and numbers. He can tell you to this day the names of all the children who were in the fourth grade when he was. He remembers the phone numbers of several of his high-school chums. He knows the birthdays of all his friends and can tell you the date on which any child of theirs was christened. He can rattle off the names of all the persons who attended the lawn fête of the First M.E. Church in Columbus in 1907. This ragbag of precise but worthless information may have helped him in his work, but I don't see how.

I find, a bit to my surprise, that there is not much else to say. Thurber goes on as he always has, walking now a little more slowly, answering fewer letters, jumping at slighter sounds. In the past ten years he has moved restlessly from one Connecticut town to another, hunting for the Great Good Place, which he conceives to be an old Colonial house, surrounded by elms and maples, equipped with all modern conveniences, and overlooking a valley. There he plans to spend his days reading *Huckleberry Finn*, raising poodles, laying down a wine cellar, playing *boules*, and talking to

16

the little group of friends which he has managed somehow to take with him into his crotchety middle age.

This book contains a selection of the stories and drawings the old boy did in his prime, a period which extended roughly from the year Lindbergh flew the Atlantic to the day coffee was rationed. He presents this to his readers with his sincere best wishes for a happy new world.

JAMES THURBER

I | *The Thurber*

Merry-Go-Round

The Lady on 142

The train was twenty minutes late, we found out when we bought our tickets, so we sat down on a bench in the little waiting room of the Cornwall Bridge station. It was too hot outside in the sun. This midsummer Saturday had got off to a sulky start, and now, at three in the afternoon, it sat, sticky and restive, in our laps.

There were several others besides Sylvia and myself waiting for the train to get in from Pittsfield: a coloured woman who fanned herself with a *Daily News*, a young lady in her twenties reading a book, a slender, tanned man sucking dreamily on the stem of an unlighted pipe. In the centre of the room, leaning against a high iron radiator, a small girl stared at each of us in turn, her mouth open, as if she had never seen people before. The place had the familiar, pleasant smell of railroad stations in the country, of something compounded of wood and leather and smoke. In the cramped space behind the ticket window, a telegraph instrument clicked intermittently, and once or twice a phone rang and the stationmaster answered it briefly. I couldn't hear what he said.

I was glad, on such a day, that we were going only as far as Gaylordsville, the third stop down the line, twenty-two minutes away. The stationmaster had told us that our tickets were the first tickets to Gaylordsville he had ever sold. I was idly pondering this small distinction when a train whistle blew in the distance. We all got to our feet, but the stationmaster came out of his cubby-hole and told us it was not our train but the 12.45 from New York, northbound. Presently the train thundered in like a hurricane and sighed ponderously to a stop. The stationmaster went out on to the platform and came back after a minute or two. The train got heavily under way again, for Canaan.

I was opening a pack of cigarettes when I heard the stationmaster talking on the phone again. This time his words came out clearly. He kept repeating one sentence. He was saying, 'Conductor Reagan on 142 has the lady the office was asking about.' The person on the other end of the line did not appear to get the meaning of the sentence. The stationmaster repeated it and hung up. For some reason, I figured that he did not understand it either.

Sylvia's eyes had the lost, reflective look they wear when she is trying to remember in what box she packed the Christmas-tree ornaments. The expressions on the faces of the coloured woman, the young lady, and the man with the pipe had not changed. The little staring girl had gone away.

Our train was not due for another five minutes, and I sat back and began trying to reconstruct the lady on 142, the lady Conductor Reagan had, the lady the office was asking about. I moved nearer to Sylvia and whispered, 'See if the trains are numbered in your timetable.' She got the timetable out of her handbag and looked at it. 'One forty-two,' she said, 'is the 12.45 from New York.' This was the train that had gone by a few minutes before. 'The woman was taken sick,' said Sylvia. 'They are probably arranging to have a doctor or her family meet her.'

The coloured woman looked around at her briefly. The young woman, who had been chewing gum, stopped chewing. The man with the pipe seemed oblivious. I lighted a cigarette and sat thinking. 'The woman on 142,' I said to Sylvia, finally, 'might be almost anything, but she definitely is not sick.' The only person who did not stare at me was the man with the pipe. Sylvia gave me her temperature-taking look, a cross between anxiety and vexation. Just then our train whistled and we all stood up. I picked up our two bags and Sylvia took the sack of string beans we had picked for the Connells.

When the train came clanking in, I said in Sylvia's ear, 'He'll sit near us. You watch.' 'Who? Who will?' she said. 'The stranger,' I told her, 'the man with the pipe.'

Sylvia laughed. 'He's not a stranger,' she said. 'He works for the Breeds.' I was certain that he didn't. Women like to place people; every stranger reminds them of somebody.

The man with the pipe was sitting three seats in front of us, across the aisle, when we got settled. I indicated him with a nod of my head. Sylvia took a book out of the top of her overnight bag and opened it. 'What's the matter with you?' she demanded. I looked around before replying. A sleepy man and woman sat across from us. Two middle-aged women in the seat in front of us were discussing the severe griping pain one of them had experienced as the result of an inflamed diverticulum. A slim, dark-eyed young woman sat in the seat behind us. She was alone.

'The trouble with women,' I began, 'is that they explain everything by illness. I have a theory that we would be celebrating the twelfth of May or even the sixteenth of April as Independence Day if Mrs Jefferson hadn't got the idea her husband had a fever and put him to bed.'

Sylvia found her place in the book. 'We've been all through that before,' she said. 'Why couldn't the woman on 142 be sick?'

That was easy. I told her. 'Conductor Reagan,' I said, 'got off the train at Cornwall Bridge and spoke to the stationmaster. "I've got the woman the office was asking about," he said.'

Sylvia cut in. 'He said "lady".'

I gave the little laugh that annoys her. 'All conductors say "lady",' I explained. 'Now, if a woman had got sick on the train, Reagan would have said, "A woman got sick on my train. Tell the office." What must have happened is that Reagan found, somewhere between Kent and Cornwall Bridge, a woman the office had been looking for.'

Sylvia didn't close her book, but she looked up. 'Maybe she got sick before she got on the train, and the office was worried,' said Sylvia. She was not giving the problem close attention.

'If the office knew she got on the train,' I said patiently, 'they wouldn't have asked Reagan to let them know if he found her. They would have told him about her when she got on.' Sylvia resumed her reading.

'Let's stay out of it,' she said. 'It isn't any of our business.'

I hunted for my Chiclets but couldn't find them. 'It might be everybody's business,' I said, 'every patriot's.'

'I know, I know,' said Sylvia. 'You think she's a spy. Well, I still think she's sick.'

I ignored that. 'Every conductor on the line has been asked to look out for her,' I said. 'Reagan found her. She won't be met by her family. She'll be met by the F.B.I.'

'Or the O.P.A.,' said Sylvia. 'Alfred Hitchcock things don't happen on the New York, New Haven & Hartford.'

I saw the conductor coming from the other end of the coach 'I'm going to tell the conductor,' I said, 'that Reagan on 142 has got the woman.'

'No, you're not,' said Sylvia. 'You're not going to get us mixed up in this. He probably knows anyway.'

The conductor, short, stocky, silvery-haired and silent, took up our tickets. He looked like a kindly Ickes. Sylvia, who had stiffened, relaxed when I let him go by without a word about the woman on 142. 'He looks exactly as if he knew where the Maltese Falcon is hidden, doesn't he?' said Sylvia, with the laugh that annoys me.

'Nevertheless,' I pointed out, 'you said a little while ago that he probably knows about the woman on 142. If she's just sick, why should they tell the conductor on *this* train? I'll rest more easily when I know that they've actually got her.'

Sylvia kept on reading as if she hadn't heard me. I leaned my head against the back of the seat and closed my eyes.

The train was slowing down noisily and a brakeman was yelling 'Kent! Kent!' when I felt a small cold pressure against my shoulder. 'Oh,' the voice of the woman in the seat behind me said, 'I've dropped my copy of *Coronet* under your seat.' She leaned closer and her voice became low and hard. 'Get off here, Mister,' she said.

'We're going to Gaylordsville,' I said.

'You and your wife are getting off here, Mister,' she said.

I reached for the suit cases on the rack. 'What do you want, for heaven's sake?' asked Sylvia.

'We're getting off here,' I told her.

'Are you *really* crazy?' she demanded. 'This is only Kent.'

'Come on, sister,' said the woman's voice. 'You take the overnight bag and the beans. You take the big bag, Mister.'

Sylvia was furious. 'I *knew* you'd get us into this,' she said to me, 'shouting about spies at the top of your voice.'

That made me angry. 'You're the one that mentioned spies,' I told her. 'I didn't.'

'You kept talking about it and talking about it,' said Sylvia.

'Come on, get off, the two of you,' said the cold, hard voice.

We got off. As I helped Sylvia down the steps, I said, 'We know too much.'

'Oh, shut up,' she said.

We didn't have far to go. A big black limousine waited a few steps away. Behind the wheel sat a heavy-set foreigner with cruel lips and small eyes. He scowled when he saw us. 'The boss don't want nobody up deh,' he said.

'It's all right, Karl,' said the woman. 'Get in,' she told us. We climbed into the back seat. She sat between us, with the gun in her hand. It was a handsome, jewelled derringer.

'Alice will be waiting for us at Gaylordsville,' said Sylvia, 'in all this heat.'

The house was a long, low, rambling building, reached at the end of a poplar-lined drive. 'Never mind the bags,' said the woman. Sylvia took the string beans and her book and we got out. Two huge mastiffs came bounding off the terrace, snarling. 'Down, Mata!' said the woman. 'Down, Pedro!' They slunk away, still snarling.

Sylvia and I sat side by side on a sofa in a large, handsomely appointed living-room. Across from us, in a chair, lounged a tall man with heavily lidded black eyes and long, sensitive fingers. Against the door through which we had entered the room leaned a thin, undersized young man, with his hands in the pockets of his coat and a cigarette hanging from his lower lip. He had a drawn, sallow face and his small, half-closed eyes stared at us incuriously. In a corner of the room, a squat, swarthy man twiddled with the dials of a radio. The woman paced up and down, smoking a cigarette in a long holder.

'Well, Gail,' said the lounging man in a soft voice, 'to what do we owe thees unexpected visit?'

Gail kept pacing. 'They got Sandra,' she said finally.

The lounging man did not change expression. 'Who got Sandra, Gail?' he asked softly.

'Reagan, on 142,' said Gail.

The squat, swarthy man jumped to his feet. 'All da time Egypt say keel dees Reagan!' he shouted. 'All da time Egypt say bomp off dees Reagan!'

The lounging man did not look at him. 'Sit down, Egypt,' he

said quietly. The swarthy man sat down. Gail went on talking.

'The punk here shot off his mouth,' she said. 'He was wise.' I looked at the man leaning against the door.

'She means you,' said Sylvia, and laughed.

'The dame was dumb,' Gail went on. 'She thought the lady on the train was sick.'

I laughed. 'She means you,' I said to Sylvia.

'The punk was blowing his top all over the train,' said Gail. 'I had to bring 'em along.'

Sylvia, who had the beans on her lap, began breaking and stringing them. 'Well, my dear lady,' said the lounging man, 'a mos' homely leetle tawtch.'

'Wozza totch?' demanded Egypt.

'Touch,' I told him.

Gail sat down in a chair. 'Who's going to rub 'em out?' she asked.

'Freddy,' said the lounging man. Egypt was on his feet again.

'Na! Na!' he shouted. 'Na de ponk! Da ponk bomp off da las' seex, seven peop'!'

The lounging man looked at him. Egypt paled and sat down.

'I thought *you* were the punk,' said Sylvia. I looked at her coldly.

'I know where I have seen you before,' I said to the lounging man. 'It was at Zagreb, in 1927. Tilden took you in straight sets, six-love, six-love, six-love.'

The man's eyes glittered. 'I theenk I bomp off thees man myself,' he said.

Freddy walked over and handed the lounging man an automatic. At this moment, the door Freddy had been leaning against burst open and in rushed the man with the pipe, shouting, 'Gail! Gail! Gail!' . . .

'Gaylordsville! Gaylordsville!' bawled the brakeman. Sylvia was shaking me by the arm. 'Quit moaning,' she said. 'Everybody is looking at you.' I rubbed my forehead with a handkerchief. 'Hurry up!' said Sylvia. 'They don't stop here long.' I pulled the bags down and we got off.

'Have you got the beans?' I asked Sylvia.

Alice Connell was waiting for us. On the way to their home in the car, Sylvia began to tell Alice about the woman on 142. I didn't say anything.

'He thought she was a spy,' said Sylvia.

They both laughed. 'She probably got sick on the train,' said Alice. 'They were probably arranging for a doctor to meet her at the station.'

'That's just what I told him,' said Sylvia.

I lighted a cigarette. 'The lady on 142,' I said firmly, 'was definitely not sick.'

'Oh, Lord,' said Sylvia, 'here we go again.'

Mr Martin bought the pack of Camels on Monday night in the most crowded cigar store on Broadway. It was theatre time and seven or eight men were buying cigarettes. The clerk didn't even glance at Mr Martin, who put the pack in his overcoat pocket and went out. If any of the staff at F. & S. had seen him buy the cigarettes, they would have been astonished, for it was generally known that Mr Martin did not smoke, and never had. No one saw him.

It was just a week to the day since Mr Martin had decided to rub out Mrs Ulgine Barrows. The term 'rub out' pleased him because it suggested nothing more than the correction of an error – in this case an error of Mr Fitweiler. Mr Martin had spent each night of the past week working out his plan and examining it. As he walked home now he went over it again. For the hundredth time he resented the element of imprecision, the margin of guesswork that entered into the business. The project as he had worked it out was casual and bold, the risks were considerable. Something might go wrong anywhere along the line. And therein lay the cunning of his scheme. No one would ever see in it the cautious, painstaking hand of Erwin Martin, head of the filing department at F. & S., of whom Mr Fitweiler had once said, 'Man is fallible but Martin isn't.' No one would see his hand, that is, unless it were caught in the act.

Sitting in his apartment, drinking a glass of milk, Mr Martin reviewed his case against Mrs Ulgine Barrows, as he had every night for seven nights. He began at the beginning. Her quacking voice and braying laugh had first profaned the halls of F. & S. on 7 March 1941 (Mr Martin had a head for dates). Old Roberts, the personnel chief, had introduced her as the newly appointed special adviser to the president of the firm, Mr Fitweiler. The woman had appalled Mr Martin instantly, but he hadn't shown it. He had given her his dry hand, a look of studious concentration, and a faint smile. 'Well,' she had said, looking at the papers on his desk, 'are you lifting the oxcart out of the ditch?' As Mr Martin recalled that moment, over his milk, he squirmed slightly. He must keep his mind on her crimes as a special adviser, not on her peccadillos as a personality. This he found difficult to do, in spite of entering an objection and sustaining it. The faults of the woman as a woman kept chattering on in his mind like an unruly witness. She had, for almost two years now, baited him. In the halls, in the elevator, even in his own office, into which she romped now and then like a circus horse, she was constantly shouting these silly questions at him. 'Are you lifting the oxcart out of the ditch? Are you tearing up the pea patch? Are you hollering down the rain barrel? Are you scraping around the bottom of the pickle barrel? Are you sitting in the catbird seat?'

It was Joey Hart, one of Mr Martin's two assistants, who had explained what the gibberish meant. 'She must be a Dodger fan,' he had said. 'Red Barber announces the Dodger games over the radio and he uses those expressions – picked 'em up down South.' Joey had gone on to explain one or two. 'Tearing up the pea patch' meant going on a rampage; 'sitting in the catbird seat' meant sitting pretty, like a batter with three balls and no strikes on him. Mr Martin dismissed all this with an effort. It had been annoying, it had driven him near to distraction, but he was too solid a man to be moved to murder by anything so childish. It was fortunate, he reflected as he passed on to the important charges against Mrs Barrows, that he had stood up under it so well. He had maintained always an outward appearance of polite tolerance. 'Why, I even believe you like the woman,' Miss Paird, his other assistant, had once said to him. He had simply smiled.

A gavel rapped in Mr Martin's mind and the case proper was resumed. Mrs Ulgine Barrows stood charged with wilful, blatant and persistent attempts to destroy the efficiency and system of F. & S. It was competent, material and relevant to review her advent and rise to power. Mr Martin had got the story from Miss Paird, who seemed always able to find things out. According to her, Mrs Barrows had met Mr Fitweiler at a party, where she had rescued him from the embraces of a powerfully built drunken man who had mistaken the president of F. & S. for a famous retired Middle Western football coach. She had led him to a sofa and somehow worked upon him a monstrous magic. The ageing gentleman had jumped to the conclusion there and then that this was a woman of singular attainments, equipped to bring out the best in him and in the firm. A week later he had introduced her into F. & S. as his special adviser. On that day confusion got its foot in the door. After Miss Tyson, Mr Brundage and Mr Bartlett had been fired and Mr Munson had taken his hat and stalked out, mailing in his resignation later, old Roberts had been emboldened to speak to Mr Fitweiler. He mentioned that Mr Munson's department had been 'a little disrupted' and hadn't they perhaps better resume the old system there? Mr Fitweiler had said certainly not. He had the greatest faith in Mrs Barrow's ideas. 'They require a little seasoning, a little seasoning, is all,' he had added. Mr Roberts had given it up. Mr Martin reviewed in detail all the changes wrought by Mrs Barrows. She had begun chipping at the cornices of the firm's edifice and now she was swinging at the foundation stones with a pickaxe.

Mr Martin came now, in his summing up, to the afternoon of Monday, 2 November 1942 – just one week ago. On that day, at 3 p.m., Mrs Barrows had bounced into his office. 'Boo!' she had yelled. 'Are you scraping around the bottom of the pickle barrel?' Mr Martin had looked at her from under his green eyeshade, saying nothing. She had begun to wander about the office, taking it in with her great, popping eyes. 'Do you really need *all* these filing cabinets?' she had demanded suddenly. Mr Martin's heart had jumped. 'Each of these files,' he had said, keeping his voice even, 'plays an indispensable part in the system of F. & S.' She had brayed at him, 'Well, don't tear up the pea patch!' and gone to the door. From there she had bawled, 'But you sure have got a lot of fine scrap in here!' Mr Martin could no longer doubt that the finger was on his beloved department. Her pickaxe was on the up-swing, poised for the first blow. It had not come yet; he had received no blue memo from the enchanted Mr Fitweiler bearing nonsensical instructions deriving from the obscene woman. But there was no doubt in Mr Martin's mind that one would be forthcoming. He must act quickly. Already a precious week had gone by. Mr Martin stood up in his living-room, still holding his milk glass. 'Gentlemen of the jury,' he said to himself, 'I demand the death penalty for this horrible person.'

The next day Mr Martin followed his routine, as usual. He polished his glasses more often and once sharpened an already sharp pencil, but not even Miss Paird noticed. Only once did he catch sight of his victim; she swept past him in the hall with a patronizing 'Hi!' At five-thirty he walked home, as usual, and had a glass of milk, as usual. He had never drunk anything stronger in his life – unless you could count ginger ale. The late Sam Schlosser, the S. of F. & S., had praised Mr Martin at a staff meeting several years before for his temperate habits. 'Our most efficient worker neither drinks nor smokes,' he had said. 'The results speak for themselves.' Mr Fitweiler had sat by, nodding approval.

Mr Martin was still thinking about that red-letter day as he walked over to the Schrafft's on Fifth Avenue near Forty-sixth Street. He got there, as he always did, at eight o'clock. He finished his dinner and the financial page of the *Sun* at a quarter to nine, as he always did. It was his custom after dinner to take a walk. This time he walked down Fifth Avenue at a casual pace. His gloved hands felt moist and warm, his forehead cold. He transferred the Camels from his overcoat to a jacket pocket. He wondered, as he did so, if they did not represent an unnecessary note of strain. Mrs Barrows smoked only Luckies. It was his idea to puff a few puffs on a Camel (after the rubbing-out), stub it out in the ashtray holding her lipstick-stained Luckies, and thus drag a small red herring across the trail. Perhaps it was not a good idea. It would take time. He might even choke, too loudly.

Mr Martin had never seen the house on West Twelfth Street where Mrs Barrows lived, but he had a clear enough picture of it. Fortunately, she had bragged to everybody about her ducky first-floor apartment in the perfectly darling three-storey red-brick. There would be no doorman or other attendants; just the tenants of the second and third floors. As he walked along, Mr Martin realized that he would get there before nine-thirty. He had considered walking north on Fifth Avenue from Schrafft's to a point from which it would take him until ten o'clock to reach the house. At that hour people were less likely to be coming in or going out. But the procedure would have made an awkward loop in the straight thread of his casualness, and he had abandoned it. It was

31

impossible to figure when people would be entering or leaving the house, anyway. There was a great risk at any hour. If he ran into anybody, he would simply have to place the rubbing-out of Ulgine Barrows in the inactive file forever. The same thing would hold true if there were someone in her apartment. In that case he would just say that he had been passing by, recognized her charming house and thought to drop in.

It was eighteen minutes after nine when Mr Martin turned into Twelfth Street. A man passed him, and a man and a woman talking. There was no one within fifty paces when he came to the house, half-way down the block. He was up the steps and in the small vestibule in no time, pressing the bell under the card that said 'Mrs Ulgine Barrows'. When the clicking in the lock started, he jumped forward against the door. He got inside fast, closing the door behind him. A bulb in a lantern hung from the hall ceiling on a chain seemed to give a monstrously bright light. There was nobody on the stairs, which went up ahead of him along the left wall. A door opened down the hall in the wall on the right. He went toward it swiftly, on tiptoe.

'Well, for God's sake, look who's here!' bawled Mrs Barrows, and her braying laugh rang out like a report of a shotgun. He rushed past her like a football tackle, bumping her. 'Hey, quit shoving!' she said, closing the door behind them. They were in her living-room, which seemed to Mr Martin to be lighted by a hundred lamps. 'What's after you?' she said. 'You're as jumpy as a goat.' He found he was unable to speak. His heart was wheezing in his throat. 'I – yes,' he finally brought out. She was jabbering and laughing as she started to help him off with his coat. 'No, no,' he said. 'I'll put it here.' He took it off and put it on a chair near the door. 'Your hat and gloves, too,' she said. 'You're in a lady's house.' He put his hat on top of the coat. Mrs Barrows seemed larger than he had thought. He kept his gloves on. 'I was passing by,' he said. 'I recognized – is there anyone here?' She laughed louder than ever. 'No,' she said, 'we're all alone. You're as white as a sheet, you funny man. Whatever *has* come over you? I'll mix you a toddy.' She started toward a door across the room. 'Scotch-and-soda be all right? But say, you don't drink, do you?' She turned and gave him her amused look. Mr Martin pulled himself together.

'Scotch-and-soda will be all right,' he heard himself say. He could hear her laughing in the kitchen.

Mr Martin looked quickly around the living-room for the weapon. He had counted on finding one there. There were handirons and a poker and something in a corner that looked like an Indian club. None of them would do. It couldn't be that way. He began to pace around. He came to a desk. On it lay a metal paper knife with an ornate handle. Would it be sharp enough? He reached for it and knocked over a small brass jar. Stamps spilled out of it and it fell to the floor with a clatter. 'Hey,' Mrs Barrows yelled from the kitchen, 'are you tearing up the pea patch?' Mr Martin gave a strange laugh. Picking up the knife, he tried its point against his left wrist. It was blunt. It wouldn't do.

When Mrs Barrows reappeared, carrying two highballs, Mr Martin, standing there with his gloves on, became acutely conscious of the fantasy he had wrought. Cigarettes in his pocket, a drink prepared for him – it was all too grossly improbable. It was more than that; it was impossible. Somewhere in the back of his mind a vague idea stirred, sprouted. 'For heaven's sake, take off those gloves,' said Mrs Barrows. 'I always wear them in the house,' said Mr Martin. The idea began to bloom, strange and wonderful. She put the glasses on a coffee table in front of a sofa and sat on the sofa. 'Come over here, you odd little man,' she said. Mr Martin went over and sat beside her. It was difficult getting a cigarette out of the pack of Camels, but he managed it. She held a match for him, laughing. 'Well,' she said, handing him his drink, 'this is perfectly marvellous. You with a drink and a cigarette.'

Mr Martin puffed, not too awkwardly, and took a gulp of the highball. 'I drink and smoke all the time,' he said. He clinked his glass against hers. 'Here's nuts to that old windbag, Fitweiler,' he said, and gulped again. The stuff tasted awful, but he made no grimace. 'Really, Mr Martin,' she said, her voice and posture changing, 'you are insulting our employer.' Mrs Barrows was now all special adviser to the president. 'I am preparing a bomb,' said Mr Martin, 'which will blow the old goat higher than hell.' He had only had a little of the drink, which was not strong. It couldn't be that. 'Do you take dope or something?' Mrs Barrows asked coldly. 'Heroin,' said Mr Martin. 'I'll be coked to the gills when I bump that old buzzard off.' 'Mr Martin!' she shouted, getting to her feet. 'That will be all of that. You must go at once.' Mr Martin took another swallow of his drink. He tapped his cigarette out in the ashtray and put the pack of Camels on the coffee table. Then he got up. She stood glaring at him. He walked over and put on his hat and coat. 'Not a word about this,' he said, and laid an index finger against his lips. All Mrs Barrows could bring out was 'Really!' Mr Martin put his hand on the doorknob. 'I'm sitting in the catbird seat,' he said. He stuck his tongue out at her and left. Nobody saw him go.

Mr Martin got to his apartment, walking, well before eleven. No one saw him go in. He had two glasses of milk after brushing his teeth, and he felt elated. It wasn't tipsiness, because he hadn't been tipsy. Anyway, the walk had worn off all effects of the whisky. He got in bed and read a magazine for a while. He was asleep before midnight.

Mr Martin got to the office at eight-thirty the next morning, as usual. At a quarter to nine, Ulgine Barrows, who had never before arrived at work before ten, swept into his office. 'I'm reporting to Mr Fitweiler now!' she shouted. 'If he turns you over to the police, it's no more than you deserve!' Mr Martin gave her a look of shocked surprise. 'I beg your pardon?' he said. Mrs Barrows snorted and bounced out of the room, leaving Miss Paird and Joey Hart staring after her. 'What's the matter with that old devil now?' asked Miss Paird. 'I have no idea,' said Mr Martin, resuming his work. The other two looked at him and then at each other. Miss Paird got up and went out. She walked slowly past the closed door of Mr Fitweiler's office. Mrs Barrows was yelling inside, but she was not braying. Miss Paird could not hear what the woman was saying. She went back to her desk.

Forty-five minutes later, Mrs Barrows left the president's office and went into her own, shutting the door. It wasn't until half an hour later that Mr Fitweiler sent for Mr Martin. The head of the filing department, neat, quiet, attentive, stood in front of the old man's desk. Mr Fitweiler was pale and nervous. He took his glasses off and twiddled them. He made a small, bruffing sound in his throat. 'Martin,' he said, 'you have been with us more than twenty years.' 'Twenty-two sir,' said Mr Martin. 'In that time,' pursued the president, 'your work and your – uh – manner have been exemplary.' 'I trust so, sir,' said Mr Martin. 'I have understood, Martin,' said Mr Fitweiler, 'that you have never taken a drink or smoked.' 'That is correct, sir,' said Mr Martin. 'Ah, yes.' Mr Fitweiler polished his glasses. 'You may describe what you did after leaving the office yesterday, Martin,' he said. Mr Martin allowed less than a second for his bewildered pause. 'Certainly, sir,' he said. 'I walked home. Then I went to Schrafft's for dinner. Afterward I walked home again. I went to bed early, sir, and read a magazine for a while. I was asleep before eleven.' 'Ah, yes,' said Mr Fitweiler again. He was silent for a moment, searching for the proper words to say to the head of the filing department. 'Mrs Barrows,' he said finally, 'Mrs Barrows has worked hard, Martin, very hard. It grieves me to report that she has suffered a severe breakdown. It has taken the form of a persecution complex accompanied by distressing hallucinations.' 'I am very sorry, sir,' said Mr Martin. 'Mrs Barrows is under the delusion,' continued Mr Fitweiler, 'that you visited her last evening and behaved yourself in an – uh – unseemly manner.' He raised his hand to silence Mr Martin's little pained outcry. 'It is the nature of these psychological diseases,' Mr Fitweiler said, 'to fix upon the least likely and most innocent party as the – uh – source of persecution. These matters are not for the lay mind to grasp, Martin. I've just had my psychiatrist, Dr Fitch, on the phone. He would not, of course, commit himself, but he made enough generalizations to substantiate my suspicions. I suggested to Mrs Barrows when she had completed her – uh – story to me this morning, that she visit Dr Fitch, for I suspected a condition at once. She flew, I regret to say, into a rage, and demanded – uh – requested that I call you on the carpet. You may not know, Martin, but Mrs Barrows had planned a reorganization of your department – subject to my approval, of course, subject to my approval. This brought you, rather than anyone else, to her mind – but again that is a phenomenon for Dr Fitch and not for us. So, Martin, I am afraid Mrs Barrows' usefulness here is at an end.' 'I am dreadfully sorry, sir,' said Mr Martin.

It was at this point that the door to the office blew open with the suddenness of a gas-main explosion and Mrs Barrows catapulted through it. 'Is the little rat denying it?' she screamed. 'He can't get away with that!' Mr Martin got up and moved discreetly to a point beside Mr Fitweiler's chair. 'You drank and smoked at my apartment,' she bawled at Mr Martin, 'and you know it! You called Mr Fitweiler an old windbag and said you were going to blow him up when you got coked to the gills on your heroin!' She stopped yelling to catch her breath and a new glint came into her popping eyes. 'If you weren't such a drab, ordinary little man,' she said, 'I'd think you'd planned it all. Sticking your tongue out, saying you were sitting in the catbird seat, because you thought no one would believe me when I told it! My God, it's really too perfect!' She brayed loudly and hysterically, and the fury was on her again. She glared at Mr Fitweiler. 'Can't you see how he has tricked us, you old fool? Can't you see his little game?' But Mr Fitweiler had been surreptitiously pressing all the buttons under the top of his desk and employees of F. & S. began pouring into the room. 'Stockton,' said Mr Fitweiler, 'you and Fishbein will take Mrs Barrows to her home. Mrs Powell, you will go with them.' Stockton, who had played a little football in high school, blocked Mrs Barrows as she made for Mr Martin. It took him and Fishbein together to force her out of the door into the hall, crowded with stenographers and office boys. She was still screaming imprecations at Mr Martin, tangled and contradictory imprecations. The hubbub finally died out down the corridor.

'I regret that this has happened,' said Mr Fitweiler. 'I shall ask you to dismiss it from your mind, Martin.' 'Yes, sir,' said Mr Martin, anticipating his chief's 'That will be all' by moving to the door. 'I will dismiss it.' He went out and shut the door, and his step was light and quick in the hall. When he entered his department he had slowed down to his customary gait, and he walked quietly across the room to the W20 file, wearing a look of studious concentration.

Memoirs of a Drudge

Mr Thurber . . . went to Ohio State University for his formal education. His informal education included . . . drudgery on several newspapers – in Columbus, in New York, and in Paris. – From *Horse Sense in American Humor*, by Walter Blair.

I don't know about that. There is, of course, a certain amount of drudgery in newspaper work, just as there is in teaching classes, tunnelling into a bank, or being President of the United States. I suppose that even the most pleasurable of imaginable occupations, that of batting baseballs through the windows of the R.C.A. Building, would pall a little as the days ran on. Seldom, it is true, do I gather my grandchildren about my knees and tell them tall tales out of my colourful years as a leg man, but I often sit in the cane-seated rocker on the back porch, thinking of the old days and cackling with that glee known only to ageing journalists. Just the other evening, when the womenfolks were washing up the supper dishes and setting them to dreen, they could hear me rocking back and forth and laughing to myself. I was thinking about the Riviera edition of the *Chicago Tribune* in southern France during the winter of 1925–6.

Seven or eight of us had been assigned to the task of getting out a little six-page newspaper, whose stories were set up in 10-point type, instead of the customary 8-point, to make life easier for everybody, including the readers. Most of our news came by wire from the Paris edition, and all we had to do was write headlines for it, a pleasurable occupation if you are not rushed, and we were never rushed. For the rest, we copied from the *Éclaireur de Nice et du Sud-Est*, a journal filled with droll and mystical stories, whose translation, far from being drudgery, was pure joy. Nice, in that indolent winter, was full of knaves and rascals, adventurers and impostors, *pochards* and *indiscrets*, whose ingenious exploits, sometimes in full masquerade costume, sometimes in the nude, were easy and pleasant to record.

We went to work after dinner and usually had the last chronicle of the diverting day written and ready for the linotypers well before midnight. It was then our custom to sit around for half an hour, making up items for the society editor's column. She was too pretty, we thought, to waste the soft southern days tracking down the arrival of prominent persons on the Azure Coast. So all she had to do was stop in at the Ruhl and the Negresco each day and pick up the list of guests who had just registered. The rest of us invented enough items to fill up the last half of her column, and a gay and romantic cavalcade, indeed, infested the littoral of our imagination. 'Lieutenant General and Mrs Pendleton Gray Winslow,' we would write, 'have arrived at their villa, Heart's Desire, on Cap d'Antibes, bringing with them their prize Burmese monkey, Thibault.' Or 'The Hon. Mr Stephen H. L. Atterbury, Chargé-d'Affaires of the American Legation in Peru, and Mrs Atterbury, the former Princess Ti Ling of Thibet are motoring to Monte Carlo from Aix-en-Provence, where they have been visiting Mr Atterbury's father, Rear Admiral A. Watson Atterbury, U.S.N., retired. Mr Stephen Atterbury is the breeder of the famous Schnauzer-Pincer, Champion Adelbert von Weigengrosse of Tamerlane, said to be valued at $15,000.' In this manner we turned out, in no time at all, and with the expenditure of very little mental energy, the most glittering column of social notes in the history of the American newspaper, either here or abroad.

As the hour of midnight struck twice, in accordance with the dreamy custom of town and church clocks in southern France, and our four or five hours of drudgery were ending, the late Frank Harris would often drop in at the *Tribune* office, and we would listen to stories of Oscar Wilde, Walt Whitman, Bernard Shaw, Emma Goldman and Frank Harris. Thus ran the harsh and exacting tenor of those days of slavery.

It is true that the languorous somnolence of our life was occasionally broken up. This would happen about one night a week, around ten o'clock, when our French composing room went on strike. The printers and their foreman, a handsome, black-bearded giant of a man, whose rages resembled the mistral, wanted to set up headlines in their own easygoing way, using whatever size type was handiest and whatever space it would fit into most easily. That is the effortless hit-or-miss system which has made a crazy quilt of French newspaper headlines for two hundred years, and André and his men could not understand why we stubbornly refused to adopt so sane and simple a method. So now and then, when he couldn't stand our stupid and inviolable headline schedules any longer, André would roar into our little city room like a storm from the Alps. Behind him in the doorway stood his linotypers, with their hats and coats on. Since the Frenchmen could comprehend no English and spoke only *Niçois*, an argot entirely meaningless to us, our arguments were carried on in shouting and gesticulating and a great deal of waving of French and American newspapers in each other's faces. After a while all the combatants on both sides would adjourn to the bar next door, still yelling and gesturing, but after four or five rounds of beer we would fall to singing old Provençal songs and new American ones, and there would be a truce for another six or seven days, everybody going back to work, still singing.

On one of those nights of battle, song and compromise, several of us defenders of the immutable American headline went back to the bar after we had got the *Tribune* to press and sat up till dawn, drinking *grog américain*. Just as the sun came up, we got on a train for Cannes, where the most talked-about international struggle of the year was to take place that afternoon, the tennis match between Suzanne Lenglen and Helen Wills. As we climbed aboard, one of my colleagues, spoiling for an argument, declared that a French translation he had read of Edgar Allen Poe's 'The Raven' was infinitely superior to the poem in the original English. How we had got around to this curious subject I have no idea, but it seemed natural enough at the time. I remember that a young reporter named Middleton visited all the compartments on the train, demanding of their sleepy and startled French occupants if they did not believe that a raven was more likely to say '*Jamais plus*' than 'Nevermore'. He returned with the claim that our fellow-passengers to a man were passionately on the side of '*Jamais plus*'. So passed a night of drudgery in the fond, far-away days of the Third Republic and the Riviera edition of the *Chicago Tribune*.

We had the long days of warm blue weather for our own, to climb the Corniche roads or wind up the mountain in a *char à bancs* to the magical streams and the million springtime flowers of St-Martin-Vésubie. Sometimes we sat the day out on the terrace of a restaurant overlooking the Bay of Angels and gave the tireless Albert suggestions as to where he might find Henry James. Albert was a young Englishman who did interviews for us with distinguished visitors to the Riviera, and he had got the curious idea that the celebrated novelist was hiding away in a *pension* somewhere between St Tropez and Mentone, rewriting 'The Golden Bowl'. We decided that Albert had got his tip about the whereabouts of the great dead man from some ageing aunt who lived in the parlours and the gardens of the past. It was one way to spend an afternoon, sitting over our glasses of vermouth-cassis, bringing back to life the poor, sensitive creator of Peter Quint and Mme de Vionnet, figuring him lost and wandering, ever so wonderfully, somewhere among the bougainvillaea and the passionflowers. Thus in fancy and in dream passed the long days of warm blue weather.

Before going to France, I worked on the Columbus *Evening Dispatch*, a fat and amiable newspaper, whose city editor seldom knew where I was and got so that he didn't care. He had a glimpse of me every day at 9 a.m., arriving at the office, and promptly at ten he saw me leave it, a sheaf of folded copy paper in my pocket and a look of enterprise in my eye. I was on my way to Marzetti's, a comfortable restaurant just down the street, where a group of us newspapermen met every morning. We would sit around for an hour drinking coffee, telling stories, drawing pictures on the table-cloth, and giving imitations of the more eminent Ohio political figures of the day, many of whom fanned their soup with their hats but had enough good, old-fashioned horse sense to realize that a proposal to shift the clocks of the state from Central to Eastern standard time was directly contrary to the will of the Lord God Almighty and that the supporters of the project would burn in hell.

After this relaxing and often stimulating interlude I would stroll out to the Carnegie Library and read the New York *World* in the periodical room. It so happened that the city offices, which I was assigned to cover, were housed at that time in the library building, the old City Hall having burned down the first night I ever attended a council meeting in it. After I had put the *World* back on its rack, only a little fragment of forenoon remained in which to gather the news, but I somehow managed the aggravating chore.

Nor were the city offices dull and colourless places. Secretary Killam of the Civil Service Commission had a tuba, on which I learned to play a few notes, an exciting and satisfying experience, as anyone who has brought forth a blast from a tuba knows. The lady dance-hall inspector was full of stories of the goings on in the more dubious clubs about town, in one of which, she reported, the boys and girls contrived the two-step without moving their feet. And the Mayor's office was frequently besieged by diverting and passionate taxpayers: an elderly gentleman who could get KDKA on the steel rims of his spectacles, a woman who was warned of the approach of earthquakes by a sharp twinge in her left side, and a lady to whom it had been revealed in a vision that the new O'Shoughnessy storage dam had not been constructed of concrete but of Cream of Wheat.

So ran the mornings away in the years of my servitude on the Columbus *Dispatch*. The afternoons, after three o'clock, I had to myself. I used to spend a great many of them at home, lying down. That tuba took quite a little out of me.

Now we come to the six months of drudgery on the New York *Evening Post*, back in the days of Sacco and Vanzetti, the Hall-Mills case, and Daddy Browning. The city editor of the paper, a gentleman with a keen eye for the frailties of men and a heart over-flowing with *misericordia*, apparently decided I did not look like a man capable of handling spot news – that is, events in the happening, such as warehouse fires and running gun fights. He therefore set me to writing what he called overnight feature stories. These were stories that could be printed anytime – tomorrow, or next week, or not at all, if the flow of important news was too heavy. They were designed to fit in between accounts of murder trials and train wrecks, to brighten the ominous page and lighten, if possible, the uneasy heart of the reader. So it came about that when other reporters were out wearing themselves down in quest of the clangorous and complicated fact, I could be observed wandering the quiet shore above the noisy torrent of contemporary history, examining the little miracles and grotesqueries of the time.

I wrote only one story a day, usually consisting of fewer than a thousand words. Most of the reporters, when they went out on assignments, first had to get their foot in the door, but the portals of the fantastic and the unique are always left open. If an astonished botanist produced a black evening primrose, or thought he had produced one, I spent the morning prowling his gardens. When a lady in the West Seventies sent in word that she was getting messages from the late Walter Savage Landor in heaven, I was sent up to see what the importunate poet had on his mind. On the occasion of the arrival in town of Major Monroe of Jacksonville, Florida, who claimed to be a hundred and seventeen years old, I walked up Broadway with him while he roundly cursed the Northern dogs who jostled him, bewailing the while the passing of Bob Lee and Tom Jackson and Joe Johnston. I studied gypsies in Canarsie and generals in the Waldorf, listened to a man talk backward, and watched a blindfolded boy play ping-pong. Put it all together and I don't know what it comes to, but it wasn't drudgery.

It was not often, in the *Post* or no *Sturm-und-Drang* phase, that I wandered farther afield than the confines of Greater New York. On the occasion of the hundred-and-fiftieth anniversary of Washington's crossing the Delaware, however, I was sent over to Trenton to report the daylong celebration. (Once in a long while I got a spot news assignment like that.) At a little past ten in the morning I discovered the hotel room which a group of the more convivial newspapermen had set up as their headquarters, and at a little past twelve I was asleep in a chair there. When I woke up it was dark, and the celebration was over. I hadn't sent anything to my paper, and by that time it was too late. I went home. The *Post*, I found out, had used the Associated Press account of what went on in Trenton.

When I got to work the next morning, the city editor came over to my desk. 'Let's see,' he said, 'what did I send you out on yesterday?' 'It didn't pan out,' I told him. 'No story.' 'The hell with it, then,' he said. 'Here, get on this – lady says there are violets growing in the snow over in Red Bank.' 'Violets don't grow in the snow,' I reminded him. 'They might in Red Bank,' he said. 'Slide on over there.' I slid instead to a bar and put in a phone call to the

Chief of Police in Red Bank. A desk sergeant answered and I asked him about the violets. 'Ain't no violence over here,' he told me, and hung up. It wasn't much to hang a story on, as we say, but I hung one on it. But first I had a few more drinks with a man I had met at the bar, very pleasant fellow, captain of a barge or something. Shortly after the strange case of the violets in the snow, I left the newspaper game and drifted into the magazine game.

And now, in closing, I wish to leave with my little readers, both boys and girls, this parting bit of advice: Stay out of the magazine game.

The Cane in the Corridor

'Funny thing about post-operative mental states,' said Joe Fletcher, rocking the big brandy glass between the palms of his hands and studying the brown tides reflectively. 'They take all kinds of curious turns.'

George Minturn moved restlessly in his chair, making a new pattern of his long legs. 'Let's go to Barney's,' he said. 'Let's go to Barney's now.'

Mrs Minturn walked over and emptied an ashtray into the fireplace as eloquently as if she were winding the clock. 'It's much too late,' she said. 'I'm sure everybody we'd want to see has left there and gone home to bed.'

Minturn finished his brandy and poured out some more.

'You remember Reginald Gardiner's imitation of wallpaper,' continued Fletcher, 'in which he presented a visual design as making a pattern of sound? Many post-operative cases make those interesting transferences. I know one man who kept drawing on a piece of paper what the ringing of a telephone *looks* like.'

'I don't want to hear about him,' said Minturn.

Fletcher drank the last of his brandy and held up his glass; after a moment his host walked over and poured in a little more.

Mrs Minturn found herself finishing her own drink and getting another one, although she seldom touched anything after dinner. 'Here's to the Washington Bridge,' she said. 'Here's to some big dam or other. Let's talk about some big dam. After all, you're an engineer, Joe.'

Fletcher lighted a cigarette, holding his brandy glass between his knees. 'Which brings up an interesting point,' he said. 'I mean, if occupational experience gives a special shape and colour to the patient's perceptions, then the theory that it is not really a hallucination but a deeper insight into reality probably falls down. For instance, if the number eighteen clangs for one patient and whistles for another – say for George here – '

Minturn spilled ashes on the lapel of his dinner coat and rubbed them into it. 'I don't want to hear any numbers,' he said thickly. 'I don't want to hear any more about it.'

His wife, who had been trying to get Fletcher's eyes but couldn't, since he continued to study his brandy, spoke up sharply. 'George is just getting over a frightful cold,' she said, 'and he's prettily easily shaken. He would worry frightfully about people, but he doesn't dare think about them. They upset him so.' Fletcher did look at her now, and smiled. She realized she had not said what she had meant to say. Something oblique but cleverly phrased and nicely pointed had got lost on its way to her tongue. 'You think you're so darn smart,' she said.

Minturn got up and began to pace. The brandy had run out. He sat down and lighted a cigarette.

'Of course, the people that doctors refer to as squashes,' pursued Fletcher, 'the invertebrates, you might say, just lie there like vegetables. It is the high-strung cases that manifest the interesting – manifestations. As you just said, Nancy, you think you're so darn smart. I mean, hospitalization moves the mind toward a false simplification. A man gets the idea that he can hold processes in his hand, the way I'm holding this glass. He lies there, you might say, pulling the easy little meanings out of life as simply as if they were daisy petals.'

'Daisy petals,' said Minturn. 'Where's brandy? Why isn't there any more brandy?'

'He gets the idea,' Fletcher went on, 'that he knows as much about life as Alfred North Whitehead or Carson McCullers.'

Minturn said, 'Oh, God.'

'Carson McCullers makes George nervous,' said Mrs Minturn, 'and you know it.'

'I ask you to remember I have scarcely seen you people since Carson McCullers began to write,' said Fletcher stiffly. 'I know "Sanctuary" upset George so he had to go away to the mountains. I *do* know that.'

'He didn't go away to the mountains at all,' said Mrs Minturn. So you *don't* know that.'

'I want to go away to the mountains now,' said Minturn. He began pacing around again, picking up things.

'There's more brandy in the kitchen, darling,' said Mrs Minturn. 'In the kitchen,' she repeated as he started upstairs.

'Oh,' said Minturn. He went out to the kitchen.

Mrs Minturn went over to Fletcher and stood looking down at him. 'It's very sweet of you, Joe, to keep harping on hospitals and sick people and mental states,' she said. 'I know why you're doing it. You're doing it because George didn't come to see you when you were in the hospital. You know very well that George is too sensitive to visit people in the hospital.'

Fletcher stood up, too. 'Is that why *you* didn't come to see me?' he asked. She was taller than he was. He sat down again.

'Yes, it was, if you want to know so much,' she said. 'George would have sensed it and he would have worried about you all the time. As it was, he *did* worry about you all the time. But he can't stand things the way you can. You know how sensitive he's always been.'

Fletcher tried to drink out of his empty glass. 'He wasn't so goddam sensitive when we were both with the Cleveland Telephone Company. He wasn't so goddam sensitive then. No, he was practically a regular guy.'

Mrs Minturn drew herself up a little higher. 'It is just quite possible, perhaps,' she said, 'that you were just not quite perceptious at that time.' She went slowly back to her chair and sat down as Minturn came in with a bottle of brandy and a corkscrew.

'Here,' he said, handing them to Fletcher. Fletcher put down his glass, inserted the corkscrew accurately into the centre of the cork, twisted it competently, and pulled out the cork. 'Wonderful thing, technology,' said Minturn, 'wonderful thing, wonderful thing. I want a drink.' Fletcher poured a great splash of brandy into his host's glass and another into his own.

'He doesn't happen to mean he *believes* in it,' said Mrs Minturn. 'The trouble with you is you can't tell when a person is allusive even.'

'You're thinking of Technocracy,' Fletcher told her, taking her glass and pouring a small quantity of brandy into it with studious precision.

'Maybe,' said Mrs Minturn, darkly, 'and just maybe not.'

'Why can't we go home now? Why can't we go home now, Nancy?' said Minturn from deep down in his chair.

'We *are* home, dear,' said Mrs Minturn. She turned to Fletcher. 'Anybody that thinks I can't appreciate a game that two can play at is definitely,' said Mrs Minturn, hiccuping, 'crazy.' She held her breath and tried counting ten slowly.

'Why don't you try bending over and drinking out of the opposite side of your glass?' asked Fletcher.

Minturn sat up a little in his chair.

'Don't have to say things like that,' he said, severely.

To compensate for her hiccups, Mrs Minturn assumed a posture of strained dignity. Minturn slid farther down into his chair. They both watched Fletcher, who had set the brandy revolving in his glass and was studying it. He took a sip of his drink. 'It is a common misconception,' he said, 'that post-operative mental states disappear on the patient's advent from the hospital. Out of the hospital, they might recur at any time, and some pretty strange phenomena could happen – as in the case of the hospitalization of a friend.'

'If you're just trying to get George down, it's not going to be of the least consequence. I can assure you of that,' said Mrs Minturn. 'He's stronger than you are in lots of more important ways.'

'Phenomena,' said Minturn.

'I'm talking of what *I* might do, not of what George might do,' said Fletcher, 'in case you consider the manifestation what you choose to call weakness.'

'Well,' said Mrs Minturn, 'I certainly do – that and meanness.'

'I want to see Mrs Trimingham,' said Minturn. 'I want to go to Bermuda.'

'I suppose it would be too much to say that you can't very well disprove what I'm saying till I say it,' said Fletcher.

'No, it wouldn't,' said Mrs Minturn. 'I don't see why we can't talk about the Grand Coolidge Dam, or something.' She laughed. 'That's really frightfully funny. It really is.' She laughed again.

Minturn had closed his eyes, but he opened them again. 'Can't say I do,' he said. 'Can't say I do.'

Fletcher went over and splashed some more brandy into Minturn's glass. 'Let us say that George is lying in the hospital,' he said. 'Now, because of a recurring phenomena, I call on him every day.'

'That's cheap,' said Mrs Minturn, 'and that's pompous.'

'It's no more pompous than it is predictable,' said Fletcher, sharply, 'It's a condition. It just so happens that it might take the turn of me calling on George every day, from the time he goes in until he gets out.'

'You can't do that,' said George. 'There's such a thing as the law.'

'Of course he can't,' said Mrs Minturn. 'Besides, George is not going to the hospital.'

'I'm not going to the hospital,' said Minturn.

'Everybody goes to the hospital sooner or later,' said Fletcher. His voice was rising.

'Nine hundred million people don't,' said Mrs Minturn, 'all the time.'

'I'm stating a pathological case!' shouted Fletcher. 'Hypothetical. George has been lying there in that bed for six weeks!'

'No,' said Minturn.

'You ought to be ashamed of yourself,' said Mrs Minturn.

'Why?' asked Fletcher. 'I'm not saying there is anything the matter with him. He's convalescing, but he can't get up.'

'Why can't I get up?' asked Minturn.

'Because you're too weak. You have no more strength than a house mouse. You feel as if you were coming apart like a cheap croquet mallet. If you tried to stand, your knees would bend the wrong way, like a flamingo's.'

'I want to go home,' mumbled Minturn.

'You *are* home,' said his wife.

'He means from the hospital,' Fletcher told her, 'in the corridors of which, by the way, you hear my cane tapping practically all the time.'

'What are *you* doing there?' said Minturn thickly.

'I come to see you every day,' said Fletcher. 'I have been to see you every day since you got there.' He had been moving around the room, and now he went back and sat down.

48

'Can't stand you calling on me every day,' said Minturn. He finished his drink and poured a new one with some effort.

'Don't worry about it, George,' said Mrs Minturn. 'We'll take you to the Mayo brothers or someplace and he'll never find out about it.'

'I don't want to go to the Mayo brothers,' said Minturn.

Fletcher sat forward in his chair. 'And what's more,' he said, 'I bring you very strange things. That's part of it. That's part of the phenomena. I bring you puzzles that won't work, linked nails that won't come apart, pigs in clover in which the little balls are glued to the bottom of the box. I bring you mystery novels in Yiddish, and artificial flowers made of wire and beads, and horehound candy.'

'Terrible, terrible rat,' said Mrs Minturn, 'terrible rat Fletcher.'

'Police find something to do about that,' said Minturn. 'Such a thing as law and order. Such a thing as malpractice.'

'And liquorice whips,' continued Fletcher, 'and the complete files of *Physical Culture* for 1931; and matchboxes that go broo-oo-oo, broo-oo-oo.'

'Broo,' said Minturn. 'I want to go to Twenty-One.'

'Terrible, terrible, terrible rat,' said Mrs Minturn.

'I see,' said Fletcher. 'You don't even feel sorry for poor old tap-tap. Tap, tap, tap, tap, tap.'

'What's that?' said Minturn.

'That's my cane in the corridor,' said Fletcher. 'You are lying there, trying to unwrassle something I have brought you, when, tap, tap, tap, here I come again.'

'Terrible rat, go home,' said Mrs Minturn.

Fletcher bowed to her gravely. 'I'm going,' he said. 'It constitutes the first occasion on which I have ever been ejected from this or any other house, but that is as it should be, I presume.'

'Don't throw anybody out,' said Minturn. 'Tap, tap, tap,' he added.

Half-way to the hall door, Fletcher turned. 'That's right, laugh,' he said. 'Tap, tap, tap, tap, tap, then.'

'Tap, tap, tap,' said Minturn from far down near the floor. A new attack of hiccups kept Mrs Minturn speechless, but she stood up as her guest went out into the hall. Minturn was still saying 'Tap, tap,' and Mrs Minturn was hiccuping, as Fletcher found his hat and coat and went out the front door into the melting snow, looking for a taxi.

The Secret Life of James Thurber

I have only dipped here and there into Salvador Dali's *The Secret Life of Salvador Dali* (with paintings by Salvador Dali and photographs of Salvador Dali), because anyone afflicted with what my grandmother's sister Abigail called 'the permanent jumps' should do no more than skitter through such an autobiography, particularly in these melancholy times.

One does not have to skitter far before one comes upon some vignette which gives the full shape and flavour of the book: the youthful dreamer of dreams biting a sick bat or kissing a dead horse, the slender stripling going into man's estate with the high hope and fond desire of one day eating a live but roasted turkey, the sighing lover covering himself with goat dung and aspic that he might give off the true and noble odour of the ram. In my flying trip through Dali I caught other glimpses of the great man: Salvador adoring a seed ball fallen from a plane tree, Salvador kicking a tiny playmate off a bridge, Salvador caressing a crutch, Salvador breaking the old family doctor's glasses with a leather-thonged mattress-beater. There would appear to be only two things in the world that revolt him (and I don't mean a long-dead hedgehog). He is squeamish about skeletons and grasshoppers. Oh, well, we all have our idiosyncrasies.

Señor Dali's memoirs have set me to thinking. I find myself muttering as I shave, and on two occasions I have swung my crutch at a little neighbour girl on my way to the post office. Señor Dali's book sells for six dollars. My own published personal history (Harper & Brothers, 1933) sold for $1.75. At the time I complained briefly about this unusual figure, principally on the ground that it represented only fifty cents more than the price asked for a book called *The Adventures of Horace the Hedgehog*, published the same month. The publishers explained that the price was a closely approximated vertical, prefigured on the basis of profitable ceiling, which in turn was arrived at by taking into consideration the effect on diminishing returns of the horizontal factor.

In those days all heads of business firms adopted a guarded kind of double talk, commonly expressed in low, muffled tones, because nobody knew what was going to happen and nobody understood what had. Big business had been frightened by a sequence of economic phenomena which had clearly demonstrated that our civilization was in greater danger of being turned off than of gradually crumbling away. The upshot of it all was that I accepted the price of $1.75. In so doing, I accepted the state of the world as a proper standard by which the price of books should be fixed. And now, with the world in ten times as serious a condition as it was in 1933, Dali's publishers set a price of six dollars on his life story. This brings me to the inescapable conclusion that the price-fixing principle, in the field of literature, is not global but personal. The trouble, quite simply, is that I told too much about what went on in the house I lived in and not enough about what went on inside myself.

Let me be the first to admit that the naked truth about me is to the naked truth about Salvador Dali as an old ukulele in the attic is to a piano in a tree, and I mean a piano with breasts. Señor Dali has the jump on me from the beginning. He remembers and describes in detail what it was like in the womb. My own earliest memory is of accompanying my father to a polling booth in Columbus, Ohio, where he voted for William McKinley.

It was a drab and somewhat battered tin shed set on wheels, and it was filled with guffawing men and cigar smoke; all in all, as far removed from the paradisiacal placenta of Salvador Dali's first recollection as could well be imagined. A fat, jolly man dandled me on his knee and said that I would soon be old enough to vote against William Jennings Bryan. I thought he meant that I could push a folded piece of paper into the slot of the padlocked box as soon as my father was finished. When this turned out not to be true, I had to be carried out of the place kicking and screaming. In my struggles I knocked my father's derby off several times. The derby was not a monstrously exciting love object to me, as practically everything Salvador encountered was to him, and I doubt, if I had that day to live over again, that I could bring myself, even in the light of exotic dedication as I now know it, to conceive an intense

52

and perverse affection for the derby. It remains obstinately in my memory as a rather funny hat, a little too large in the crown, which gave my father the appearance of a tired, sensitive gentleman who had been persuaded against his will to take part in a game of charades.

We lived on Champion Avenue at the time, and the voting booth was on Mound Street. As I set down these names, I begin to perceive an essential and important difference between the infant Salvador and the infant me. This difference can be stated in terms of environment. Salvador was brought up in Spain, a country coloured by the legends of Hannibal, El Greco, and Cervantes. I was brought up in Ohio, a region steeped in the tradition of Coxey's Army, the Anti-Saloon League, and William Howard Taft. It is only natural that the weather in little Salvador's soul should have been stirred by stranger winds and enveloped in more fantastic mists than the weather in my own soul. But enough of mewling apology for my lacklustre early years. Let us get back to my secret life, such as it was, stopping just long enough to have another brief look at Señor Dali on our way.

Salvador Dali's mind goes back to a childhood half imagined and half real, in which the edges of actuality were sometimes less sharp than the edges of dream. He seems somehow to have got the idea that this sets him off from Harry Spencer, Charlie Doakes, I. Feinberg, J. J. McNaboe, Willie Faulkner, Herbie Hoover, and me. What Salvie had that the rest of us kids didn't was the perfect scenery, characters, and costumes for his desperate little rebellion against the clean, the conventional, and the comfortable. He put perfume on his hair (which would have cost him his life in, say, Bayonne, N.J., or Youngstown, Ohio), he owned a lizard with two tails, he wore silver buttons on his shoes, and he knew, or imagined he knew, little girls named Galuchka and Dullita. Thus he was born half-way along the road to paranoia, the soft Poictesme of his prayers, the melting Oz of his oblations, the capital, to put it so that you can see what I am trying to say, of his heart's desire. Or so, anyway, it must seem to a native of Columbus, Ohio, who, as a youngster, bought his twelve-dollar suits at the F. & R. Lazarus Co., had his hair washed out with Ivory soap, owned a bull terrier with only one tail, and played (nicely and a bit diffidently) with little girls named Irma and Betty and Ruby.

Another advantage that the young Dali had over me, from the standpoint of impetus toward paranoia, lay in the nature of the adults who peopled his real world. There was, in Dali's home town of Figueras, a family of artists named Pitchot (musicians, painters, and poets), all of whom adored the ground that the *enfant terrible* walked on. If one of them came upon him throwing himself from a high rock – a favourite relaxation of our hero – or hanging by his feet with his head immersed in a pail of water, the wild news was spread about the town that greatness and genius had come to Figueras. There was a woman who put on a look of maternal interest when Salvador threw rocks at her. The mayor of the town fell dead one day at the boy's feet. A doctor in the community (not the one he had horsewhipped) was seized of a fit and attempted to beat him up. (The contention that the doctor was out of his senses at the time of the assault is Dali's, not mine.)

The adults around me when I was in short pants were neither so glamorous nor so attentive. They consisted mainly of eleven maternal great-aunts, all Methodists, who were staunch believers in physic, mustard plaster, and Scripture, and it was part of their dogma that artistic tendencies should be treated in the same way as hiccups or hysterics. None of them was an artist, unless you can count Aunt Lou, who wrote sixteen-stress verse, with hit-and-miss rhymes, in celebration of people's birthdays or on the occasion of great national disaster. It never occurred to me to bite on a bat in my aunts' presence or to throw stones at them. There was one escape, though: my secret world of idiom.

Two years ago my wife and I, looking for a house to buy, called on a firm of real-estate agents in New Milford. One of the members of the firm, scrabbling through a metal box containing many keys, looked up to say, 'The key to the Roxbury house isn't here.' His partner replied, 'It's a common lock. A skeleton will let you in.' I was suddenly once again five years old, with wide eyes and open mouth. I pictured the Roxbury house as I would have pictured it as a small boy, a house of such dark and nameless horrors as have never crossed the mind of our little bat-biter.

It was of sentences like that, nonchalantly tossed off by real-estate dealers, great-aunts, clergymen, and other such prosaic persons that the enchanted private world of my early boyhood was made. In this world, businessmen who phoned their wives to say that they were tied up at the office sat roped to their swivel chairs, and probably gagged, unable to move or speak, except somehow, miraculously, to telephone; hundreds of thousands of businessmen tied to their chairs in hundreds of thousands of offices in every city of my fantastic cosmos. An especially fine note about the binding of all the businessmen in all the cities was that whoever did it always did it around five o'clock in the afternoon.

Then there was the man who left town under a cloud. Sometimes I saw him all wrapped up in the cloud, and invisible, like a cat in a burlap sack. At other times it floated, about the size of a sofa, three or four feet above his head, following him wherever he went. One could think about the man under the cloud before going to sleep; the image of him wandering around from town to town was a sure soporific.

Not so the mental picture of a certain Mrs Huston, who had been terribly cut up when her daughter died on the operating table. I could see the doctors too vividly, just before they set upon Mrs Huston with their knives, and I could hear them. 'Now, Mrs Huston, will we get up on the table like a good girl, or will we have to be put there?' I could usually fight off Mrs Huston before I went to sleep, but she frequently got into my dreams, and sometimes she still does.

I remember the grotesque creature that came to haunt my meditations when one evening my father said to my mother, 'What did Mrs Johnson say when you told her about Betty?' and my mother replied, 'Oh, she was all ears.' There were many other wonderful figures in the secret, surrealist landscapes of my youth: the old lady who was always up in the air, the husband who did not seem to be able to put his foot down, the man who lost his head during a fire but was still able to run out of the house yelling, the young lady who was, in reality, a soiled dove. It was a world that, of necessity, one had to keep to oneself and brood over in silence, because it would fall to pieces at the touch of words. If you brought it out into the light of actual day and put it to the test of questions, your parents would try to laugh the miracles away, or they would take your temperature and put you to bed. (Since I always ran a temperature, whenever it was taken, I was put to bed and left there all alone with Mrs Huston.)

Such a world as the world of my childhood is, alas, not year-proof. It is a ghost that, to use Henley's words, gleams, flickers, vanishes away. I think it must have been the time my little Cousin Frances came to visit us that it began surely and forever to dissolve. I came into the house one rainy dusk and asked where Frances was. 'She is,' said our cook, 'up in the front room crying her heart out.' The fact that a person could cry so hard that his heart would come out of his body, as perfectly shaped and glossy as a red velvet pin-cushion, was news to me. For some reason I had never heard the expression, so common in American families whose hopes and dreams run so often counter to attainment. I went upstairs and opened the door of the front room. Frances, who was three years older than I, jumped up off the bed and ran past me, sobbing, and down the stairs.

My search for her heart took some fifteen minutes. I tore the bed apart and kicked up the rugs and even looked in the bureau drawers. It was no good. I looked out the window at the rain and the darkening sky. My cherished mental image of the man under the cloud began to grow dim and fade away. I discovered that, all alone in a room, I could face the thought of Mrs Huston with cold equanimity. Downstairs, in the living-room, Frances was still crying. I began to laugh.

Ah there, Salvador!

Recollections of the Gas Buggy

Footnotes to An Era for the Future Historian

Now that the humorous magazines have taken to printing drawings of horses rearing at the sight of an automobile, and of children exclaiming as a car goes by, 'What is that thing, Mamma? Mamma, what is that thing, huh, Mamma?,' it is perhaps not out of place to prepare some small memorial in advance of the passing of the motor-car. It appears to have reached, on its way backward to oblivion, what corresponds roughly to the year 1903.

I think that no one has drawn a darker or more vivid picture of the approaching doom of the gas engine than Mrs Robertson, the aged coloured washerwoman whose prophecies and pronouncements I have the privilege of listening to every Monday morning. Mrs Robertson is, for my money, an extremely sound woman, although admittedly my judgement of soundness has sometimes been questioned.

Some of the opinions of Mrs Robertson which I recall offhand are these: 'If you don't pay no mind to diseases, they will go away.' 'The night was made partly for rest and partly as a punishment for the sinful.' And 'The government only allows you to keep furniture for two months.' This last conviction grows out of Mrs Robertson's habit of buying furniture on the instalment plan and failing to keep up her payments longer than six or seven weeks, with the result that the things are repossessed. She looks upon this recurring ritual in her domestic life as a form of federal taxation.

Mrs Robertson's beliefs and feelings about the future of the automobile (which I have been leading up to) go like this: the oil supplies of the world are being dried up in order to prevent future wars. This will also put an end forever to pleasure driving, but that is all right because, if people kept on riding in cars, they would soon lose the use of both legs, and the life of Man would pass from the earth.

If Mrs Robertson is right in her predictions, I should like to set down my own few unique experiences with gas-driven vehicles before I forget them. They may possibly serve as footnotes to the work of some future historian, lightening a little the dolorous annals of the automobile.

Let me admit, to begin with, that the automobile and I were never in tune with each other. There was a fundamental incompatibility between us that amounted at times almost to chemical repulsion. I have felt the headlights of an automobile following me the way the eyes of a cat follow the ominous activities of a neighbour's dog. Some of the machines I have owned have seemed to me to bridle slightly when I got under the wheel. Neither the motor-car nor myself would greatly mourn if one of us were suddenly extinguished.

Years ago, an aunt of my father's came to visit us one winter in Columbus, Ohio. She enjoyed the hallucination, among others, that she was able to drive a car. I was riding with her one December day when I discovered to my horror, that she thought the red and green lights on the traffic signals had been put up by the municipality as a gay and expansive manifestation of the Yuletide spirit. Although we finally reached home safely, I never completely recovered from the adventure, and could not be induced, after that day, to ride in a car on holidays.

When I got an automobile of my own and began to drive it, I brought to the enterprise a magnificent ignorance of the workings of a gas engine, and a profound disinterest in its oily secrets. On several occasions, worried friends of an engineering turn of mind attempted to explain the nature of gas engines to me, but they succeeded only in losing me in a mechanical maze of terminology. I developed the notion that the gas engine was more soundly constructed than I was. I elaborate this point only to show you on what unequal terms the motor car and I were brought together.

Out of my long and dogged bouts with automobiles of various makes, there comes back to me now only one truly pleasurable experience. There may have been others, but I doubt it. I was driving in the British Isles in 1938, and came one day to a sudden, coughing stop in a far and lonely section of Scotland. The car had run out of gas in the wilderness. This car's gasoline gauge had a trick of mounting toward 'Full' instead of sinking toward 'Empty' when the tank was running low, one of many examples of pure cussedness of which it was capable. There I was, miles from any village, with not even a farmhouse in sight. On my left was a thick wood, out of which the figure of a man suddenly appeared. He asked me what was the matter, and I said I had run out of petrol. 'It just happens,' he told me, 'that I have a can of petrol.' With that, he went back into the woods, and came out again with a five-gallon can of gasoline. He put it in the tank for me, I thanked him, paid for it, and drove on.

Once when I was telling this true but admittedly remarkable story, at a party in New York, a bright-eyed young woman exclaimed, 'But when the man emerged from the lonely woods, miles away from any village, far from the nearest farmhouse, carrying a five-gallon can of gasoline, why didn't you ask him how he happened to be there with it?' I lighted a cigarette. 'Madam,' I said, 'I was afraid he would vanish.' She gave a small laugh and moved away from me. Everybody always does.

Another experience I had in England the same year helped to shake the faith of at least one Briton in the much-vaunted Yankee affinity for machinery. The battery of my car had run down in a village about twenty miles from York, my destination. I put in a call to a garage and a young mechanic showed up presently in a wrecking car. He said he would give me a tow for a few yards. I was to let the clutch in and out (or out and in, whichever it is) and start the engine that way. It is a device as old as the automobile itself, and years before I had managed it successfully. Any child or old lady can do it.

So he attached a rope to the back of his car and the front of mine, and we were off. I kept letting the clutch out and in (or in and out) madly, but nothing happened. The garage man kept stopping every 500 yards or so and coming back to consult with me. He was profoundly puzzled. It was farther than he had ever dragged a car in his life. We must have gone, in this disheartening manner about a third of the way to York. Finally he got out for the seventh time and said to me, 'What gear have you got her in?' I didn't have her in any gear. I had her in neutral. She had been in neutral all the while.

Now, as any child or old lady knows, you have to have her in gear. If she is in neutral, it is like trying to turn on the electric lights when there are no bulbs in the sockets. The garage mechanic looked at me with the special look garage mechanics reserve for me. It is a mixture of incredulity, bewilderment, and distress. I put her in low gear, he gave me a short haul, and she started. I paid him and, as I drove off, I could see him in the rear-view mirror, standing in the road still staring after me with that look.

After I had got back to America (safe and sound, to the surprise of my friends), I produced this same expression on the face of a garage man in Connecticut one afternoon. I had driven the same car from Newtown to Litchfield on a crisp October day. It happened that I was just getting over an attack of grippe, and still running a temperature of a couple of degrees. The car, out of plain devilry, began to run one, too. The red fluid in the engine gauge on the dashboard started to rise alarmingly. It got to the point marked 'Danger'. I drove into a garage in a pretty jumpy state of mind. A garage man looked at the gauge and said the thermostat was clogged – or something of the kind. I was standing outside the car, staring at the dashboard and its, to me, complicated dials, when I noticed to my horror that one of them registered 1650. I pointed a shaking finger at it and said to the mechanic, 'That dial shouldn't be registering as high as all that, should it?' He gave me the same look I had got from the man in England. 'That's your radio dial, Mac,' he said. 'You got her set at WQXR.'

I got into the car and drove home. The garage man stared after me until I was out of sight. He is probably still telling it around.

My temperature rose a degree that night, and I developed a theory about my automobile. The thing possessed, I decided, a certain antic intelligence, akin to that of a six-months-old poodle. It had run a temperature that afternoon out of mischief and mockery, because I was running one. It had deliberately betrayed me in the Scottish wilderness that other afternoon, by running its gasoline gauge toward 'Full' instead of 'Empty'. I began to wonder what I had done to the car to arouse its malice. Finally I put my finger on it. The car had probably never forgiven me for an incident that had occurred at the border between Belgium and France one day in 1937.

We had stopped at the Belgium customs on our way into France.

60

A customs man leaned into the car, glanced at the mileage recorded on the speedometer, and said something in French. I thought he said I would have to pay one franc for every kilometre the car had travelled. I was loudly indignant in French and in English. The car had gone about 35,000 miles. I figured this out in kilometres, and it came roughly to 55,000. Changing that figure into francs and then into dollars, still loudly and angrily, I estimated I would have to pay around $1,800 to the Belgian customs. The customs man kept trying to get a word in, and so did my wife, but I roared on to my peroration. I shouted that the car had not cost one half of $1,800 when it was new, and even then it hadn't been worth a third of that. I announced that I would not pay as much as fifty dollars to drive the car into Oz or Never-Never Land (*Jamais-Jamais Pays*).

The engine, which had been running, stopped. The customs man finally got in a word. Dismissing me as obviously insane, he spoke to my wife. He shouted that he had said nothing about $1,800 or even eight dollars. He had simply made some small comment on the distance the car had gone. As far as he was concerned, we could drive it to *Jamais-Jamais Pays* and stay there. He turned on his heel and stalked away, and I started the motor. It took quite a while. The car was acting up. The night my fever rose, I thought I knew why. It had resented the slighting remarks I made about its value and had determined to get even with me.

It got even with me in more ways than I have described.

Whenever I tried to put chains on a tyre, the car would maliciously wrap them around a rear axle. If I parked it ten feet from a fire plug and went into a store, it would be only five feet from the plug when I came out. If it saw a nail in the road, the car would swerve and pick the nail up. Once, driving into a bleak little town in the Middle West, I said aloud, 'I'd hate to be stuck in this place.' The car promptly burned out a bearing, and I was stuck there for two days.

If Mrs Robertson is right in her prophecy, and the gas engine is really on the way out, it will be no dire blow for me. I will move within roller-skating distance of a grocery, a drugstore, a church, a library, and a movie house. If the worst comes to the worst, I could even walk.

2 | From *My World*
and *Welcome to it*

What Do You Mean It Was Brillig?

I was sitting at my typewriter one afternoon several weeks ago, staring at a piece of blank white paper, when Della walked in. 'They are here with the reeves,' she said. It did not surprise me that they were. With a coloured woman like Della in the house it would not surprise me if they showed up with the toves. In Della's afternoon it is always brillig; she could outgrabe a mome rath on any wabe in the world. Only Lewis Carroll would have understood Della completely. I try hard enough. 'Let them wait a minute,' I said. I got out the big Century Dictionary and put it on my lap and looked up 'reeve'. It is an interesting word, like all of Della's words; I found out that there are four kinds of reeves. 'Are they here with strings of onions?' I asked. Della said they were not. 'Are they here with enclosures or pens for cattle, poultry, or pigs; sheepfolds?' Della said no sir. 'Are they here with administrative officers?' From a little nearer the door Della said no again. 'Then they've got to be here,' I said, 'with some females of the Common European sandpiper.' These scenes of ours take as much out of Della as they do out of me, but she is not a woman to be put down by a crazy man with a dictionary. 'They are here with the reeves for the windas,' said Della with brave stubbornness. Then, of course, I understood what they were there with: they were with the Christmas wreaths for the windows. 'Oh *those* reeves!' I said. We were both greatly relieved; we both laughed. Della and I never quite reach the breaking point; we just come close to it.

Della is a New England coloured woman with nothing of the South in her accent; she doesn't say 'd' for 'th' and she pronounces her 'r's. Hearing her talk in the next room, you might not know at first that she was coloured. You might not know till she said some such thing as 'Do you want cretonnes for the soup tonight?' (She makes wonderful cretonnes for the soup.) I have not found out much about Della's words, but I have learned a great deal about her background. She told me one day that she has three brothers and that one of them works into a garage and another works into an

T – T.T.C. – C

incinerator where they burn the refuge. The one that works into the incinerator has been working into it since the Armitage. That's what Della does to you; she gives you incinerator perfectly and then she comes out with the Armitage. I spent most of an hour one afternoon trying to figure out what was wrong with the Armitage; I thought of Armistead and armature and Armentières, and when I finally hit on Armistice it sounded crazy. It still does. Della's third and youngest brother is my favourite; I think he'll be yours, too, and everybody else's. His name is Arthur and it seems that he has just passed, with commendably high grades, his silver-service eliminations. Della is delighted about that, but she is not half so delighted about it as I am.

Della came to our house in Connecticut some months ago, trailing her glory of cloudiness. I can place the date for you approximately: it was while there were still a great many fletchers about. 'The lawn is full of fletchers,' Della told me one morning, shortly after she arrived, when she brought up my orange juice. 'You mean neighbours?' I said. 'This early?' By the way she laughed I knew that fletchers weren't people; at least not people of flesh and blood. I got dressed and went downstairs and looked up the word in the indispensable Century. A fletcher, I found, is a man who makes arrows. I decided, but without a great deal of conviction, that there couldn't be any arrow-makers on my lawn at that hour in the morning and at this particular period in history. I walked cautiously out the back door and around to the front of the house – and there they were. I don't know many birds but I do know flickers. A flicker is a bird which, if it were really named fletcher, would be called flicker by all the coloured cooks in the United States. Out of a mild curiosity I looked up 'flicker' in the dictionary and I discovered that he is a bird of several aliases. When Della brought my toast and coffee into the dining-room I told her about this. 'Fletchers,' I said, 'are also golden-winged woodpecker, yellowhammers, and high-holders.' For the first time Della gave me the look that I was to recognize later, during the scene about the reeves. I have become very familiar with that look and I believe I know the thoughts that lie behind it. Della was puzzled at first because I work at home instead of in an office, but I think she has it figured out now. This man, she thinks, used to work into an office like anybody else, but he had to be sent to an institution; he got well enough to come home from the institution, but he is still not well enough to go back to the office. I could have avoided all these suspicions, of course, if I had simply come out in the beginning and corrected Della when she got words wrong. Coming at her obliquely with a dictionary only enriches the confusion; but I wouldn't have it any other way. I share with Della a form of escapism that is the most mystic and satisfying flight from actuality I have ever known. It may not always comfort me, but it never ceases to beguile me.

Every Thursday when I drive Della to Waterbury in the car for her day off, I explore the dark depths and the strange recesses of her nomenclature. I found out that she had been married for ten years but was now divorced; that is, her husband went away one day and never came back. When I asked her what he did for a living, she said he worked into a dove-wedding. 'Into a what?' I asked. 'Into a dove-wedding,' said Della. It is one of the words I haven't figured out yet, but I am still working on it. 'Where are you from, Mr Thurl?' she asked me one day. I told her Ohio, and she said, 'Ooooh, to be sure!' as if I had given her a clue to my crazy definitions, my insensitivity to the ordinary household nouns, and my ignorance of the commoner migratory birds. 'Semantics, Ohio,' I said. 'Why, there's one of them in Massachusetts, too,' said Della. 'The one I mean,' I told her, 'is bigger and more confusing.' 'I'll bet it is,' said Della.

Della told me the other day that she had had only one sister, a beautiful girl who died when she was twenty-one. 'That's too bad,' I said. 'What was the matter?' Della had what was the matter at her tongue's tip. 'She got tuberculosis from her teeth,' she said, 'and it went all through her symptom.' I didn't know what to say to that except that my teeth were all right but that my symptom could probably be easily gone all through. 'You work too much with your brain,' said Della. I knew she was trying to draw me out about my brain and what had happened to it so that I could no longer work into an office, but I changed the subject. There is no doubt that Della is considerably worried about my mental condition. One morning when I didn't get up till noon because I had been writing letters until three o'clock, Della told my wife at breakfast what was the matter with me. 'His mind works so fast his body can't keep up with it,' she said. This diagnosis has shaken me not a little. I have decided to sleep longer and work less. I know exactly what will happen to me if my mind gets so far ahead of my body that my body can't catch up with it. They will come with a reeve and this time it won't be a red-and-green one for the window, it will be a black one for the door.

The Secret Life of Walter Mitty

'We're going through!' The Commander's voice was like thin ice breaking. He wore his full-dress uniform, with the heavily braided white cap pulled down rakishly over one cold grey eye. 'We can't make it, sir. It's spoiling for a hurricane, if you ask me.' 'I'm not asking you, Lieutenant Berg,' said the Commander. 'Throw on the power lights! Rev her up to 8,500! We're going through!' The pounding of the cylinders increased: ta-pocketa-pocketa-pocketa *pocketa-pocketa*. The Commander stared at the ice forming on the pilot window. He walked over and twisted a row of complicated dials. 'Switch on No. 8 auxiliary!' he shouted. 'Switch on No. 8 auxiliary!' repeated Lieutenant Berg. 'Full strength in No. 3 turret!' shouted the Commander. 'Full strength in No. 3 turret!' The crew, bending to their various tasks in the huge, hurtling eight-engined Navy hydroplane, looked at each other and grinned. 'The Old Man'll get us through,' they said to one another. 'The Old Man ain't afraid of Hell!'

'Not so fast! You're driving too fast!' said Mrs Mitty. 'What are you driving so fast for?'

'Hmm?' said Walter Mitty. He looked at his wife, in the seat beside him, with shocked astonishment. She seemed grossly unfamiliar, like a strange woman who had yelled at him in a crowd. 'You were up to fifty-five,' she said. 'You know I don't like to go more than forty. You were up to fifty-five.' Walter Mitty drove on toward Waterbury in silence, the roaring of the SN 202 through the worst storm in twenty years of Navy flying fading in the remote, intimate airways of his mind. 'You're tensed up again,' said Mrs Mitty .'It's one of your days. I wish you'd let Dr Renshaw look you over.'

Walter Mitty stopped the car in front of the building where his wife went to have her hair done. 'Remember to get those overshoes while I'm having my hair done,' she said. 'I don't need overshoes,' said Mitty. She put her mirror back into her bag. 'We've been all through that,' she said, getting out of the car. 'You're not a young man any longer.' He raced the engine a little. 'Why don't you wear your gloves? Have you lost your gloves?' Walter Mitty reached in a pocket and brought out the gloves. He put them on, but after she had turned and gone into the building and he had driven on to a red light, he took them off again. 'Pick it up, brother!' snapped a cop as the light changed, and Mitty hastily pulled on his gloves and lurched ahead. He drove around the streets aimlessly for a time, and then he drove past the hospital on his way to the parking lot.

. . . 'It's the millionaire banker, Wellington McMillan,' said the pretty nurse. 'Yes?' said Walter Mitty, removing his gloves slowly. 'Who has the case?' 'Dr Renshaw and Dr Benbow, but there are two specialists here, Dr Remington from New York and Mr Pritchard-Mitford from London. He flew over.' A door opened down a long, cool corridor and Dr Renshaw came out. He looked distraught and haggard. 'Hello, Mitty,' he said. 'We're having the devil's own time with McMillan, the millionaire banker and close personal friend of Roosevelt. Obstreosis of the ductal tract. Tertiary. Wish you'd take a look at him.' 'Glad to,' said Mitty.

In the operating room there were whispered introductions: 'Dr Remington, Dr Mitty. Mr Pritchard-Mitford, Dr Mitty.' 'I've read your book on streptothricosis,' said Pritchard-Mitford, shaking hands. 'A brilliant performance, sir.' 'Thank you,' said Walter Mitty. 'Didn't know you were in the States, Mitty,' grumbled Remington. 'Coals to Newcastle, bringing Mitford and me up here for a tertiary,' 'You are very kind,' said Mitty. A huge, complicated machine, connected to the operating table, with many tubes and wires, began at this moment to go pocketa-pocketa-pocketa. 'The new anaesthetizer is giving way!' shouted an interne. 'There is no one in the East who knows how to fix it!' 'Quiet, man!' said Mitty, in a low, cool voice. He sprang to the machine, which was now going pocketa-pocketa-queep-pocketa-queep. He began fingering delicately a row of glistening dials. 'Give me a fountain-pen!' he snapped. Someone handed him a fountain-pen. He pulled a faulty piston out of the machine and inserted the pen in its place. 'That will hold for ten minutes,' he said. 'Get on with the operation.' A nurse hurried over and whispered to Renshaw, and Mitty saw the man turn pale. 'Coreopsis has set in,' said Renshaw nervously. 'If you would take over,

70

Mitty?' Mitty looked at him and at the craven figure of Benbow, who drank, and at the grave, uncertain faces of the two great specialists. 'If you wish,' he said. They slipped a white gown on him; he adjusted a mask and drew on thin gloves; nurses handed him shining . . .

'Back it up, Mac! Look out for that Buick!' Walter Mitty jammed on the brakes. 'Wrong lane, Mac,' said the parking-lot attendant, looking at Mitty closely. 'Gee. Yeh,' muttered Mitty. He began cautiously to back out of the lane marked 'Exit Only.' 'Leave her sit there,' said the attendant. 'I'll put her away.' Mitty got out of the car. 'Hey, better leave the key.' 'Oh,' said Mitty, handing the man the ignition key. The attendant vaulted into the car, backed it up with insolent skill, and put it where it belonged.

They're so damn cocky, thought Walter Mitty, walking along Main Street; they think they know everything. Once he had tried to take his chains off, outside New Milford, and he had got them wound around the axles. A man had had to come out in a wrecking car and unwind them, a young, grinning garageman. Since then Mrs Mitty always made him drive to a garage to have the chains taken off. The next time, he thought, I'll wear my right arm in a sling; they won't grin at me then. I'll have my right arm in a sling and they'll see I couldn't possibly take the chains off myself. He kicked at the slush on the sidewalk. 'Overshoes,' he said to himself, and he began looking for a shoe store.

When he came out into the street again, with the overshoes in a box under his arm, Walter Mitty began to wonder what the other thing was his wife had told him to get. She had told him twice, before they set out from their house for Waterbury. In a way he hated these weekly trips to town – he was always getting something wrong. Kleenex, he thought, Squibb's, razor blades? No. Toothpaste, toothbrush, bicarbonate, carborundum, initiative and referendum? He gave it up. But she would remember it. 'Where's the what's-its-name?' she would ask. 'Don't tell me you forgot the what's-its-name.' A newsboy went by shouting something about the Waterbury trial.

. . . 'Perhaps this will refresh your memory.' The District Attorney suddenly thrust a heavy automatic at the quiet figure on the witness stand. 'Have you ever seen this before?' Walter

Mitty took the gun and examined it expertly. 'This is my Webley-Vickers 50.80,' he said calmly. An excited buzz ran around the courtroom. The judge rapped for order. 'You are a crack shot with any sort of firearms, I believe?' said the District Attorney, insinuatingly. 'Objection!' shouted Mitty's attorney. 'We have shown that the defendant could not have fired the shot. We have shown that he wore his right arm in a sling on the night of the fourteenth of July.' Walter Mitty raised his hand briefly and the bickering attorneys were stilled. 'With any known make of gun,' he said evenly, 'I could have killed Gregory Fitzhurst at three hundred feet *with my left hand*.' Pandemonium broke loose in the courtroom. A woman's scream rose above the bedlam and suddenly a lovely, dark-haired girl was in Walter Mitty's arms. The District Attorney struck at her savagely. Without rising from his chair, Mitty let the man have it on the point of the chin. 'You miserable cur!' ...

'Puppy biscuit,' said Walter Mitty. He stopped walking and the buildings of Waterbury rose up out of the misty courtroom and surrounded him again. A woman who was passing laughed. 'He said "Puppy biscuit",' she said to her companion. 'That man said "Puppy biscuit" to himself.' Walter Mitty hurried on. He went into an A. & P., not the first one he came to but a smaller one farther up the street. 'I want some biscuit for small, young dogs,' he said to the clerk. 'Any special brand, sir?' The greatest pistol shot in the world thought a moment. 'It says "Puppies Bark for It" on the box,' said Walter Mitty.

His wife would be through at the hairdresser's in fifteen minutes, Mitty saw in looking at his watch, unless they had trouble drying it; sometimes they had trouble drying it. She didn't like to get to the hotel first; she would want him to be there waiting for her as usual. He found a big leather chair in the lobby, facing a window, and he put the overshoes and the puppy biscuit on the floor beside it. He picked up an old copy of *Liberty* and sank down into the chair. 'Can Germany Conquer the World Through the Air?' Walter Mitty looked at the pictures of bombing planes and of ruined streets.

... 'The cannonading has got the wind up in young Raleigh,

sir,' said the sergeant. Captain Mitty looked up at him through tousled hair. 'Get him to bed,' he said wearily. 'With the others. I'll fly alone.' 'But you can't, sir,' said the sergeant anxiously. 'It takes two men to handle that bomber and the Archies are pounding hell out of the air. Von Richtman's circus is between here and Saulier.' 'Somebody's got to get that ammunition dump,' said Mitty. 'I'm going over. Spot of brandy?' He poured a drink for the sergeant and one for himself. War thundered and whined around the dugout and battered at the door. There was a rending of wood and splinters flew through the room. 'A bit of a near thing,' said Captain Mitty carelessly. 'The box barrage is closing in,' said the sergeant. 'We only live once, Sergeant,' said Mitty, with his faint, fleeting smile. 'Or do we?' He poured another brandy and tossed it off. 'I never see a man could hold his brandy like you, sir,' said the sergeant. 'Begging your pardon, sir.' Captain Mitty stood up and strapped on his huge Webley-Vickers automatic. 'It's forty kilometres through hell, sir,' said the sergeant. Mitty finished one last brandy. 'After all,' he said softly, 'what isn't?' The pounding of the cannon increased; there was the rat-tat-tatting of machine-guns, and from somewhere came the menacing pocketa-pocketa-pocketa of the new flame-throwers. Walter Mitty walked to the door of the dugout humming 'Auprès de Ma Blonde'. He turned and waved to the sergeant. 'Cheerio!' he said. . . .

Something struck his shoulder. 'I've been looking all over this hotel for you,' said Mrs Mitty. 'Why do you have to hide in this old chair? How did you expect me to find you?' 'Things close in,' said Walter Mitty vaguely. 'What?' Mrs Mitty said. 'Did you get the what's-its-name? The puppy biscuit? What's in that box?' 'Overshoes,' said Mitty. 'Couldn't you have put them on in the store?' 'I was thinking,' said Walter Mitty. 'Does it ever occur to you that I am sometimes thinking?' She looked at him. 'I'm going to take your temperature when I get you home,' she said.

They went out through the revolving doors that made a faintly derisive whistling sound when you pushed them. It was two blocks to the parking lot. At the drugstore on the corner she said, 'Wait here for me. I forgot something. I won't be a minute.' She was more than a minute. Walter Mitty lighted a cigarette. It began to rain, rain with sleet in it. He stood up against the wall of the drugstore, smoking. . . . He put his shoulders back and his heels together. 'To hell with the handkerchief,' said Walter Mitty scornfully. He took one last drag on his cigarette and snapped it away. Then, with that faint, fleeting smile playing about his lips, he faced the firing squad; erect and motionless, proud and disdainful, Walter Mitty the Undefeated, inscrutable to the last.

Here Lies Miss Groby

Miss Groby taught me English composition thirty years ago. It wasn't what prose said that interested Miss Groby; it was the way prose said it. The shape of a sentence crucified on a blackboard (parsed, she called it) brought a light to her eye. She hunted for Topic Sentences and Transitional Sentences the way little girls hunt for white violets in springtime. What she loved most of all were Figures of Speech. You remember her. You must have had her, too. Her influence will never die out of the land. A small schoolgirl asked me the other day if I could give her an example of metonymy. (There are several kinds of metonymies, you may recall, but the one that will come to mind most easily, I think, is Container for the Thing Contained.) The vision of Miss Groby came clearly before me when the little girl mentioned the old, familiar word. I saw her sitting at her desk, taking the rubber band off the roll-call cards, running it back upon the fingers of her right hand, and surveying us all separately with quick little henlike turns of her head.

Here lies Miss Groby, not dead, I think, but put away on a shelf with the other T squares and rulers whose edges had lost their certainty. The fierce light that Miss Groby brought to English literature was the light of Identification. Perhaps, at the end, she could no longer retain the dates of the birth and death of one of the Lake poets. That would have sent her to the principal of the school with her resignation. Or perhaps she could not remember, finally, exactly how many Cornishmen there were who had sworn that Trelawny should not die, or precisely how many springs were left to Housman's lad in which to go about the woodlands to see the cherry hung with snow.

Verse was one of Miss Groby's delights because there was so much in both its form and content that could be counted. I believe she would have got an enormous thrill out of Wordsworth's famous lines about Lucy if they had been written this way:

A violet by a mossy stone
Half hidden from the eye,
Fair as a star when ninety-eight
Are shining in the sky.

It is hard for me to believe that Miss Groby ever saw any famous work of literature from far enough away to know what it meant. She was forever climbing up the margins of books and crawling between their lines, hunting for the little gold of phrase, making marks with a pencil. As Palamides hunted the Questing Beast, she hunted the Figure of Speech. She hunted it through the clangorous halls of Shakespeare and through the green forests of Scott.

Night after night, for homework, Miss Groby set us to searching in *Ivanhoe* and *Julius Caesar* for metaphors, similes, metonymies, apostrophes, personifications, and all the rest. It got so that figures of speech jumped out of the pages at you, obscuring the sense and pattern of the novel or play you were trying to read. 'Friends, Romans, countrymen, lend me your ears.' Take that, for instance. There is an unusual but perfect example of Container for the Thing Contained. If you read the funeral oration unwarily – that is to say, for its meaning – you might easily miss the C.F.T.T.C. Antony is, of course, not asking for their ears in the sense that he wants them cut off and handed over; he is asking for the function of those ears, for their power to hear, for, in a word, the thing they contain.

At first I began to fear that all the characters in Shakespeare and Scott were crazy. They confused cause with effect, the sign for the thing signified, the thing held for the thing holding it. But after a while I began to suspect that it was I myself who was crazy. I would find myself lying awake at night saying over and over, 'The thinger for the thing contained'. In a great but probably misguided attempt to keep my mind on its hinges, I would stare at the ceiling and try to think of an example of the Thing Contained for the Container. It struck me as odd that Miss Groby had never thought of that inversion. I finally hit on one, which I still remember. If a woman were to grab up a bottle of Grade A and say to her husband, 'Get away from me or I'll hit you with the milk,' that would be a Thing Contained for the Container. The next day in class I raised my hand and brought my curious discovery straight out before Miss

Groby and my astonished schoolmates. I was eager and serious about it and it never occurred to me that the other children would laugh. They laughed loudly and long. When Miss Groby had quieted them she said to me rather coldly, 'That was not really amusing, James.' That's the mixed-up kind of thing that happened to me in my teens.

In later years I came across another excellent example of this figure of speech in a joke long since familiar to people who know vaudeville or burlesque (or radio, for that matter). It goes something like this:

A: What's your head all bandaged up for?
B: I got hit with some tomatoes.
A: How could that bruise you up so bad?
B: These tomatoes were in a can.

I wonder what Miss Groby would have thought of that one.

I dream of my old English teacher occasionally. It seems that we are always in Sherwood Forest and that from far away I can hear Robin Hood winding his silver horn.

'Drat that man for making such a racket on his cornet!' cries Miss Groby. 'He scared away a perfectly darling Container for the Thing Contained, a great, big, beautiful one. It leaped right back into its context when that man blew that cornet. It was the most wonderful Container for the Thing Contained I ever saw here in the Forest of Arden.'

'This is Sherwood Forest,' I say to her.

'That doesn't make any difference at all that I can see,' she says to me.

Then I wake up, tossing and moaning.

The Man Who Hated Moonbaum

After they had passed through the high, grilled gate they walked for almost a quarter of a mile, or so it seemed to Tallman. It was very dark; the air smelled sweet; now and then leaves brushed against his cheek or forehead. The little, stout man he was following had stopped talking, but Tallman could hear him breathing. They walked on for another minute. 'How we doing?' Tallman asked, finally. 'Don't ask me questions!' snapped the other man. 'Nobody asks me questions! You'll learn.' The hell I will, thought Tallman, pushing through the darkness and the fragrance and the mysterious leaves; the hell I will, baby; this is the last time you'll ever see me. The knowledge that he was leaving Hollywood within twenty-four hours gave him a sense of comfort.

There was no longer turf or gravel under his feet; there was something that rang flatly: tile, or flagstones. The little man began to walk more slowly and Tallman almost bumped into him. 'Can't we have a light?' said Tallman. 'There you go!' shouted his guide. 'Don't get me screaming! What are you trying to do to me?' 'I'm not trying to do anything to you,' said Tallman. 'I'm trying to find out where we're going.'

The other man had come to a stop and seemed to be groping around. 'First it's wrong uniforms,' he said, 'then it's red fire – red fire in Scotland, red fire three hundred years ago! I don't know why I ain't crazy!' Tallman could make out the other man dimly, a black, gesturing blob. 'You're doing all right,' said Tallman. Why did I ever leave the Brown Derby with this guy? he asked himself. Why did I ever let him bring me to his house – if he has a house? Who the hell does he think he is?

Tallman looked at his wrist watch; the dial glowed wanly in the immense darkness. He was a little drunk, but he could see that it was half past three in the morning. 'Not trying to do anything to me, he says!' screamed the little man. 'Wasn't his fault! It's never anybody's fault! They give me ten thousand dollars' worth of Sam Browne belts for Scotch Highlanders and it's nobody's fault!'

Tallman was beginning to get his hangover headache. 'I want a light!' he said. 'I want a drink! I want to know where the hell I am!' 'That's it! Speak out!' said the other. 'Say what you think! I like a man who knows where he is. We'll get along.' 'Contact!' said Tallman. 'Camera! Lights! Get out that hundred-year-old brandy you were talking about.'

The response to this was a soft flood of rose-coloured radiance; the little man had somehow found a light switch in the dark. God knows where, thought Tallman; probably on a tree. They were in a courtyard paved with enormous flagstones which fitted together with mosaic perfection. The light revealed the dark stones of a building which looked like the Place de la Concorde side of the Crillon. 'Come on, you people!' said the little man. Tallman looked behind him, half expecting to see the shadowy forms of Scottish Highlanders, but there was nothing but the shadows of trees and of oddly shaped plants closing in on the courtyard. With a key as small as a dime, the little man opened a door that was fifteen feet high and made of wood six inches thick.

Marble stairs tumbled down like Niagara into a grand canyon of a living-room. The steps of the two men sounded sharp and clear on the stairs, died in the soft depths of an immensity of carpet in the living-room. The ceiling towered above them. There were high-lights on dark wood medallions, on burnished shields, on silver curves and edges. On one wall a forty-foot tapestry hung from the ceiling to within a few feet of the floor. Tallman was looking at this when his companion grasped his arm. 'The second rose!' he said. 'The second rose from the right!' Tallman pulled away. 'One of us has got to snap out of this, baby,' he said. 'How about that brandy?' 'Don't interrupt me!' shouted his host. 'That's what Whozis whispers to What's-His-Name – greatest love story in the world, if I do say so myself – king's wife mixed up in it – knights riding around with spears – Whozis writes her a message made out of twigs bent together to make words: "I love you" – sends it floating down a stream past her window – they got her locked in – goddamnedest thing in the history of pictures. Where was I? Oh – "Second rose from the right," she says. Why? Because she seen it twitch, she seen it move. What's-His-Name is bending over her, kissing her maybe. He whirls around and shoots an arrow at the

79

rose – second from the right, way up high there – down comes the whole tapestry, weighs eleven hundred pounds, and out rolls this spy, shot through the heart. What's-His-Name sent him to watch the lovers.' The little man began to pace up and down the deep carpet. Tallman lighted a fresh cigarette from his glowing stub and sat down in an enormous chair. His host came to a stop in front of the chair and shook his finger at its occupant.

'Look,' said the little man. 'I don't know who you are and I'm telling you this. You could ruin me, but I got to tell you. I get Moonbaum here – I get Moonbaum himself here – you can ask Manny or Sol – I get the best arrow shot in the world here to fire that arrow for What's-His-Name – '

'Tristram,' said Tallman. 'Don't prompt me!' bellowed the little man. 'For Tristram. What happens? Do I know he's got arrows you shoot bears with? Do I know he ain't got caps on 'em? If I got to know that, why do I have Mitnik? Moonbaum is sitting right there – the tapestry comes down and out rolls this guy, shot through the heart – only the arrow is in his stomach. So what happens? So Moonbaum laughs! That makes Moonbaum laugh! The greatest love story in the history of pictures, and Moonbaum laughs!' The little man raced over to a large chest, opened it, took out a cigar, stuck it in his mouth, and resumed his pacing. 'How do you like it?' he shouted. 'I love it,' said Tallman. 'I love every part of it. I always have.' The little man raised his hands above his head. 'He loves it! He hears one – maybe two – scenes, and he loves every part of it! Even Moonbaum don't know how it comes out, and you love every part of it!' The little man was standing before Tallman's chair again, shaking his cigar at him. 'The story got around,' said Tallman. 'These things leak out. Maybe you talk when you're drinking. What about that brandy?'

The little man walked over and took hold of a bell rope on the wall, next to the tapestry. 'Moonbaum laughs like he's dying,' he said. 'Moonbaum laughs like he's seen Chaplin.' He dropped the bell rope. 'I hope you really got that hundred-year-old brandy,' said Tallman. 'Don't keep telling me what you hope!' howled the little man. 'Keep listening to what I hope!' He pulled the bell rope savagely. 'Now we're getting somewhere,' said Tallman. For the first time the little man went to a chair and sat down; he chewed on his unlighted cigar. 'Do you know what Moonbaum wants her called?' he demanded, lowering his heavy lids. 'I can guess,' said Tallman. 'Isolde.' 'Birds of a feather!' shouted his host. 'Horses of the same colour! Isolde! Name of God, man, you can't call a woman Isolde! What do I want her called?' 'You have me there,' said Tallman. 'I want her called Dawn,' said the little man, getting up out of his chair. 'It's short, ain't it? It's sweet, ain't it? You can say it, can't you?' 'To get back to that brandy,' said Tallman, 'who is supposed to answer that bell?' 'Nobody is supposed to answer it,' said the little man. 'That don't ring, that's a fake bell rope; it don't ring anywhere. I got it to remind me of an idea Moonbaum ruined. Listen: Louisiana mansion – guy with seven daughters – old-Southern-colonel stuff – Lionel Barrymore could play it – we open on a room that looks like a million dollars – Barrymore crosses and pulls the bell rope. What happens?' 'Nothing,' said Tallman. 'You're crazy!' bellowed the little man. 'Part of the wall falls in! Out flies a crow – in walks a goat, maybe – the place has gone to seed, see? It's just a hulk of its former self, it's a shallows!' He turned and walked out of the room. It took him quite a while.

When he came back, he was carrying a bottle of brandy and two huge brandy glasses. He poured a great deal of brandy into each glass and handed one to Tallman. 'You and Mitnik!' he said, scornfully. 'Pulling walls out of Southern mansions. Crows you give me, goats you give me! What the hell kind of effect is that?' 'I could have a bad idea,' said Tallman, raising his glass. 'Here's to Moonbaum. May he maul things over in his mind all night and never get any spontanuity into 'em.' 'I drink nothing to Moonbaum,' said the little man. 'I hate Moonbaum. You know where they catch that crook – that guy has a little finger off one hand and wears a glove to cover it up? What does Moonbaum want? Moonbaum wants the little finger to *flap*! What do I want? I want it stuffed. What do I want it stuffed with? Sand. Why?' 'I know,' said Tallman. 'So that when he closes his hand over the head of his cane, the little finger sticks out stiffly, giving him away.' The little man seemed to leap into the air; his brandy splashed out of his glass. 'Suitcase!' he screamed. 'Not cane! Suitcase! He grabs hold of a suitcase!' Tallman didn't say anything, he closed his eyes and sipped his brandy, it was wonderful brandy. He looked up presently to find his host staring at him with a resigned expression in his eyes. 'All right, then, suitcase,' the little man said. 'Have it suitcase. We won't fight about details. I'm trying to tell you my story. I don't tell my stories to everybody.' 'Richard Harding Davis stole that finger gag – used it in *Gallegher*,' said Tallman. 'You could sue him.' The little man walked over to his chair and flopped into it. 'He's beneath me,' he said. 'He's beneath me like the dirt. I ignore him.'

Tallman finished his brandy slowly. His host's chin sank upon his chest; his heavy eyelids began to close. Tallman waited several minutes and then tiptoed over to the marble stairs. He took off his shoes and walked up the stairs, carefully. He had the heavy door open when the little man shouted at him. 'Birds of a feather, all of you!' he shouted. 'You can tell Moonbaum I said so! Shooting guys out of tapestries!' 'I'll tell him,' said Tallman. 'Good night. The brandy was wonderful.' The little man was not listening. He was pacing the floor again, gesturing with an empty brandy glass in one hand and the unlighted cigar in the other. Tallman stepped out into the cool air of the courtyard and put on one shoe and laced it. The heavy door swung shut behind him with a terrific crash. He picked up the other shoe and ran wildly toward the trees and the oddly shaped plants. It was daylight now. He could see where he was going.

The Macbeth Murder Mystery

'It was a stupid mistake to make,' said the American woman I had met at my hotel in the English lake country, 'but it was on the counter with the other Penguin books – the little sixpenny ones, you know, with the paper covers – and I supposed of course it was a detective story. All the others were detective stories. I'd read all the others, so I bought this one without really looking at it carefully. You can imagine how mad I was when I found it was Shakespeare.' I murmured something sympathetically. 'I don't see why the Penguin-books people had to get out Shakespeare plays in the same size and everything as the detective stories,' went on my companion. 'I think they have different-coloured jackets,' I said. 'Well, I didn't notice that,' she said. 'Anyway, I got real comfy in bed that night and all ready to read a good mystery story and here I had *The Tragedy of Macbeth* – a book for high-school students. Like *Ivanhoe*,' 'Or *Lorna Doone*,' I said. 'Exactly,' said the American lady. 'And I was just crazy for a good Agatha Christie, or something. Hercule Poirot is my favourite detective.' 'Is he the rabbity one?' I asked. 'Oh, no,' said my crime-fiction expert. 'He's the Belgian one. You're thinking of Mr Pinkerton, the one that helps Inspector Bull. He's good, too.'

Over her second cup of tea my companion began to tell the plot of a detective story that had fooled her completely – it seems it was the old family doctor all the time. But I cut in on her. 'Tell me,' I said. 'Did you read *Macbeth*?' 'I *had* to read it,' she said. 'There wasn't a scrap of anything else to read in the whole room.' 'Did you like it?' I asked. 'No, I did not,' she said decisively. 'In the first place, I don't think for a moment that Macbeth did it.' I looked at her blankly. 'Did what?' I asked. 'I don't think for a moment that he killed the King,' she said. 'I don't think the Macbeth woman was mixed up in it, either. You suspect them the most, of course, but those are the ones that are never guilty – or shouldn't be, anyway.' 'I'm afraid,' I began, 'that I – ' 'But don't you see?' said the American lady. 'It would spoil everything if you could figure out right away who did it. Shakespeare was too smart for that. I've read that people never *have* figured out *Hamlet*, so it isn't likely Shakespeare would have made *Macbeth* as simple as it seems.' I thought this over while I filled my pipe. 'Who do you suspect?' I asked, suddenly. 'Macduff,' she said, promptly. 'Good God!' I whispered, softly.

'Oh Macduff did it, all right,' said the murder specialist. 'Hercule Poirot would have got him easily.' 'How did you figure it out?' I demanded. 'Well,' she said, 'I didn't right away. At first I suspected Banquo. And then, of course, he was the second person killed. That was good right in there, that part. The person you suspect of the first murder should always be the second victim.' 'Is that so?' I murmured. 'Oh, yes,' said my informant. 'They have to keep surprising you. Well, after the second murder I didn't know *who* the killer was for a while.' 'How about Malcolm and Donalbain, the King's sons?' I asked. 'As I remember it, they fled right after the first murder. That looks suspicious.' 'Too suspicious,' said the American lady. 'Much too suspicious. When they flee, they're never guilty. You can count on that.' 'I believe,' I said, 'I'll have a brandy,' and I summoned the waiter. My companion leaned toward me, her eyes bright, her teacup quivering. 'Do you know who discovered Duncan's body?' she demanded. I said I was sorry, but I had forgotten. 'Macduff discovers it,' she said, slipping into the historical present. 'Then he comes running downstairs and shouts, "Confusion has broke open the Lord's anointed temple" and "Sacrilegious murder has made his masterpiece" and on and on like that.' The good lady tapped me on the knee. 'All that stuff was rehearsed,' she said. 'You wouldn't say a lot of stuff like that, offhand, would you – if you had found a body?' She fixed me with a glittering eye. 'I – ' I began. 'You're right!' she said. 'You wouldn't! Unless you had practiced it in advance. "My God, there's a body in here!" is what an innocent man would say.' She sat back with a confident glare.

I thought for a while. 'But what do you make of the Third Murderer?' I asked. 'You know, the Third Murderer has puzzled *Macbeth* scholars for three hundred years.' 'That's because they never thought of Macduff,' said the American lady. 'It was Macduff, I'm certain. You couldn't have one of the victims murdered by two ordinary thugs – the murderer always has to be somebody important.' 'But what about the banquet scene?' I asked, after a moment. 'How do you account for Macbeth's guilty actions there, when Banquo's ghost came in and sat in his chair?' The lady leaned forward and tapped me on the knee again. 'There wasn't any ghost,' she said. 'A big, strong man like that doesn't go around seeing ghosts – especially in a brightly lighted banquet hall with dozens of people around. Macbeth was *shielding somebody*!' 'Who was he shielding?' I asked. 'Mrs Macbeth, of course,' she said. 'He thought she did it and he was going to take the rap himself. The husband always does that when the wife is suspected.' 'But what,' I demanded, 'about the sleepwalking scene, then?' 'The same thing, only the other way around,' said my companion. 'That time *she* was shielding *him*. She wasn't asleep at all. Do you remember where it says, "Enter Lady Macbeth with a taper"?' 'Yes,' I said. 'Well, people who walk in their sleep *never carry lights*!' said my fellow-traveller. 'They have a second sight. Did you ever hear of a sleepwalker carrying a light?' 'No,' I said, 'I never did.' 'Well, then, she wasn't asleep. She was acting guilty to shield Macbeth.' 'I think,' I said, 'I'll have another brandy,' and I called the waiter. When he brought it, I drank it rapidly and rose to go. 'I believe,' I said, 'that you have got hold of something. Would you lend me that *Macbeth*? I'd like to look it over tonight. I don't feel, somehow, as if I'd ever really read it.' 'I'll get it for you,' she said. 'But you'll find that I am right.'

I read the play over carefully that night, and the next morning, after breakfast, I sought out the American woman. She was on the putting green, and I came up behind her silently and took her arm. She gave an exclamation. 'Could I see you alone?' I asked, in a low voice. She nodded cautiously and followed me to a secluded spot. 'You've found out something?' she breathed. 'I've found out,' I said, triumphantly, 'the name of the murderer!' 'You mean it wasn't Macduff?' she said. 'Macduff is as innocent of those murders,' I said, 'as Macbeth and the Macbeth woman.' I opened the copy of the play, which I had with me, and turned to Act II, Scene 2. 'Here,' I said, 'you will see where Lady Macbeth says, "I laid their daggers ready. He could not miss 'em. Had he not resembled my father as he slept, I had done it." Do you see?' 'No,' said the American woman, bluntly, 'I don't.' 'But it's simple!' I exclaimed. 'I wonder I didn't see it years ago. The reason Duncan resembled Lady Macbeth's father as he slept is that *it actually was her father*!' 'Good God!' breathed my companion, softly. 'Lady Macbeth's father killed the King,' I said, 'and, hearing someone coming, thrust the body under the bed and crawled into the bed himself.' 'But,' said the lady, 'you can't have a murderer who only appears in the story once. You can't have that.' 'I know that,' I said, and I turned to Act II, Scene 4. 'It says here, "Enter Ross with an old Man." Now, that old man is never identified and it is my contention he was old Mr Macbeth, whose ambition it was to make his daughter Queen. There you have your motive.' 'But even then,' cried the American lady, 'he's still a minor character!' 'Not,' I said, gleefully, 'when you realize that he was also *one of the weird sisters in disguise*!' 'You mean one of the three witches?' 'Precisely,' I said. 'Listen to this speech of the old man's. "On Tuesday last, a falcon towering in her pride of place, was by a mousing owl hawk'd at and kill'd." Who does that sound like?' 'It sounds like the way the three witches talk,' said my companion, reluctantly. 'Precisely!' I said again. 'Well,' said the American woman, 'maybe you're right, but – ' 'I'm sure I am,' I said. 'And do you know what I'm going to do now?' 'No,' she said. 'What?' 'Buy a copy of *Hamlet*,' I said, 'and solve *that*!' My companion's eye brightened. 'Then,' she said, 'you don't think Hamlet did it?' 'I am,' I said, 'absolutely positive he didn't.' 'But who,' she demanded, 'do you suspect?' I looked at her cryptically. 'Everybody,' I said, and disappeared into a small grove of trees as silently as I had come.

A Ride with Olympy

Olympy Sementzoff called me '*Monsieur*' because I was the master of the Villa Tamisier and he was the gardener, the Russian husband of the French caretaker, Maria. I called him '*Monsieur*', too, because I could never learn to call any man Olympy and because there was a wistful air of *ancien régime* about him. He drank Bénédictine with me and smoked my cigarettes; he also as you will see, drove my car. We conversed in French, a language alien to both of us, but more alien to me than to him. He said '*gauche*' for both 'right' and 'left' when he was upset, but when I was upset I was capable of flights that put the French people on their guard, wide-eyed and wary. Once, for instance, when I cut my wrist on a piece of glass I ran into the lobby of a hotel shouting in French, 'I am sick with a knife!' Olympy would have known what to say (except that it would have been his left wrist in any case) but he wouldn't have shouted: his words ran softly together and sounded something like the burbling of water over stones. Often I did not know what he was talking about; rarely did he know what I was talking about. There was a misty, far-away quality about this relationship, in French, of Russia and Ohio. The fact that the accident Olympy and I were involved in fell short of catastrophe was, in view of everything, something of a miracle.

Olympy and Maria 'came with' the villa my wife and I rented on Cap d'Antibes. Maria was a deep-bosomed, large-waisted woman, as persistently pleasant as Riviera weather in a good season; no mistral ever blew in the even climate of her temperament. She must have been more than forty-five but she was as strong as a root; once when I had trouble getting a tough cork out of a wine bottle she took hold and whisked it out as if it had been a maidenhair fern. On Sundays her son came over from the barracks in Antibes and we all had a glass of white Bordeaux together, sometimes the Sementzoffs' wine, sometimes our own. Her son was eighteen and a member of the Sixth Regiment of Chasseurs Alpins, a tall, sombre boy, handsome in his uniform and cape. He was an *enfant du premier lit,* as the French say. Maria made her first bed with a sergeant of the army who was *cordonnier* for his regiment during the war and seemed somehow to have laid by quite a little money. After the war the sergeant-shoemaker resigned from the army, put his money in investments of some profoundly mysterious nature in Indo-China, and lost it all. '*Il est mort,*' Maria told us, '*de chagrin.*' Grief over his ill-fortune brought on a decline; the *chagrin,* Maria said, finally reached his brain, and he died at the age of thirty-eight. Maria had to sell their house to pay the taxes, and go to work.

Olympy Sementzoff, Maria's second husband, was shy, not very tall, and wore a beard; in his working clothes you didn't notice much more than that. When he was dressed for Sunday – he wore a fine double-breasted jacket – you observed that his mouth was sensitive, his eyes attractively sad, and that he wore his shyness with a certain air. He worked in a boat factory over near Cannes – Maria said that he was a *spécialiste de bateaux*; odd jobs about the villa grounds he did on his off days. It was scarcely light when he got up in the morning, for he had to be at work at seven; it was almost dark when he got home. He was paid an incredibly small amount for what he did at the factory and a handful of sous each month for what he did about the grounds. When I gave him a hundred francs for some work he had done for me in the house – he could repair anything from a drain to a watch – he said, '*Oh, monsieur, c'est trop!*' '*Mais non, monsieur,*' said I. '*Ce n'est pas beaucoup.*' He took it finally, after an exchange of bows and compliments.

The elderly wife of the Frenchman from whom we rented the villa told us, in a dark whisper, that Olympy was a White Russian and that there was perhaps a *petit mystère* about him, but we figured this as her own fanciful bourgeois alarm. Maria did not make a mystery out of her husband. There was the Revolution, most of Olympy's brothers and sisters were killed – one knew how that was – and he escaped. He was, of course, an exile and must not go back. If she knew just who he was in Russia and what he had done, she didn't make it very clear. He was in Russia and he escaped; she had married him thirteen years before; *et puis, voilà!* It would have been nice to believe that there was the blood of the Czars in

Olympy, but if there was anything to the ancient legend that all the stray members of the Imperial House took easily and naturally to driving a taxi, that let Olympy out. He was not a born chauffeur, as I found out the day I came back from our automobile ride on foot and – unhappily for Maria – alone.

Olympy Sementzoff rose to and from his work in one of those bastard agglomerations of wheels, motor, and superstructure that one saw only in France. It looked at first glance like the cockpit of a cracked-up plane. Then you saw that there were two wheels in front and a single wheel in back. Except for the engine – which Maria said was a 'Morgan *moteur*' – and the wheels and tyres, it was handmade. Olympy's boss at the boat factory had made most of it, but Olympy himself had put on the *ailes*, or fenders, which were made of some kind of wood. The strange canopy that served as a top was Maria's proud handiwork; it seemed to have been made of canvas and kitchen aprons. The thing had a right-hand drive. When the *conducteur* was in his seat he was very low to the ground: you had to bend down to talk to him. There was a small space beside the driver in which another person could sit, or crouch. The whole affair was not much larger than an overturned cabinet victrola. It got bouncingly under way with all the racket of a dog fight and in full swing was capable of perhaps thirty miles an hour. The contraption had cost Olympy three thousand francs, or about a hundred dollars. He had driven it for three years and was hand in glove with its mysterious mechanism. The gadgets on the dash and on the floorboard, which he pulled or pushed to make the thing go, seemed to include fire tongs, spoons, and doorknobs. Maria miraculously managed to squeeze into the seat beside the driver in an emergency, but I could understand why she didn't want to drive to the Nice Carnival in the 'Morgan'. It was because she didn't that I suggested Olympy should take her over one day in my Ford sedan. Maria had given us to understand that her *mari* could drive any car – he could be a chauffeur if he wanted to, a *bon* chauffeur. All I would have to do, *voyez-vous*, was to take Olympy for a turn around the Cap so that he could get the hang of the big car. Thus it was that one day after lunch we set off.

Half a mile out of Antibes on the shore road, I stopped the car and changed places with Olympy, letting the engine run. Leaning forward, he took a tense grip on a steering wheel much larger than he was used to and too far away from him. I could see that he was nervous. He put his foot on the clutch, tentatively, and said, '*Embrayage?*' He had me there. My knowledge of French automotive terms is inadequate and volatile. I was forced to say I didn't know. I couldn't remember the word for clutch in any of the three languages, French, Italian and German, in which it was given in my *Motorist's Guide* (which was back at the villa). Somehow '*embrayage*' didn't sound right for clutch (it is, though). I knew it wouldn't do any good for an American writer to explain in French to a Russian boat specialist the purpose that particular pedal served; furthermore, I didn't really know. I compromised by putting my left foot on the brake. '*Frein,*' I said. '*Ah,*' said Olympy, unhappily. This method of indicating what something might be by demonstrating what it wasn't had a disturbing effect. I shifted my foot to the accelerator – or rather pointed my toe at it – and suddenly the word for that, even the French for gasoline, left me. I was growing a little nervous myself. '*Benzina,*' I said, in Italian finally. '*Ah?*' said Olympy. Whereas we had been one remove from reality to begin with, we were now two, or perhaps three, removes. A polyglot approach to the fine precision of a gas engine is roundabout and dangerous. We both lost a little confidence in each other. I suppose we should have given up right then, but we didn't.

Olympy decided the extra pedal was the *embrayage*, shifted into low from neutral, and the next thing I knew we were making a series of short forward bounds like a rabbit leaping out of a wheat field to see where he is. This form of locomotion takes a lot out of a man and car. The engine complained in loud, rhythmic whines. And then Olympy somehow got his left foot on the starter and there was a familiar undertone of protest; this set his right foot to palpitating on the accelerator and the rabbit-jumps increased in scope. Abandoning my search for the word for starter, I grabbed his left knee and shouted '*Ça commence!*' Just what was commencing Olympy naturally couldn't figure – probably some habitual and ominous idiosyncrasy of the machinery. He gave me a quick, pale look. I shut off the ignition, and we discussed the starter situation, breathing a little heavily. He understood what it was finally, and presently we were lurching ahead again, Olympy holding her in low gear, like a wrestler in a clinch, afraid to risk shifting into second. He tried it at last and with a jamming jolt and a roar we went into reverse: the car writhed like a tortured leopard and the engine quit.

I was puzzled and scared, and so was Olympy. Only a foolish pride in masculine fortitude kept us going. I showed him the little jog to the right you have to make to shift into second and he started the engine and we were off again, jolting and lurching. He made the shift, finally, with a noise like lightning striking a foundry – and veered swoopingly to the right. We barely missed a series of staunch granite blocks, set in concrete, that mark ditches and soft shoulders. We whisked past a pole. The leaves of a vine hanging on a wall slapped at me through the window. My voice left me. I was fascinated and paralyzed by the swift passes disaster was making at my head. At length I was able to grope blindly toward the ignition switch, but got my wrist on the klaxon button. When I jerked my arm away, Olympy began obediently sounding the horn. We were riding on the edge of a ditch. I managed somehow to shut off the ignition and we rolled to a stop. Olympy, unused to a left-hand drive, had forgotten there was a large portion of the car to his right, with me in it. I told him, '*A gauche, à gauche, toujours à gauche!*' '*Ah,*' said Olympy, but there was no comprehension in him. I could see he didn't know we had been up against the vines of villa walls: intent on the dark problem of gear shifting, he had been oblivious of where the car and I had been. There was a glint in his eye now. He was determined to get the thing into high on his next attempt; we had come about half a mile in the lower gears.

The road curved downhill as it passed Eden Roc and it was here that an elderly English couple, unaware of the fact that hell was loose on the highway, were walking. Olympy was in second again, leaning forward like a racing bicycle rider. I shouted at him to look out, he said '*Oui*' – and we grazed the old man and his wife. I glanced back in horror: they were staring at us, mouths and eyes wide, unable to move or make a sound. Olympy raced on to a new peril: a descending hairpin curve, which he negotiated in some far-fetched manner, with me hanging on to the emergency brake. The road straightened out, I let go the brake, and Olympy slammed into high with the desperate gesture of a man trying to clap his hat over a poised butterfly. We began to whiz: Olympy hadn't counted on a fast pickup. He whirled around a car in front of us with a foot to spare. '*Lentement!*' I shouted, and then '*Gauche!*' as I began to get again the whimper of poles and walls in my ears. '*Ça va mieux, maintenant,*' said Olympy, quietly. A wild thought ran through my head that maybe this was the way they used to drive in Russia in the old days.

Ahead of us now was one of the most treacherous curves on the Cap. The road narrowed and bent, like a croquet wicket, around a high stone wall that shut off your view of what was coming. What was coming was usually on the wrong side of the road, so it wouldn't do to shout '*Gauche!*' now. We made the turn all right. There was a car coming, but it was well over on its own side. Olympy apparently didn't think so. He whirled the wheel to the right, didn't take up the play fast enough in whirling it back, and there was a tremendous banging crash, like a bronze monument falling. I had a glimpse of Olympy's right hand waving around like the hand of a man hunting for something under a table. I didn't know what his feet were doing. We were still moving, heavily, with a ripping noise and a loud roar. '*Poussez le phare!*' I shouted, which means 'push the headlight!' '*Ah-h-h-h,*' said Olympy. I shut off the ignition and pulled on the hand brake, but we had already stopped. We got out and looked at the pole we had sideswiped and at the car. The right front fender was crumpled and torn and the right back one banged up, but nothing else had been hurt. Olympy's face was so stricken when he looked at me that I felt I had to cheer him up. '*Il fait beau,*' I announced, which is to say that the weather is fine. It was all I could think of.

I started for a garage that Olympy knew about. At the first street we came to he said '*Gauche*' and I turned left. '*Ah, non,*' said Olympy. '*Gauche,*' and he pointed the other way. 'You mean *droit*?' I asked, just that way. '*Ah!*' said Olympy. '*C'est bien ça!*' It was as if he had thought of something he hadn't been able to remember for days. That explained a great deal.

I left Olympy and the car at the garage; he said he would walk back. One of the garage men drove me into Juan-les-Pins and I walked home from there – and into a look of wild dismay in

Maria's eyes. I hadn't thought about that: she had seen us drive away together and here I was, alone. '*Où est votre mari?*' I asked her, hurriedly. It was something of a failure as a reassuring beginning. I had taken the question out of her own mouth, so I answered it. 'He has gone for a walk,' I told her. Then I tried to say that her husband was *bon*, but I pronounced it *beau*, so that what I actually said was that her husband was handsome. She must have figured that he was not only dead but laid out. There was a *mauvais quart d'heure* for both of us before the drooping figure of Olympy finally appeared. He explained sadly to Maria that the mechanism of the Ford is strange and curious compared to the mechanism of the Morgan. I agreed with him. Of course, he protested, he would pay for the repairs to the car, but Maria and I both put down that suggestion. Maria's idea of my work was that I was paid by the City of New York and enjoyed a tremendous allowance. Olympy got forty francs a day at the boat factory.

That night, at dinner, Maria told us that her *mari* was pacing up and down in their little bedroom at the rear of the house. He was in a state. I didn't want an attack of *chagrin* to come on him as it had on the *cordonnier* and perhaps reach his brain. When Maria was ready to go we gave her a handful of cigarettes for Olympy and a glass of Bénédictine. The next day, at dawn, I hear the familiar *tintamarre* and *hurlement* and *brouhaha* of Olympy's wonderful contraption getting under way once more. He was off to the boat factory and his forty francs a day, his dollar and thirty cents. It would have cost him two weeks' salary to pay for the fenders, but he would have managed it somehow. When I went down to breakfast, Maria came in from the kitchen with a large volume, well fingered and full of loose pages, which she handed to me. It was called *Le Musée d'Art* and subtitled *Galerie des Chefs-d'œuvre et Précis de l'Histoire de l'Art au XIXe Siècle, en France et à l'Étranger* (*1000 gravures, 58 planches hors texte*). A present to *Monsieur* from Olympy Sementzoff, with his compliments. The incident of the automobile was thus properly rounded off with an exchange of presents: cigarettes, Bénédictine, and *Le Musée d'Art*. It seemed to me the way such things should always end, but perhaps Olympy and I were ahead of our day – or behind it.

3

From *Let Your Mind Alone*

Destructive Forces in Life

The mental efficiency books go into elaborate detail about how to attain Masterful Adjustment, as one of them calls it, but it seems to me the problems they set up, and knock down, are in the main unimaginative and pedestrian: the little fusses at the breakfast table, the routine troubles at the office, the familiar anxieties over money and health – the welter of workaday annoyances which all of us meet with and usually conquer without extravagant wear and tear. Let us examine, as a typical instance, a brief case history presented by the learned Mr David Seabury, author of *What Makes Us Seem So Queer, Unmasking Our Minds, Keep Your Wits, Growing Into Life* and *How to Worry Successfully*. I select it at random. 'Frank Fulsome,' writes Mr Seabury, 'flung down the book with disgust and growled an insult at his wife. That little lady put her hands to her face and fled from the room. She was sure Frank must hate her to speak so cruelly. Had she known it, he was not really speaking to her at all. The occasion merely gave vent to a pent-up desire to "punch his fool boss in the jaw".' This is, I believe, a characteristic Seabury situation. Many of the women in his treatises remind you of nobody so much as Ben Bolt's Alice, who 'wept with delight when you gave her a smile, and trembled with fear at your frown'. The little ladies most of us know would, instead of putting their hands to their faces and fleeing from the room, come right back at Frank Fulsome. Frank would perhaps be lucky if he didn't get a punch in the jaw himself. In any case, the situation would be cleared up in approximately three minutes. This 'had she known' business is not as common among wives today as Mr Seabury seems to think it is. The Latent Content (as the psychologists call it) of a husband's mind is usually as clear to the wife as the Manifest Content, frequently much clearer.

I could cite a dozen major handicaps to Masterful Adjustmen, which the thought technicians never touch upon, a dozen situations not so easy of analysis and solution as most of theirs. I will, however, content myself with one. Let us consider the case of a man of my acquaintance who had accomplished Discipline of Mind, overcome the Will to Fail, mastered the Technique of Living – had, in a word, practically attained Masterful Adjustment – when he was called on the phone one afternoon about five o'clock by a man named Bert Scursey. The other man, whom I shall call Harry Conner, did not answer the phone, however; his wife answered it. As Scursey told me the story later, he had no intention when he dialled the Conners' apartment at the Hotel Graydon of doing more than talk with Harry. But, for some strange reason, when Louise Conner answered, Bert Scursey found himself pretending to be, and imitating the voice of, a coloured woman. This Scursey is by way of being an excellent mimic, and a coloured woman is one of the best things he does.

'Hello,' said Mrs Conner. In a plaintive voice, Scursey said, 'Is dis heah Miz Commah?' 'Yes, this is Mrs Conner,' said Louise. 'Who is speaking?' 'Dis heah's Edith Rummum,' said Scursey. 'Ah used wuck for yo frens was nex doah yo place a Sou Norwuck.' Naturally, Mrs Conner did not follow this, and demanded rather sharply to know who was calling and what she wanted. Scursey, his voice soft with feigned tears, finally got it over to his friend's wife that he was one Edith Rummum, a coloured maid who had once worked for some friends of the Conners' in South Norwalk, where they had lived some years before. 'What is it you want, Edith?' asked Mrs Conner, who was completely taken in by the impostor (she could not catch the name of the South Norwalk friends, but let that go). Scursey – or Edith, rather – explained in a pitiable, hesitant way that she was without work or money and that she didn't know what she was going to do; Rummum, she said, was in the gaolhouse because of a cutting scrape on a roller-coaster. Now, Louise Conner happened to be a most kind-hearted person, as Scursey well knew, so she said that she could perhaps find some laundry work for Edith to do. 'Yessum,' said Edith. 'Ah laundas.' At this point, Harry Conner's voice, raised in the room behind his wife, came clearly to Scursey, saying, 'Now, for God's sake, Louise, don't go giving our clothes out to somebody you never saw or heard of in your life.' This interjection of Conner's was in firm keeping with a theory of logical behaviour which he had got out of the Mind and Personality books. There was no Will to Weakness here, no Desire to Have His Shirts Ruined, no False Sympathy for the Coloured Woman Who Has Not Organized Her Life.

But Mrs Conner who often did not listen to Mr Conner, in spite of his superior mental discipline, prevailed.* 'Where are you now, Edith?' she asked. This disconcerted Scursey for a moment, but he finally said, 'Ah's jes rounda corna, Miz Commah.' 'Well, you come over to the Hotel Graydon,' said Mrs Conner. 'We're in Apartment 7-A on the seventh floor.' 'Yessm,' said Edith. Mrs Conner hung up and so did Scursey. He was now, he realized, in something of a predicament. Since he did not possess a streamlined mind, as Dr Mursell has called it, and had definitely a Will to Confuse, he did not perceive that his little joke had gone far enough. He wanted to go on with it, which is a characteristic of wool-gatherers, pranksters, wags, wishfulfillers, and escapists generally. He enjoyed fantasy as much as reality, probably even more, which is a sure symptom of Regression, Digression and Analogical Redintegration. What he finally did, therefore, was to call back the Conners and get Mrs Conner on the phone again. 'Jeez, Miz Commah,' he said, with a hint of panic in his voice, 'Ah cain' fine yo apottoman!' 'Where are you, Edith?' she asked. 'Lawd, Ah doan know,' said Edith. 'Ah's on *some* floah in de Hotel Graydon.' 'Well, listen, Edith, you took the elevator, didn't you?' 'Das whut Ah took,' said Edith, uncertainly. 'Well, you go back to the elevator and tell the boy you want off at the seventh floor. I'll meet you at the elevator.' 'Yessm,' said Edith, with even more uncertainty. At this point, Conner's loud voice, speaking to his wife, was again heard by Scursey. 'Where in the hell is she calling from?' demanded Conner, who had developed Logical Reasoning. 'She must have wandered into somebody else's apartment if she is calling you from this building, for God's sake!' Whereupon, having no desire to explain where Edith was calling from, Scursey hung up.

After an instant of thought, or rather Disintegrated Phantasmagoria, Scursey rang the Conners again. He wanted to prevent Louise from going out to the elevator and checking up with the

* This sometimes happens even when the husband is mentally disciplined and the wife is not.

operator. This time, as Scursey had hoped, Harry Conner answered, having told his wife that he would handle this situation. 'Hello!' shouted Conner, irritably. 'Who is this?' Scursey now abandoned the role of Edith and assumed a sharp, fussy, masculine tone. 'Mr Conner,' he said, crisply, 'this is the office. I am afraid we shall have to ask you to remove this coloured person from the building. She is blundering into other people's apartments, using their phones. We cannot have that sort of thing, you know, at the Graydon.' The man's words and his tone infuriated Conner. 'There are a lot of sort of things I'd like to see you not have at the Graydon!' he shouted. 'Well, please come down to the lobby and do something about this situation,' said the man, nastily. 'You're damned right I'll come down!' howled Conner. He banged down the receiver.

Bert Scursey sat in a chair and gloated over the involved state of affairs which he had created. He decided to go over to the Graydon, which was just up the street from his own apartment, and see what was happening. It promised to have all the confusion which his disorderly mind so deplorably enjoyed. And it did have. He found Conner in a tremendous rage in the lobby, accusing an astonished assistant manager of having insulted him. Several persons in the lobby watched the curious scene. 'But, Mr Conner,' said the assistant manager, a Mr Bent, 'I have no idea what you are talking about.' 'If you listen, you'll find out!' bawled Harry Conner. 'In the first place, this coloured woman's coming to the hotel was no idea of mine. I've never seen her in my life and I don't want to see her! I want to go to my *grave* without seeing her!' He had forgotten what the Mind and Personality books had taught him: never raise your voice in anger, always stick to the point. Naturally, Mr Bent could only believe that his guest had gone out of his mind. He decided to humour him. 'Where is this – ah – coloured woman, Mr Conner?' he asked, warily. He was somewhat pale and was fiddling with a bit of paper. A dabbler in psychology books himself, he knew that coloured women are often Sex Degradation symbols, and he wondered if Conner had not fallen out of love with his wife without realizing it. (This theory, I believe, Mr Bent has clung to ever since, although the Conners are one of the happiest couples in the country.) 'I don't know where she is!' cried Conner. 'She's up on some other floor phoning my wife! *You* seemed to know all about it! I had nothing to do with it! I opposed it from the start! But I want no insults from you no matter *who* opposed it!' 'Certainly not, certainly not,' said Mr Bent, backing slightly away. He began to wonder what he was going to do with this maniac.

At this juncture Scursey, who had been enjoying the scene at a safe distance, approached Conner and took him by the arm 'What's the matter, old boy?' he asked. 'H'lo, Bert,' said Conner, sullenly. And then, his eyes narrowing, he began to examine the look on Scursey's face. Scursey is not good at dead-panning; he is only good on the phone. There was a guilty grin on his face. 'You –' said Conner, bitterly, remembering Scursey's pranks of mimicry, and he turned on his heel, walked to the elevator, and, when Scursey tried to get in too, shoved him back into the lobby. That was the end of the friendship between the Conners and Bert Scursey. It was more than that. It was the end of Harry Conner's stay at the Graydon. It was, in fact, the end of his stay in New York City. He and Louise live in Oregon now, where Conner accepted a less important position than he had held in New York because the episode of Edith had turned him against Scursey, Mr Bent, the Graydon, and the whole metropolitan area.

Anybody can handle the Frank Fulsomes of the world, but is there anything to be done about the Bert Scurseys? Can we so streamline our minds that the antics of the Scurseys roll off them like water off a duck's back? I don't think so. I believe the authors of the inspirational books don't think so, either, but are afraid to attack the subject. I imagine they have been hoping nobody would bring it up. Hardly anybody goes through life without encountering his Bert Scursey and having his life – and his mind – accordingly modified. I have known a dozen Bert Scurseys. I have often wondered what happened to some of their victims. There was, for example, the man who rang up a waggish friend of mine by mistake, having got a wrong number. 'Is this the Shu-Rite Shoestore?' the caller asked, querulously. 'Shu-Rite Shoestore, good morning!' said my friend, brightly. 'Well,' said the other, 'I just called up to say that the shoes I bought there a week ago are shoddy. They're made, by God, of cardboard. I'm going to bring them in and show you. I want satisfaction!' 'And you shall have it!' said my friend. 'Our shoes are, as you say, shoddy. There have been many complaints, many complaints. Our shoes, I am afraid, simply go to pieces on the foot. We shall, of course, refund your money.' I know another man who was always being routed out of bed by people calling a certain rail-road which had a similar phone number. 'When can I get a train to Buffalo?' a sour-voiced woman demanded one morning about seven o'clock. 'Not till two a.m. tomorrow, Madam,' said this man. 'But that's ridiculous!' cried the woman, 'I know,' said the man, 'and we realize that. Hence we include, in the regular fare, a taxi which will call for you in plenty of time to make the train. Where do you live?' The lady, slightly mollified, told him an address in the Sixties. 'We'll have a cab there at one-thirty, Madam,' he said. 'The driver will handle your baggage.' 'Now I can count on that?' she said. 'Certainly, Madam,' he told her. 'One-thirty, sharp.'

Just what changes were brought about in that woman's character by that call, I don't know. But the thing might have altered the colour and direction of her life, the pattern of her mind, the whole fabric of her nature. Thus we see that a person might build up a streamlined mind, a mind awakened to a new life, a new discipline, only to have the whole works shot to pieces by so minor and unpredictable a thing as a wrong telephone number. On the other hand, the undisciplined mind would never have the fortitude to consider a trip to Buffalo at two in the morning, nor would it have the determination to seek redress from a shoestore which had sold it a faulty pair of shoes. Hence the undisciplined mind runs far less chance of having its purpose thwarted, its plans distorted, its whole scheme and system wrenched out of line. The undisciplined mind, in short, is far better adapted to the confused world in which we live today than the streamlined mind. This is, I am afraid, no place for the streamlined mind.

With the disappearance of the gas mantle and the advent of the short circuit, man's tranquillity began to be threatened by everything he put his hand on. Many people believe that it was a sad day indeed when Benjamin Franklin tied that key to a kite string and flew the kite in a thunderstorm; other people believed that if it hadn't been Franklin, it would have been someone else. As, of course, it was in the case of the harnessing of steam and the invention of the gas engine. At any rate, it has come about that so-called civilized man finds himself today surrounded by the myriad mechanical devices of a technological world. Writers of books on how to control your nerves, how to conquer fear, how to cultivate calm, how to be happy in spite of everything, are of several minds as regards the relation of man and the machine. Some of them are prone to believe that the mind and body, if properly disciplined, can get the upper hand of this mechanized existence. Others merely ignore the situation and go on to the profitable writing of more facile chapters of inspiration. Still others attribute the whole menace of the machine to sex, and so confuse the average reader that he cannot always be certain whether he has been knocked down by an automobile or is merely in love.

Dr Bisch, the Be-Glad-You're-Neurotic man, has a remarkable chapter which deals, in part, with man, sex, and the machine. He examines the case of three hypothetical men who start across a street on a red light and get in the way of an oncoming automobile. A dodges successfully; B stands still, 'accepting the situation with calm and resignation', thus becoming one of my favourite heroes in modern belles-lettres; and C hesitates, wavers, jumps backward and forward, and finally runs head on into the car. To lead you through Dr Bisch's complete analysis of what was wrong with B and C would occupy your whole day. He mentions what the McDougallians would say ('Instinct!'), what the Freudians would retort ('Complexes!'), and what the behaviourists would shout ('Conditioned reflexes!'). He also brings in what the physiologists would say – deficient thyroid, hypoadrenal functioning, and so on. The average sedentary man of our time who is at all suggestible must emerge from this chapter believing that his chances of surviving a combination of instinct, complexes, reflexes, glands, sex, and present-day traffic conditions are about equal to those of a one-legged blind man trying to get out of a labyrinth.

Let us single out what Dr Bisch thinks the Freudians would say about poor Mr C, who ran right into the car. He writes, '"Sex hunger," the Freudians would declare. "Always keyed up and irritable because of it. Undoubtedly suffers from insomnia and when he does sleep his dream life must be productive, distorted, and possibly frightening. Automobile unquestionably has sex significance for him . . . to C the car is both enticing and menacing at one and the same time. . . . A thorough analysis is indicated. . . . It might take months. But then, the man needs an analysis as much as food. He is heading for a complete nervous collapse."' It is my studied opinion, not to put too fine a point on it, that Mr C is heading for a good mangling, and that if he gets away with only a nervous collapse, it will be a miracle.

I have not always, I am sorry to say, been able to go the whole way with the Freudians, or even a very considerable distance. Even though, as Dr Bisch says, 'One must admit that the Freudians have had the best of it thus far. At least they have received the most publicity.' It is in matters like their analysis of men and machines, of Mr C and the automobile, that the Freudians and I part company. Of course, the analysis above is simply Dr Bisch's idea of what the Freudians would say, but I think he has got it down pretty well. Dr Bisch himself leans toward the Freudian analysis of Mr C, for he says in this same chapter, 'An automobile bearing down upon you may be a sex symbol at that, you know, especially if you dream it.' It is my contention, of course, that even if you dream it, it is probably not a sex symbol, but merely an automobile bearing down upon you. And if it bears down upon you in real life, I am sure it is an automobile. I have seen the same behaviour that characterized Mr C displayed by a squirrel (Mr S) that lives in the grounds of my house in the country. He is a fairly tame squirrel, happily mated and not sex-hungry, if I am any judge, but nevertheless he frequently runs out toward my automobile

104

when I start down the driveway, and then hesitates, wavers, jumps forward and backward, and occasionally would run right into the car except that he is awfully fast on his feet and that I always hurriedly put on the brakes of the 1935 V-8 Sex Symbol that I drive.

I have seen this same behaviour in the case of rabbits (notoriously uninfluenced by any sex symbols save those of other rabbits), dogs, pigeons, a doe, a young hawk (which flew at my car), a blue heron that I encountered on a country road in Vermont, and once, near Paul Smiths in the Adirondacks, a fox. They all acted exactly like Mr C. The hawk, unhappily, was killed. All the others escaped with nothing worse, I suppose, than a complete nervous collapse. Although I cannot claim to have been conversant with the private life and the secret compulsions, the psychoneuroses and the glandular activities of all these animals, it is nevertheless my confident and unswervable belief that there was nothing at all the matter with any one of them. Like Mr C, they suddenly saw a car swiftly bearing down upon them, got excited, and lost their heads. I do not believe, you see, there was anything the matter with Mr C, either. But I do believe that, after a thorough analysis lasting months, with a lot of harping on the incident of the automobile, something might very well come to be the matter with him. He might even actually get to suffering from the delusion that he believes automobiles are sex symbols.

It seems to me worthy of note that Dr Bisch, in reciting the reactions of three persons in the face of an oncoming car, selected three men. What would have happened had they been Mrs A, Mrs B, and Mrs C? You know as well as I do: all three of them would have hesitated, wavered, jumped forward and backward, and finally run head on into the car if some man hadn't grabbed them. (I used to know a motorist who, every time he approached a woman standing on a kerb preparing to cross the street, shouted, 'Hold it, stupid!') It is not too much to say that, with a car bearing down upon them, ninety-five women out of a hundred would act like Mr C – or Mr S., the squirrel, or Mr F, the fox. But it is certainly too much to say that ninety-five out of every hundred women look upon an automobile as a sex symbol. For one thing, Dr Bisch points out that the automobile serves as a sex symbol because of the 'mechanical principle involved'. But only one woman in a thousand really knows anything about the mechanical principle involved in an automobile. And yet, as I have said, ninety-five out of a hundred would hesitate, waver, and jump, just as Mr C did. I think we have the Freudians here. If we haven't proved our case with rabbits and a blue heron, we have certainly proved it with women.

To my notion, the effect of the automobile and of other mechanical contrivances on the state of our nerves, minds and spirits is a problem which the popular psychologists whom I have dealt with know very little about. The sexual explanation of the relationship of man and the machine is not good enough. To arrive at the real explanation, we have to begin very far back, as far back as Franklin and the kite, or at least as far back as a certain man and woman who appear in a book of stories written more than sixty years ago by Max Adeler. One story in this book tells about a housewife who bought a combination ironing-board and card table, which some New England genius had thought up in his spare time. The husband, coming home to find the devilish contraption in the parlour, was appalled. 'What is that thing?' he demanded. His wife explained that it was a card table, but that if you pressed a button underneath, it would become an ironing board. Whereupon she pushed the button and the table leaped a foot into the air, extended itself, and became an ironing-board. The story goes on to tell how the thing finally became so finely sensitized that it would change back and forth if you merely touched it – you didn't have to push the button. The husband stuck it in the attic (after it had leaped up and struck him a couple of times while he was playing euchre), and on windy nights it could be heard flopping and banging around, changing from a card table to an ironing board and back. The story serves as one example of our dread heritage of annoyance, shock, and terror arising out of the nature of mechanical contrivances *per se*. The mechanical principle involved in this damnable invention had, I believe, no relationship to sex whatsoever. There are certain analysts who see sex in anything, even a leaping ironing board, but I think we can ignore these scientists.

No man (to go on) who has wrestled with a self-adjusting card table can ever be quite the man he once was. If he arrives at the state where he hesitates, wavers, and jumps at every mechanical device he encounters, it is not, I submit, because he recognizes the enticements of sex in the device, but only because he recognizes the menace of the machine as such. There might very well be, in every descendant of the man we have been discussing, an inherited desire to jump at, and conquer, mechanical devices before they have a chance to turn into something twice as big and twice as menacing. It is not reasonable to expect that his children and their children will have entirely escaped the stigma of such traumata. I myself will never be the man I once was, nor will my descendants probably ever amount to much, because of a certain experience I had with an automobile.

I had gone out to the barn of my country place, a barn which was used both as a garage and a kennel, to quiet some large black poodles. It was 1 a.m. of a pitch-dark night in winter and the poodles had apparently been terrified by some kind of a prowler, a tramp, a turtle, or perhaps a fiend of some sort. Both my poodles and I myself believed, at the time, in fiends, and still do. Fiends who materialize out of nothing and nowhere, like winged pigweed or Russian thistle. I had quite a time quieting the dogs, because their panic spread to me and mine spread back to them again, in a kind of vicious circle. Finally, a hush as ominous as their uproar fell upon them, but they kept looking over their shoulders, in a kind of apprehensive way. 'There's nothing to be afraid of,' I told them as firmly as I could, and just at that moment the klaxon of my car, which was just behind me, began to shriek. Everybody has heard a klaxon on a car suddenly begin to sound; I understand it is a short-circuit that causes it. But very few people have heard one scream behind them while they were quieting six or eight alarmed poodles in the middle of the night in an old barn. I jump now whenever I hear a klaxon, even the klaxon on my own car when I push the button intentionally. The experience has left its mark. Everybody, from the day of the jumping card table to the day of the screaming klaxon, has had similar shocks. You can see the result, entirely unsuperinduced by sex, in the strained faces and muttering lips of people who pass you on the streets of great, highly mechanized cities. There goes a man who picked up one of those trick matchboxes that whir in your hands; there goes a woman who tried to change a fuse without turning off the current; and yonder toddles an ancient who cranked an old Reo with the spark advanced. Every person carries in his consciousness the old scar, or the fresh wound, of some harrowing misadventure with a contraption of some sort. I know people who would not deposit a nickel and a dime in a cigarette-vending machine and push the lever even if a diamond necklace came out. I know dozens who would not climb into an aeroplane even if it didn't move off the ground. In none of these people have I discerned what I would call a neurosis, an 'exaggerated' fear; I have discerned only a natural caution in a world made up of gadgets that whir and whine and whiz and shriek and sometimes explode.

I should like to end with the case history of a friend of mine in Ohio named Harvey Lake. When he was only nineteen, the steering bar of an old electric runabout broke off in his hand, causing the machine to carry him through a fence and into the grounds of the Columbus School for Girls. He developed a fear of automobiles, trains, and every other kind of vehicle that was not pulled by a horse. Now, the psychologists would call this a complex and represent the fear as abnormal, but I see it as a purely reasonable apprehension. If Harvey Lake had, because he was catapulted into the grounds of the Columbus School for Girls, developed a fear of girls, I would call that a complex; but I don't call his normal fear of machines a complex. Harvey Lake never in his life got into a plane (he died in a fall from a porch), but I do not regard that as neurotic, either, but only sensible.

I have, to be sure, encountered men with complexes. There was, for example, Marvin Belt. He had a complex about aeroplanes that was quite interesting. He was not afraid of machinery, or of high places, or of crashes. He was simply afraid that the pilot of any plane he got into might lose his mind. 'I imagine myself high over Montana,' he once said to me, 'in a huge, perfectly safe tri-motored plane. Several of the passengers are dozing, others are reading, but I am keeping my eyes glued on the door to the cockpit. Suddenly the pilot steps out of it, a wild light in his eyes, and in a falsetto like that of a little girl he says to me, "Conductor, will you please let me off at One-Hundred-and-Twenty-fifth Street?"' 'But,' I said to Belt, 'even if the pilot does go crazy, there is still

108

the co-pilot.' 'No, there isn't,' said Belt. 'The pilot has hit the co-pilot over the head with something and killed him.' Yes, the psychoanalysts can have Marvin Belt. But they can't have Harvey Lake, or Mr C, or Mr S, or Mr F, or, while I have my strength, me.

The Breaking Up of the Winships

The trouble that broke up the Gordon Winships seemed to me, at first, as minor a problem as frost on a window-pane. Another day, a touch of sun, and it would be gone. I was inclined to laugh it off, and, indeed, as a friend of both Gordon and Marcia, I spent a great deal of time with each of them, separately, trying to get them to laugh it off, too – with him at his club, where he sat drinking Scotch and smoking too much, and with her in their apartment, that seemed so large and lonely without Gordon and his restless moving around and his quick laughter. But it was no good; they were both adamant. Their separation has lasted now more than six months. I doubt very much that they will ever go back together again.

It all started one night at Leonardo's, after dinner, over their Bénédictine. It started innocently enough, amiably even, with laughter from both of them, laughter that froze finally as the clock ran on and their words came out sharp and flat and stinging. They had been to see *Camille*. Gordon hadn't liked it very much. Marcia had been crazy about it because she is crazy about Greta Garbo. She belongs to that considerable army of Garbo admirers whose enchantment borders almost on fanaticism and sometimes even touches the edges of frenzy. I think that, before everything happened, Gordon admired Garbo, too, but the depth of his wife's conviction that here was the greatest figure ever seen in our generation on sea or land, on screen or stage, exasperated him that night. Gordon hates (or used to) exaggeration, and he respects (or once did) detachment. It was his feeling that detachment is a necessary thread in the fabric of a woman's charm. He didn't like to see his wife get herself 'into a sweat' over anything and, that night at Leonardo's, he unfortunately used that expression and made that accusation.

Marcia responded, as I get it, by saying, a little loudly (they had gone on to Scotch and soda), that a man who had no abandon of feeling and no passion for anything was not altogether a man, and that his so-called love of detachment simply covered up a lack of critical appreciation and understanding of the arts in general. Her sentences were becoming long and wavy, and her words formal. Gordon suddenly began to pooh-pooh her; he kept saying 'Pooh!' (an annoying mannerism of his, I have always thought). He wouldn't answer her arguments or even listen to them. That, of course, infuriated her. 'Oh, pooh to you, too!' she finally more or less shouted. He snapped at her, 'Quiet, for God's sake! You're yelling like a prizefight manager!' Enraged at that, she had recourse to her eyes as weapons and looked steadily at him for a while with the expression of one who is viewing a small and horrible animal, such as a horned toad. They then sat in moody and brooding silence for a long time, without moving a muscle, at the end of which, getting a hold on herself, Marcia asked him, quietly enough, just exactly what actor on the screen or on the stage, living or dead, he considered greater than Garbo. Gordon thought a moment and then said, as quietly as she had put the question, 'Donald Duck'. I don't believe that he meant it at the time, or even thought that he meant it. However that may have been, she looked at him scornfully and said that that speech just about perfectly represented the shallowness of his intellect and the small range of his imagination. Gordon asked her not to make a spectacle of herself – she had raised her voice slightly – and went on to say that her failure to see the genius of Donald Duck proved conclusively to him that she was a woman without humour. That, he said, he had always suspected; now, he said, he knew it. She had a great desire to hit him, but instead she sat back and looked at him with her special Mona Lisa smile, a smile rather more of contempt than, as in the original, of mystery. Gordon hated that smile, so he said that Donald Duck happened to be exactly ten times as great as Garbo would ever be and that anybody with a brain in his head would admit it instantly. Thus the Winships went on and on, their resentment swelling, their sense of values blurring, until it ended up with her taking a taxi home alone (leaving her vanity bag and one glove behind her in the restaurant) and with him making the rounds of the late places and rolling up to his club around dawn. There, as he got out, he asked his taxi-driver which he liked better, Greta Garbo or Donald Duck, and the driver said he liked Greta Garbo best. Gordon said to him, bitterly, 'Pooh to you, too, my good friend!' and went to bed.

The next day, as is usual with married couples, they were both contrite, but behind their contrition lay sleeping the ugly words each had used and the cold glances and the bitter gestures. She phoned him, because she was worried. She didn't want to be, but she was. When he hadn't come home, she was convinced he had gone to his club, but visions of him lying in a gutter or under a table, somehow horribly mangled, haunted her, and so at eight o'clock she called him up. Her heart lightened when he said, 'Hullo,' gruffly: he was alive, thank God! His heart may have lightened a little, too, but not very much, because he felt terrible. He felt terrible and he felt that it was her fault that he felt terrible. She said that she was sorry and that they had both been very silly, and he growled something about he was glad she realized *she'd* been silly, anyway. That attitude put a slight edge on the rest of her words. She asked him shortly if he was coming home. He said sure he was coming home; it was his home, wasn't it? She told him to go back to bed and not be such an old bear, and hung up.

The next incident occurred at the Clarkes' party a few days later. The Winships had arrived in fairly good spirits to find themselves in a buzzing group of cocktail-drinkers that more or less revolved around the tall and languid figure of the guest of honour, an eminent lady novelist. Gordon late in the evening won her attention and drew her apart for one drink together and, feeling a little high and happy at that time, as is the way with husbands, mentioned lightly enough (he wanted to get it out of his subconscious), the argument that he and his wife had had about the relative merits of Garbo and Duck. The tall lady, lowering her cigarette-holder, said, in the spirit of his own gaiety, that she could count her in on his side. Unfortunately, Marcia Winship, standing some ten feet away, talking to a man with a beard, caught not the spirit but only a few of the words of the conversation, and jumped to the conclusion that her husband was deliberately reopening the old wound, for the purpose of humiliating her in public. I think that in another moment Gordon might have brought her over, and put his arm around her, and admitted his 'defeat' – he was feeling pretty fine.

But when he caught her eye, she gazed through him, freezingly, and his heart went down. And then his anger rose.

Their fight, naturally enough, blazed out again in the taxi they took to go home from the party. Marcia wildly attacked the woman novelist (Marcia had had quite a few cocktails), defended Garbo, excoriated Gordon, and laid into Donald Duck. Gordon tried for a while to explain exactly what had happened, and then he met her resentment with a resentment that mounted even higher, the resentment of the misunderstood husband. In the midst of it all she slapped him. He looked at her for a second under lowered eyelids and then said, coldly, if a bit fuzzily, 'This is the end, but I want you to go to your grave knowing that Donald Duck is *twenty times* the artist Garbo will ever be, the longest day you, or she, ever live, if you *do* – and I can't understand, with so little to live for, why you should!' Then he asked the driver to stop the car, and he got out, in wavering dignity. 'Caricature! Cartoon!' she screamed after him. 'You and Donald Duck both, you –' The driver drove on.

The last time I saw Gordon – he moved his things to the club the next day, forgetting the trousers to his evening clothes and his razor – he had convinced himself that the point at issue between him and Marcia was one of extreme importance involving both his honour and his integrity. He said that now it could never be wiped out and forgotten. He said that he sincerely believed Donald Duck was as great a creation as any animal in all the works of Lewis Carroll, probably even greater, perhaps much greater. He was drinking and there was a wild light in his eye. I reminded him of his old love of detachment, and he said to the hell with detachment. I laughed at him, but he wouldn't laugh. 'If,' he said, grimly, 'Marcia persists in her silly belief that that Swede is great and that Donald Duck is merely a caricature, I cannot conscientiously live with her again. I believe that he is great, that the man who created him is a genius, probably our only genius. I believe, further, that Greta Garbo is just another actress. As God is my judge, I believe that! What does she expect me to do, go whining back to her and pretend that I think Garbo is wonderful and that Donald Duck is simply a cartoon? Never!' He gulped down some Scotch straight. 'Never!' I could not ridicule him out of his obsession. I left him and went over to see Marcia.

I found Marcia pale, but calm, and as firm in her stand as Gordon was in his. She insisted that he had deliberately tried to humiliate her before that gawky so-called novelist, whose clothes were the dowdiest she had ever seen and whose affectations obviously covered up a complete lack of individuality and intelligence. I tried to convince her that she was wrong about Gordon's attitude at the Clarkes' party, but she said she knew him like a book. Let him get a divorce and marry that creature if he wanted to. They can sit around all day, she said, and all night, too, for all I care, and talk about their precious Donald Duck, the damn comic strip! I told Marcia that she shouldn't allow herself to get so worked up about a trivial and nonsensical matter. She said it was not silly and nonsensical to her. It might have been once, yes, but it wasn't now. It had made her see Gordon clearly for what he was, a cheap, egotistical, resentful cad who would descend to ridicule his wife in front of a scrawny, horrible stranger who could not write and never would be able to write. Furthermore, her belief in Garbo's greatness was a thing she could not deny and would not deny, simply for the sake of living under the same roof with Gordon Winship. The whole thing was part and parcel of her integrity as a woman and as an – as an, well, as a woman. She could go to work again; he would find out.

There was nothing more that I could say or do. I went home. That night, however, I found that I had not really dismissed the whole ridiculous affair, as I hoped I had, for I dreamed about it. I had tried to ignore the thing, but it had tunnelled deeply into my subconscious. I dreamed that I was out hunting with the Winships and that, as we crossed a snowy field, Marcia spotted a rabbit and, taking quick aim, fired and brought it down. We all ran across the snow toward the rabbit, but I reached it first. It was quite dead, but that was not what struck horror into me as I picked it up. What struck horror into me was that it was a white rabbit and was wearing a vest and carrying a watch. I woke up with a start. I don't know whether that dream means that I am on Gordon's side or on Marcia's. I don't want to analyse it. I am trying to forget the whole miserable business.

The Admiral on the Wheel

When the coloured maid stepped on my glasses the other morning, it was the first time they had been broken since the late Thomas A. Edison's seventy-ninth birthday. I remember that day well, because I was working for a newspaper then and I had been assigned to go over to West Orange that morning and interview Mr Edison. I got up early and, in reaching for my glasses under the bed (where I always put them), I found that one of my more sober and reflective Scotch terriers was quietly chewing them. Both tortoiseshell temples (the pieces that go over your ears) had been eaten and Jeannie was toying with the lenses in a sort of jaded way. It was in going over to Jersey that day, without my glasses, that I realized that the disadvantages of defective vision (bad eyesight) are at least partially compensated for by its peculiar advantages. Up to that time I had been in the habit of going to bed when my glasses were broken and lying there until they were fixed again. I had believed I could not go very far without them, not more than a block, anyway, on account of the danger of bumping into things, getting a headache, losing my way. None of those things happened, but a lot of others did. I saw the Cuban flag flying over a national bank, I saw a gay old lady with a grey parasol walk right through the side of a truck, I saw a cat roll across a street in a small striped barrel, I saw bridges rise lazily into the air, like balloons.

I suppose you have to have just the right proportion of sight to encounter such phenomena: I seem to remember that oculists have told me I have only two-fifths vision without what one of them referred to as 'artificial compensation' (glasses). With three-fifths vision or better, I suppose the Cuban flag would have been an American flag, the gay old lady a garbage man with a garbage can on his back, the cat a piece of butcher's paper blowing in the wind, the floating bridges smoke from tugs, hanging in the air. With perfect vision, one is extricably trapped in the workaday world, a prisoner of reality, as lost in the commonplace America of 1937 as Alexander Selkirk was lost on his lonely island. For the hawk-eyed

115

person life has none of those soft edges which for me blur into fantasy; for such a person an electric welder is merely an electric welder, not a radiant fool setting off a sky-rocket by day. The kingdom of the partly blind is a little like Oz, a little like Wonderland, a little like Poictesme. Anything you can think of, and a lot you never would think of, can happen there.

For three days after the maid, in cleaning the apartment, stepped on my glasses – I had not put them far enough under the bed – I worked at home and did not go uptown to have them fixed. It was in this period that I made the acquaintance of a remarkable Chesapeake spaniel. I looked out my window and after a moment spotted him, a noble, silent dog lying on a ledge above the entrance to a brownstone house in lower Fifth Avenue. He lay there, proud and austere, for three days and nights, sleepless, never eating, the perfect watchdog. No ordinary dog could have got up on the high ledge above the doorway, to begin with; no ordinary people would have owned such an animal. The ordinary people were the people who walked by the house and did not see the dog. Oh, I got my glasses fixed finally and I know that now the dog has gone, but I haven't looked to see what prosaic object occupies the spot where he so staunchly stood guard over one of the last of the old New York houses on Fifth Avenue; perhaps an unpainted flowerbox or a cleaning cloth dropped from an upper window by a careless menial. The moment of disenchantment would be too hard; I never look out that particular window any more.

Sometimes at night, even with my glasses on, I see strange and unbelievable sights, mainly when I am riding in an automobile which somebody else is driving (I never drive myself at night out of fear that I might turn up at the portals of some mystical monastery and never return). Only last summer I was riding with someone along a country road when suddenly I cried at him to look out. He slowed down and asked me sharply what was the matter. There is no worse experience than to have someone shout at you to look out for something you don't see. What this driver didn't see and I did see (two-fifths vision works a kind of magic in the night) was a little old admiral in full-dress uniform riding a bicycle at right angles to the car I was in. He might have been starlight behind a tree, or a billboard advertising Moxie; I don't know – we were quickly past the place he rode out of; but I would recognize him if I saw him again. His beard was blowing in the breeze and his hat was set at a rakish angle, like Admiral Beatty's. He was having a swell time. The gentleman who was driving the car has been, since that night, a trifle stiff and distant with me. I suppose you can hardly blame him.

To go back to my daylight experiences with the naked eye, it was me, in case you have heard the story, who once killed fifteen white chickens with small stones. The poor beggars never had a chance. This happened many years ago when I was living at Jay, New York. I had a vegetable garden some seventy feet behind the house, and the lady of the house had asked me to keep an eye on it in my spare moments and to chase away any chickens from neighbouring farms that came pecking around. One morning, getting up from my typewriter, I wandered out behind the house and saw that a flock of white chickens had invaded the garden. I had, to be sure, misplaced my glasses for the moment but I could still see well enough to let the chickens have it with ammunition from a pile of stones that I kept handy for the purpose. Before I could be stopped, I had riddled all the tomato plants in the garden, over the tops of which the lady of the house had, the twilight before, placed newspapers and paper bags to ward off the effects of frost. It was one of the darker experiences of my dimmer hours.

Some day, I suppose, when the clouds are heavy and the rain is coming down and the pressure of realities is too great, I shall deliberately take my glasses off and go wandering out into the streets. I daresay I may never be heard of again (I have always believed it was Ambrose Bierce's vision and not his whim that caused him to wander into oblivion). I imagine I'll have a remarkable time, wherever I end up.

A Couple of Hamburgers

It had been raining for a long time, a slow, cold rain falling out of iron-coloured clouds. They had been driving since morning and they still had a hundred and thirty miles to go. It was about three o'clock in the afternoon. 'I'm getting hungry,' she said. He took his eyes off the wet, winding road for a fraction of a second and said, 'We'll stop at a dog-wagon.' She shifted her position irritably. 'I wish you wouldn't call them *dog*-wagons,' she said. He pressed the klaxon button and went around a slow car. 'That's what they are,' he said 'Dog-wagons.' She waited a few seconds '*Decent* people call them *diners*,' she told him, and added, 'Even if you call them diners, I don't like them.' He speeded up a hill. 'They have better stuff than most restaurants,' he said. 'Anyway, I want to get home before dark and it takes too long in a restaurant. We can stay our stomachs with a couple hamburgers.' She lighted a cigarette and he asked her to light one for him. She lighted one deliberately and handed it to him. 'I wish you wouldn't say "stay our stomachs",' she said. 'You know I hate that. It's like "sticking to your ribs". You say that all the time.' He grinned. 'Good old American expressions, both of them,' he said. 'Like sow belly. Old pioneer term, sow belly.' She sniffed. 'My ancestors were pioneers, too. You don't have to be vulgar just because you were a pioneer.' 'Your ancestors never got as far west as mine did,' he said. 'The real pioneers travelled on their sow belly and got somewhere.' He laughed loudly at that. She looked out at the wet trees and signs and telephone poles going by. They drove on for several miles without a word; he kept chortling every now and then.

'What's that funny sound?' she asked, suddenly. It invariably made him angry when she heard a funny sound. 'What funny sound?' he demanded. 'You're always hearing funny sounds.' She laughed briefly. 'That's what you said when the bearing burned out,' she reminded him. 'You'd never have noticed it if it hadn't been for me.' 'I noticed it, all right,' he said. 'Yes,' she said. 'When it was too late.' She enjoyed bringing up the subject of the burned-

118

out bearing whenever he got to chortling. 'It was too late when *you* noticed it, as far as that goes,' he said. Then, after a pause, 'Well, what does it sound like *this* time? All engines make a noise running, you know.' 'I know all about that,' she answered. 'It sounds like – it sounds like a lot of safety pins being jiggled around in a tumbler.' He snorted. 'That's your imagination. Nothing gets the matter with a car that sounds like a lot of safety-pins. I happen to know that.' She tossed away her cigarette. 'Oh, sure,' she said. 'You always happen to know everything.' They drove on in silence.

'I want to stop somewhere and get something to *eat*!' she said loudly. 'All right, all right!' he said. 'I been watching for a dog-wagon, haven't I? There hasn't been any. I can't make you a dog-wagon.' The wind blew rain in on her and she put up the window on her side all the way. 'I won't stop at just any old diner,' she said. 'I won't stop unless it's a cute one.' He looked around at her. 'Unless it's a *what* one?' he shouted. 'You know what I mean,' she said. 'I mean a decent, clean one where they don't slosh things at you. I hate to have a lot of milky coffee sloshed at me.' 'All right,' he said. 'We'll find a cute one, then. You pick it out. I wouldn't know. I might find one that was cunning but not cute.' That struck him as funny and he began to chortle again. 'Oh, shut up,' she said.

Five miles farther along they came to a place called Sam's Diner. 'Here's one,' he said, slowing down. She looked it over. 'I don't want to stop there,' she said. 'I don't like the ones that have nicknames.' He brought the car to a stop at one side of the road 'Just what's the matter with the ones that have nicknames?' he asked with edgy, mock interest. 'They're always Greek ones,' she told him. 'They're always Greek one's,' he repeated after her. He set his teeth firmly together and started up again. After a time, 'Good old Sam, the Greek,' he said, in a singsong. 'Good old Connecticut Sam Beardsley, the Greek.' 'You didn't see his name,' she snapped. 'Winthrop, then,' he said. 'Old Samuel Cabot Winthrop, the Greek dog-wagon man.' He was getting hungry.

On the outskirts of the next town she said, as he slowed down, 'It looks like a factory kind of town.' He knew that she meant she wouldn't stop there. He drove on through the place. She lighted a cigarette as they pulled out into the open again. He slowed down and lighted a cigarette for himself. 'Factory kind of town than

I am!' he snarled. It was ten miles before they came to another town. 'Torrington,' he growled. 'Happen to know there's a dog-wagon here because I stopped in it once with Bob Combs. Damn cute place, too, if you ask me.' 'I'm not asking you anything,' she said, coldly. 'You think you're *so* funny. I think I know the one you mean,' she said, after a moment. 'It's right in the town and it sits at an angle from the road. They're never so good, for some reason.' He glared at her and almost ran up against the kerb. 'What the hell do you mean "sits at an angle from the road"?' he cried. He was very hungry now. 'Well, it isn't silly,' she said, calmly. 'I've noticed the ones that sit at an angle. They're cheaper, because they fitted them into funny little pieces of ground. The big ones parallel to the road are the best.' He drove right through Torrington, his lips compressed. 'Angle from the road, for God's sake!' he snarled, finally. She was looking out her window.

On the outskirts of the next town there was a diner called The Elite Diner. 'This looks – ' she began. 'I see it, I see it!' he said. 'It doesn't happen to look any cuter to me than any goddam – ' she cut him off. 'Don't be such a sorehead, for Lord's sake,' she said. He pulled up and stopped beside the diner, and turned on her. 'Listen,' he said, grittingly, 'I'm going to put down a couple of hamburgers in this place even if there isn't one single inch of chintz or cretonne in the whole – ' ' 'Oh, be still,' she said. 'You're just hungry and mean like a child. Eat your old hamburgers, what do I care?' Inside the place they sat down on stools and the counterman walked over to them, wiping up the counter top with a cloth as he did so. 'What'll it be, folks?' he said. 'Bad day, ain't it? Except for ducks.' 'I'll have a couple of – ' began the husband, but his wife cut in. 'I just want a pack of cigarettes,' she said. He turned around slowly on his stool and stared at her as she put a dime and a nickel in the cigarette machine and ejected a package of Lucky Strikes. He turned to the counterman again. 'I want a couple of hamburgers,' he said. 'With mustard and lots of onion. *Lots* of onion!' She hated onions. 'I'll wait for you in the car,' she said. He didn't answer and she went out.

He finished his hamburgers and his coffee slowly. It was terrible coffee. Then he went out to the car and got in and drove off, slowly humming 'Who's Afraid of the Big Bad Wolf?' After a

120

mile or so, 'Well,' he said, 'What was the matter with the Elite Diner, milady?' 'Didn't you *see* that cloth the man was wiping the counter with?' she demanded. 'Ugh!' She shuddered. 'I didn't happen to want to eat any of the counter,' he said. He laughed at that comeback. 'You didn't even notice it,' she said. 'You never notice anything. It was filthy.' 'I noticed they had some damn fine coffee in there,' he said. 'It was swell.' He knew she loved good coffee. He began to hum his tune again; then he whistled it; then he began to sing it. She did not show her annoyance, but she knew that he knew she was annoyed. 'Will you be kind enough to tell me what time it is?' she asked. 'Big *bad* wolf, big *bad* wolf – five minutes o' five – tum-dee-*doo*-dee-dum-m-m.' She settled back in her seat and took a cigarette from her case and tapped it on the case. 'I'll wait till we get home,' she said. 'If you'll be kind enough to speed up a little.' He drove on at the same speed. After a time he gave up the 'Big Bad Wolf' and there was deep silence for two miles. Then suddenly he began to sing, very loudly, *H*-A-double-R-*I*-G-A-N *spells Harrr*-i-gan – ' She gritted her teeth. She hated that worse than any of his songs except 'Barney Google'. He would go on to 'Barney Google' pretty soon, she knew. Suddenly she leaned slightly forward. The straight line of her lips began to curve up ever so slightly. She heard the safety-pins in the tumbler again. Only now they were louder, more insistent, ominous. He was singing too loud to hear them. 'Is a *name* that *shame* has never been con-*nec*-ted with – *Harrr*-i-gan, that's *me*!' She relaxed against the back of the seat, content to wait.

Written after reading several recent novels about the deep south and confusing them a little – as the novelists themselves do – with *Tobacco Road* and *God's Little Acre*.

Old Nate Birge sat on the rusted wreck of an ancient sewing-machine in front of Hell Fire, which was what his shack was known as among the neighbours and to the police. He was chewing on a splinter of wood and watching the moon come up lazily out of the old cemetery in which nine of his daughters were lying, only two of whom were dead. He began to mutter to himself. 'Bateman be comin' back any time now wid a thousan' dollas fo' his ol' pappy,' said Birge. 'Bateman ain' goin' let his ol' pappy starve nohow.' A high, cracked voice spoke inside the house, in a toneless singsong. 'Bateman see you in hell afore he do anything 'bout it,' said the voice. 'Who dat?' cried Birge, standing up. 'Who dat sayin' callumy 'bout Bateman? Good gahd amighty!' He sat down quickly again. His feet hurt him, since he had gangrene in one of them and Bless-Yo-Soul, the cow, had stepped on the other one that morning in Hell Hole, the pasture behind Hell Fire. A woman came to the door with a skillet in her hand. Elviry Birge was thin and emaciated and dressed in a tattered old velvet evening gown. 'You oughtn' speak thataway 'bout Bateman at thisatime,' said Birge. 'Bateman's a good boy. He go 'way in 1904 to make his pappy a thousan' dollas.' 'Thuh hell wuth thut,' said Elviry, even more tonelessly than usual. 'Bateman ain' going' brang we-all no thousan' dollas. Bateman got heself a place fo' dat thousan' dollas.' She shambled back into the house. 'Elviry's gone crazy,' muttered Birge to himself.

A large woman with a heavy face walked into the littered yard, followed by a young man dressed in a tight blue suit. The woman carried two suitcases; the young man was smoking a cigarette and running a pocket comb through his hair. 'Who dat?' demanded Birge, peering into the dark. 'It's me, yore Sister Sairy,' said the large woman. 'An' tuckered as a truck horse.' The young man

hrew his cigarette on the ground and spat at its burning end.
Mom shot a policeman in Chicago,' he said, sulkily, 'an' we hadda
beat it.' 'Whut you shoot a policeman fo', Sairy?' demanded
Birge, who had not seen his sister for twenty years. 'Gahdam it,
you cain' go 'round doin' that!' 'That'll be one o' Ramsay's jokes,'
said Sairy. 'Ramsay's a hand for jokes, he is. Seems like that's all
he is a hand for.' 'Ah, shut yore trap before I slap it shut,' said
Ramsay. He had never been in the deep South before and he didn't
like it. 'When do we eat?' he asked. 'Ev'body goin' 'round
shootin' policemen,' muttered Birge, hobbling about the yard.
'Seem lak ev'body shootin' policeman 'cept Bateman. Bateman,
he's a good boy.' Elvry came to the door again, still carrying the
skillet; as they had had no food since Coolidge's first term, she
used it merely as a weapon. 'Whut's ut?' she asked, frowning into
the dark. The moon, grown tired, had sunk back into the cemetery
again. 'Come ahn out, cackle-puss, an' find out,' said Ramsay.
'Look heah, boy!' cried Birge. 'I want me more rev'rence outa you,
gahdam it!' 'Hello, Elvry,' said Sairy, sitting on one of her suitcases. 'We come to visit you. Ain't you glad!' Elvry didn't move
from the doorway.

'We-all thought you-all was in *She*cago,' said Elvry, in her
toneless voice. 'We-all was in all Chicago,' said Ramsay, 'but we-
all is here all, now all.' He spat. 'Dam ef he ain' right, too,' said
Birge, chuckling. 'Lawdy gahd! You bring me a thousan' dollas,
boy?' he asked, suddenly. 'I ain't brought nobody no thousand
dollers,' growled Ramsay. 'Whine you make yerself a thousand
dollers, you old buzzard?' 'Don' lem call me buzzard, Elvry!'
shouted Birge. 'Cain' you hit him wid somethin'? Hit him wid dat
skillet!' Elvry made for Ramsay with her skillet, but he wrested it
away from her and struck her over the head with it. The impact
made a low, dull sound, like *sponk*. Elvry fell unconscious, and
Ramsay sat down on her, listlessly. 'Hell va place ya got here,' he
said.

At this juncture a young blonde girl, thin and emaciated but
beautiful in the light of the moon (which had come up again), ran
into the yard. 'Wheah you bin, gal?' demanded Birge. 'Faith is
crazy,' he said to the others, 'an' they ain' nobody knows why,
'cause I give her a good Christian upbringin' ef evah a man did.

Look heah, gal, yo' Aunt Sairy heah fo' a visit, gahdam it, an'
nobody home to welcome her. All my daughters 'cept Prudence
bin gone fo' two weeks now. Prudence, she bin gone fo' two yeahs.'
Faith sat down on the stoop. 'Clay an' me bin settin' fire to the
auditorium,' she said. Birge began whittling at a stick. 'Clay's he
third husban',' he said. '"Pears lak she should pay some 'tention
to her fifth husban', or leastwise her fo'th, but she don'. I don'
understan' wimmin. Seem lak ev'body settin' fire to somethin'
ev'time I turn my back. Wonder any buildin's standin' in the
whole gahdam United States. You see anythin' o' Bateman, gal?'
'I ain' seen anything' o' anybody,' said Faith. 'Now that is a bald
face lie by a daughter I brought up in the feah o' hell fire,' said
Birge. 'Look heah, gal, you cain' set fire to no buildin' 'thout you
see somebody. Gahd's love give that truth to this world. Speak to
yo' Aunt Sairy, gal. She jest kill hesef a *po*liceman in *She*cago.'
'Did you kill a policeman, Aunt Sairy?' Faith asked her. Sairy
didn't answer her, but she spoke to Ramsay. 'You sit on the
suitcase an' let me sit on Elviry a while,' she said. 'Do as yo'
Motha tells you boy,' said Birge. 'Ah, shut up!' said Ramsay
smoking.

Ben Turnip, a half-witted neighbour boy with double pneu
monia, came into the yard, wearing only overalls. 'Ah seed you'a
was a-settin',' he said, bursting into high, toneless laughter. 'Heah'
Bateman! Heah's Bateman!' cried Birge, hobbling with many a
painful gahdam over to the newcomer. 'You bring me a thousan'
dollas, Bateman?' Elviry came to, pushed Ramsay off her, an'
got up. 'That ain' Bateman, you ol' buzzard,' she said scornfully.
'That's only Ben Turnip an' him turned in the haid, too, lak hi
Motha afore him.' 'Go 'long woman,' said Birge. 'I recken
know moan son. You bring yo' ol' pappy a thousan' dollas
Bateman?' 'Ah seed you-all was a-settin',' said Ben Turnip. Sud
denly he became very excited, his voice rising to a high singsong
'He-settin', I-settin', you-settin', we-settin',' he screamed. 'Deed
a-bye, deed-a-bye, deed-a-bye, die!' 'Bateman done gone crazy,'
mumbled Birge. He went back and sat down on the sewin
machine. 'Seem lak ev'body gone crazy. Now, that's a pity,' h
said, sadly. 'Nuts,' said Ramsay.

'S'pose you-all did see me a-settin',' said Ben Turnip, belliger

124

ently. 'Whut uv ut? Cain' Ah set?' 'Sho, sho, set yoself, Bateman,' said Birge. 'I'll whang ovah his haid wid Elviry's skillet fust pusson say anything 'bout you settin'. Set yoself.' Ben sat down on the ground and began digging with a stick. 'I done brong you a thousan' dollas,' said Ben. Birge leaped from his seat. 'Glory gahd to Hallerlugie!' he shouted. 'You heah de man, Elviry? Bateman done . . .'

If you keep on long enough it turns into a novel.

Doc Marlowe

I was too young to be other than awed and puzzled by Doc Marlowe when I knew him. I was only sixteen when he died. He was sixty-seven. There was that vast difference in our ages and there was a vaster difference in our backgrounds. Doc Marlowe was a medicine-show man. He had been a lot of other things, too: a circus man, the proprietor of a concession at Coney Island, a saloon-keeper; but in his fifties he had travelled around with a tent-show troupe made up of a Mexican named Chickalilli, who threw knives, and a man called Professor Jones, who played the banjo. Doc Marlowe would come out after the entertainment and harangue the crowd and sell bottles of medicine for all kinds of ailments. I found out all this about him gradually, toward the last, and after he died. When I first knew him, he represented the Wild West to me, and there was nobody I admired so much.

I met Doc Marlowe at old Mrs Willoughby's rooming-house. She had been a nurse in our family, and I used to go and visit her over week-ends sometimes, for I was very fond of her. I was about eleven years old then. Doc Marlowe wore scarred leather leggings, a bright-coloured bead vest that he said he got from the Indians, and a ten-gallon hat with kitchen matches stuck in the band, all the way round. He was about six feet four inches tall, with big shoulders, and a long, drooping moustache. He let his hair grow long, like General Custer's. He had a wonderful collection of Indian relics and six-shooters, and he used to tell me stories of his adventures in the Far West. His favourite expressions were 'Hay, boy!' and 'Hay, boy-gie!', which he used the way some people now use 'Hot dog!' or 'Doggone!' He told me once that he had killed an Indian chief named Yellow Hand in a tomahawk duel on horseback. I thought he was the greatest man I had ever seen. It wasn't until he died and his son came on from New Jersey for the funeral that I found out he had never been in the Far West in his life. He had been born in Brooklyn.

Doc Marlowe had given up the road when I knew him, but he

still dealt in what he called 'medicines'. His stock in trade was a liniment that he had called Snake Oil when he travelled around. He changed the name to Blackhawk Liniment when he settled in Columbus. Doc didn't always sell enough of it to pay for his bed and board, and old Mrs Willoughby would sometimes have to 'trust' him for weeks at a time. She didn't mind, because his liniment had taken a bad kink out of her right limb that had bothered her for thirty years. I used to see people whom Doc had massaged with Blackhawk Liniment move arms and legs that they hadn't been able to move before he 'treated' them. His patients were day labourers, wives of streetcar conductors, and people like that. Sometimes they would shout and weep after Doc had massaged them, and several got up and walked around who hadn't been able to walk before. One man hadn't turned his head to either side for seven years before Doc soused him with Blackhawk. In half an hour he could move his head as easily as I could move mine. 'Glory be to God!' he shouted. 'It's the secret qualities in the ointment, my friend,' Doc Marlowe told him, suavely. He always called the liniment ointment.

News of his miracles got around by word of mouth among the poorer classes of town – he was not able to reach the better people (the 'tony folks', he called them) – but there was never a big enough sale to give Doc a steady income. For one thing, people thought there was more magic in Doc's touch than in his liniment, and, for another, the ingredients of Blackhawk cost so much that his profits were not very great. I know, because I used to go to the wholesale chemical company once in a while for him and buy his supplies. Everything that went into the liniment was standard and expensive (and well-known, not secret). A man at the company told me he didn't see how Doc could make much money on it at thirty-five cents a bottle. But even when he was very low in funds Doc never cut out any of the ingredients or substituted cheaper ones. Mrs Willoughby had suggested it to him once, she told me, when she was helping him 'put up a batch', and he had got mad. 'He puts a heap of store by that liniment being right up to the mark,' she said.

Doc added to his small earnings, I discovered, by money he made gambling. He used to win quite a few dollars on Saturday nights at Freck's saloon, playing poker with the marketman and the rail-roaders who dropped in there. It wasn't for several years that I found out Doc cheated. I had never heard about marked cards until he told me about them and showed me his. It was one rainy afternoon, after he had played seven-up with Mrs Willoughby and old Mr Peiffer, another roomer of hers. They had played for small stakes (Doc wouldn't play cards unless there was some money up, and Mrs Willoughby wouldn't play if very much was up). Only twenty or thirty cents had changed hands in the end. Doc had won it all. I remember my astonishment and indignation when it dawned on me that Doc had used the marked cards in playing the old lady and the old man. 'You didn't cheat *them*, did you?' I asked him. 'Jimmy, my boy,' he told me, 'the man that calls the turn wins the money.' His eyes twinkled and he seemed to enjoy my anger. I was outraged, but I was helpless. I knew I could never tell Mrs Willoughby about how Doc had cheated her at seven-up. I liked her, but I liked him, too. Once he had given me a whole dollar to buy fireworks with on the Fourth of July.

I remember once, when I was staying at Mrs Willoughby's, Doc Marlowe was roused out of bed in the middle of the night by a poor woman who was frantic because her little girl was sick. This woman had had the sciatica driven out of her by his liniment, she reminded Doc. He placed her then. She had never been able to pay him a cent for his liniment or his 'treatments', and he had given her a great many. He got up and dressed, and went over to her house. The child had colic, I suppose. Doc couldn't have had any idea what was the matter, but he sopped on liniment; he sopped on a whole bottle. When he came back home, two hours later, he said he had 'relieved the distress'. The little girl had gone to sleep and was all right the next day, whether on account of Doc Marlowe or in spite of him I don't know. 'I want to thank you, Doctor,' said the mother, tremulously, when she called on him that afternoon. He gave her another bottle of liniment, and he didn't charge her for it or for his 'professional call'. He used to massage, and give liniment to, a lot of sufferers who were too poor to pay. Mrs Willoughby told him once that he was too generous and too easily taken in. Doc laughed – and winked at me, with the twinkle in his eye that he had had when he told me how he had cheated the old lady at cards.

Once I went for a walk with him out Town Street on a Saturday afternoon. It was a warm day, and after a while I said I wanted a soda. Well, he said, he didn't care if he took something himself. We went into a drugstore, and I ordered a chocolate soda and he had a lemon phosphate. When we had finished, he said, 'Jimmy, my son, I'll match you to see who pays for the drinks.' He handed me a quarter and he told me to toss the quarter and he would call the turn. He called heads and won. I paid for the drinks. It left me with a dime.

I was fifteen when Doc got out his pamphlets, as he called them. He had eased the misery of the life of a small-time printer and the grateful man had given him a special price on two thousand advertising pamphlets. There was very little in them about Blackhawk Liniment. They were mostly about Doc himself and his 'Life in the Far West'. He had gone out to Franklin Park one day with a photographer – another of his numerous friends – and there the photographer took dozens of pictures of Doc, a lariat in one hand, a six-shooter in the other. I had gone along. When the pamphlets came out, there were the pictures of Doc, peering around trees, crouching behind bushes, whirling the lariat, aiming the gun. 'Dr H. M. Marlowe Hunting Indians' was one of the captions. 'Dr H. M. Marlowe after Hoss-Thieves' was another one. He was very proud of the pamphlets and always had a sheaf with him. He would pass them out to people on the street.

Two years before he died Doc got hold of an ancient, wheezy Cadillac somewhere. He aimed to start travelling around again, he said, but he never did, because the old automobile was so worn out it wouldn't hold up for more than a mile or so. It was about this time that a man named Hardman and his wife came to stay at Mrs Willoughby's. They were farm people from around Lancaster who had sold their place. They got to like Doc because he was so jolly, they said, and they enjoyed his stories. He treated Mrs Hardman for an old complaint in the small of her back and wouldn't take any money for it. They thought he was a fine gentleman. Then there came a day when they announced that they were going to St Louis, where they had a son. They talked some of settling in St Louis. Doc Marlowe told them they ought to buy a nice auto cheap and drive out, instead of going by train – it wouldn't cost much and they could see the country, give themselves a treat. Now, he knew where they could pick up just such a car.

Of course, he finally sold them the decrepit Cadillac – it had been stored away somewhere in the back of a garage whose owner kept it there for nothing because Doc had relieved his mother of a distress in the groins, as Doc explained it. I don't know just how the garage man doctored up the car, but he did. It actually chugged along pretty steadily when Doc took the Hardmans out for a trial spin. He told them he hated to part with it, but he finally let them have it for a hundred dollars. I knew, of course, and so did Doc, that it couldn't last many miles.

Doc got a letter from the Hardmans in St Louis ten days later. They had had to abandon the old junk pile in West Jefferson, some fifteen miles out of Columbus. Doc read the letter aloud to me, peering over his glasses, his eyes twinkling, every now and then punctuating the lines with 'Hay, boy!' and 'Hay, boy-gie!' 'I just want you to know, Dr Marlowe,' he read, 'what I think of low-life swindlers like you [Hay, boy!] and that it will be a long day before I put my trust in a two-faced lyer and imposture again [Hay, boy-gie!]. The garage man in W. Jefferson told us your old rattle-trap had been doctored up just to fool us. It was a low down dirty trick as no swine would play on a white man [Hay, boy!].' Far from being disturbed by the letter, Doc Marlowe was plainly amused. He took off his glasses, after he finished it and laughed, his hand to his brow and his eyes closed. I was pretty mad, because I had liked the Hardmans, and because they had liked him. Doc Marlowe put the letter carefully back into its envelope and tucked it away in his inside coat pocket, as if it were something precious. Then he picked up a pack of cards and began to lay out a solitaire hand. 'Want to set in a little seven-up game, Jimmy?' he asked me. I was furious. 'Not with a cheater like you!' I shouted, and stamped out of the room, slamming the door. I could hear him chuckling to himself behind me.

The last time I saw Doc Marlowe was just a few days before he died. I didn't know anything about death, but I knew that he was dying when I saw him. His voice was very faint and his face was drawn; they told me he had a lot of pain. When I got ready to

130

eave the room, he asked me to bring him a tin box that was on his ureau. I got it and handed it to him. He poked around in it for a while with unsteady fingers and finally found what he wanted. He anded it to me. It was a quarter, or rather it looked like a quarter, ut it had heads on both sides. 'Never let the other fella call the urn, Jimmy, my boy,' said Doc, with a shadow of his old twinkle and the echo of his old chuckle. I still have the two-headed quarter. 'or a long time I didn't like to think about it, or about Doc Marlowe, but I do now.

The Wood Duck

Mr Krepp, our vegetable man, had told us we might find some cider out the New Milford road a way – we would come to a sign saying 'Morris Plains Farm' and that would be the place. So we got into the car and drove down the concrete New Milford road, which is black in the centre with the dropped oil of a million cars. It's a main-trunk highway; you can go fifty miles an hour on it except where warning signs limit you to forty or, near towns, thirty-five, but nobody ever pays any attention to these signs. Even then, in November, dozens of cars flashed past us with a high, ominous whine, their tyres roaring rubberly on the concrete. We found Morris Plains Farm without any trouble. There was a big white house to the left of the highway; only a few yards off the road a small barn had been made into a roadside stand, with a dirt driveway curving up to the front of it. A spare, red-cheeked man stood in the midst of baskets and barrels of red apples and glass jugs of red cider. He was waiting on a man and a woman. I turned into the driveway – and put the brakes on hard. I had seen, just in time, a duck.

It was a small, trim duck, and even I, who know nothing about wild fowl, knew that this was no barnyard duck, this was a wild duck. He was all alone. There was no other bird of any kind around, not even a chicken. He was immensely solitary. With none of the awkward waddling of a domestic duck, he kept walking busily around in the driveway, now and then billing up water from a dirty puddle in the middle of the drive. His obvious contentment, his apparently perfect adjustment to his surroundings, struck me as something of a marvel. I got out of the car and spoke about it to a man who had driven up behind me in a rattly sedan. He wore a leather jacket and high, hard boots, and I figured he would know what kind of duck this was. He did. 'That's a wood duck,' he said. 'It dropped in here about two weeks ago, Len says, and's been here ever since.'

The proprietor of the stand, in whose direction my informant

132

had nodded as he spoke, helped his customers load a basket of apples into their car and walked over to us. The duck stepped, with a little flutter of its wings, into the dirty puddle, took a small, unconcerned swim, and got out again, ruffling its feathers. 'It's rather an odd place for a wood duck, isn't it?' asked my wife. Len grinned and nodded; we all watched the duck. 'He's a banded duck,' said Len. 'There's a band on his leg. The state game commission sends out a lot of 'em. This'n lighted here two weeks ago – it was on a Saturday – and he's been around ever since.' 'It's funny he wouldn't be frightened away, with all the cars going by and all the people driving in,' I said. Len chuckled. 'He seems to like it here,' he said. The duck wandered over to some sparse grass at the edge of the road, aimlessly, but with an air of settled satisfaction. 'He's tame as anything,' said Len. 'I guess they get tame when them fellows band 'em.' The man in the leather jacket said, ''Course they haven't let you shoot wood duck for a long while and that might make 'em tame, too.' 'Still,' said my wife (we forgot about the cider for the moment), 'it's strange he would stay here, right on the road almost.' 'Sometimes,' said Len, reflectively, 'he goes round back o' the barn. But mostly he's here in the drive.' 'But don't they,' she asked, 'let them loose in the woods after they're banded? I mean, aren't they supposed to stock up the forests?' 'I guess they're supposed to,' said Len, chuckling again, 'But 'pears this'n didn't want to.'

An old Ford truck lurched into the driveway and two men in the seat hailed the proprietor. They were hunters, big, warmly dressed, heavily shod men. In the back of the truck was a large bird dog. He was an old pointer and he wore an expression of remote disdain for the world of roadside commerce. He took no notice of the duck. The two hunters said something to Len about cider, and I was just about to chime in with my order when the accident happened. A car went by the stand at fifty miles an hour, leaving something scurrying in its wake. It was the duck, turning over and over on the concrete. He turned over and over swiftly, but lifelessly, like a thrown feather duster, and then he lay still. 'My God,' I cried, 'they've killed your duck, Len!' The accident gave me a quick feeling of anguished intimacy with the bereaved man. 'Oh, now,' he wailed. 'Now, that's awful!' None of us for a moment moved. Then the two hunters walked toward the road, slowly, self-consciously, a little embarrassed in the face of this quick incongruous ending of a wild fowl's life in the middle of a concrete highway. The pointer stood up, looked after the hunters, raised his ears briefly, and then lay down again.

It was the man in the leather jacket finally who walked out to the duck and tried to pick it up. As he did so, the duck stood up. He looked about him like a person who has been abruptly wakened and doesn't know where he is. He didn't ruffle his feathers. 'Oh, he isn't quite *dead*!' said my wife. I knew how she felt. We were going to have to see the duck die; somebody would have to kill him, finish him off. Len stood beside us. My wife took hold of his arm. The man in the leather jacket knelt down, stretched out a hand, and the duck moved slightly away. Just then, out from behind the barn, limped a setter dog, a lean white setter dog with black spots. His right back leg was useless and he kept it off the ground. He stopped when he saw the duck in the road and gave it a point, putting his head out, lifting his front leg, maintaining a wavering, marvellous balance on two legs. He was like a drunken man drawing a bead with a gun. This new menace, this anticlimax, was too much. I think I yelled.

What happened next happened as fast as the automobile accident. The setter made his run, a limping, wobbly run, and he was in between the men and the bird before they saw him. The duck flew, got somehow off the ground a foot or two, and tumbled into the grass of the field across the road, the dog after him. It seemed crazy, but the duck could fly – a little, anyway. 'Here, here,' said Len, weakly. The hunters shouted, I shouted, my wife screamed. 'He'll kill him! He'll *kill* him!' The duck flew a few yards again, the dog at his tail. The dog's third plunge brought his nose almost to the duck's tail, and then one of the hunters tackled the animal and pulled him down and knelt in the grass, holding him. We all breathed easier. My wife let go Len's arm.

Len started across the road after the duck, who was fluttering slowly, waveringly, but with a definite purpose, toward a wood that fringed the far side of the field. The bird was dazed, but a sure, atavistic urge was guiding him; he was going home. One of the hunters joined Len in his pursuit. The other came back across the

134

road, dragging the indignant setter; the man in the leather jacket walked beside them. We all watched Len and his companion reach the edge of the wood and stand there, looking; they had followed the duck through the grass slowly, so as not to alarm him; he had been alarmed enough. 'He'll never come back,' said my wife. Len and the hunter finally turned and came back through the grass. The duck had got away from them. We walked out to meet them at the edge of the concrete. Cars began to whiz by in both directions. I realized, with wonder, that all the time the duck, and the hunters, and the setter were milling around in the road, not one had passed. It was as if traffic had been held up so that our little drama could go on. 'He couldn't o' been much hurt,' said Len. 'Likely just grazed and pulled along in the wind of the car. Them fellows don't look out for anything. It's a sin.' My wife had a question for him. 'Does your dog always chase the duck?' she asked. 'Oh, that ain't my dog,' said Len. 'He just comes around.' The hunter who had been holding the setter now let him go, and he slunk away. The pointer, I noticed, lay with his eyes closed. 'But doesn't the duck mind the dog?' persisted my wife. 'Oh, he minds him,' said Len. 'But the dog's never really hurt him none yet. There's always somebody around.'

We drove away with a great deal to talk about (I almost forgot the cider). I explained the irony, I think I explained the profound symbolism, of a wild duck's becoming attached to a roadside stand. My wife strove simply to understand the duck's viewpoint. She didn't get anywhere. I knew even then, in the back of my mind, what would happen. We decided, after a cocktail, to drive back to the place and find out if the duck had returned. My wife hoped it wouldn't be there, on account of the life it led in the driveway; I hoped it wouldn't because I felt that would be, somehow, too pat an ending. Night was falling when we started off again for Morris Plains Farm. It was a five-mile drive and I had to put my bright lights on before we got there. The barn door was closed for the night. We didn't see the duck anywhere. The only thing to do was to go up to the house and inquire. I knocked on the door and a young man opened it. 'Is – is the proprietor here?' I asked. He said no, he had gone to Waterbury. 'We wanted to know,' my wife said, 'whether the duck came back.' 'What?' he asked, a little startled, I thought. Then, 'Oh, the duck. I saw him around the driveway when my father drove off.' He stared at us, waiting. I thanked him and started back to the car. My wife lingered, explaining, for a moment. 'He thinks we're crazy,' she said, when she got into the car. We drove on a little distance. 'Well,' I said, 'he's back.' 'I'm glad he is, in a way,' said my wife. 'I hated to think of him all alone out there in the woods.'

4

From *The Middle-Aged Man on the Flying Trapeze*

The Departure of Emma Inch

Emma Inch looked no different from any other middle-aged, thin woman you might glance at in the subway or deal with across the counter of some small store in a country town, and then forget forever. Her hair was drab and unabundant, her face made no impression on you, her voice I don't remember – it was just a voice. She came to us with a letter of recommendation from some acquaintance who knew that we were going to Martha's Vineyard for the summer and wanted a cook. We took her because there was nobody else, and she seemed all right. She had arrived at our hotel in Forty-fifth Street the day before we were going to leave and we got her a room for the night, because she lived way uptown somewhere. She said she really ought to go back and give up her room, but I told her I'd fix that.

Emma Inch had a big scuffed brown suitcase with her, and a Boston bull terrier. His name was Feely. Feely was seventeen years old and he grumbled and growled and snuffled all the time, but we needed a cook and we agreed to take Feely along with Emma Inch, if she would take care of him and keep him out of the way. It turned out to be easy to keep Feely out of the way because he would lie grousing anywhere Emma put him until she came and picked him up again. I never saw him walk. Emma had owned him, she said, since he was a pup. He was all she had in the world, she told us, with a mist in her eyes. I felt embarrassed but not touched. I didn't see how anybody could love Feely.

I didn't loose any sleep about Emma Inch and Feely the night of the day they arrived, but my wife did. She told me next morning that she had lain awake a long time thinking about the cook and her dog, because she felt kind of funny about them. She didn't know why. She just had a feeling that they were kind of funny. When we were all ready to leave – it was about three o'clock in the afternoon, for we had kept putting off the packing – I phoned Emma's room, but she didn't answer. It was getting late and we felt nervous – the Fall River boat would sail in about two hours.

139

We couldn't understand why we hadn't heard anything from Emma and Feely. It wasn't until four o'clock that we did. There was a small rap on the door of our bedroom and I opened it and Emma and Feely were there, Feely in her arms, snuffing and snaffling, as if he had been swimming a long way.

My wife told Emma to get her bag packed, we were leaving in a little while. Emma said her bag *was* packed, except for her electric fan, and she couldn't get that in. 'You won't need an electric fan at the Vineyard,' my wife told her. 'It's cool there, even during the day, and it's almost cold at night. Besides, there is no electricity in the cottage we are going to.' Emma Inch seemed distressed. She studied my wife's face. 'I'll have to think of something else then,' she said. 'Mebbe I could let the water run all night.' We both sat down and looked at her. Feely's asthmatic noises were the only sounds in the room for a while. 'Doesn't that dog ever stop that?' I asked, irritably. 'Oh, he's just talking,' said Emma. 'He talks all the time, but I'll keep him in my room and he won't bother you none.' 'Doesn't he bother you?' I asked. 'He *would* bother me,' said Emma 'at night, but I put the electric fan on and keep the light burning. He don't make so much noise when it's light, because he don't snore. The fan kind of keeps me from noticing him. I put a piece of cardboard, like, where the fan hits it and then I don't notice Feely so much. Mebbe I could let the water run in my room all night instead of the fan.' I said 'Hmmm' and got up and mixed a drink for my wife and me – we had decided not to have one till we got on the boat, but I thought we'd better have one now. My wife didn't tell Emma there would be no running water in her room at the Vineyard.

'We've been worried about you, Emma,' I said. 'I phoned your room but you didn't answer.' 'I never answer the phone,' said Emma, 'because I always get a shock. I wasn't there anyways. I couldn't sleep in that room. I went back to Mrs McCoy's on Seventy-eighth Street.' I lowered my glass. 'You went back to Seventy-eighth Street last *night*?' I demanded. 'Yes, sir,' she said. 'I had to tell Mrs McCoy I was going away and wouldn't be there any more for a while – Mrs McCoy's the landlady. Anyways, I never sleep in a hotel.' She looked around the room. 'They burn down,' she told us.

It came out that Emma Inch had not only gone back to Seventy-eighth Street the night before but had walked all the way, carrying Feely. It had taken her an hour or two, because Feely didn't like to be carried very far at a time, so she had had to stop every block or so and put him down on the sidewalk for a while. It had taken her just as long to walk back to our hotel, too; Feely, it seems, never got up before afternoon – that's why she was so late. She was sorry. My wife and I finished our drinks, looking at each other, and at Feely.

Emma Inch didn't like the idea of riding to Pier 14 in a taxi, but after ten minutes of cajoling and pleading she finally got in. 'Make it go slow,' she said. We had enough time, so I asked the driver to take it easy. Emma kept getting to her feet and I kept pulling her back on to the seat. 'I never been in an automboile before,' she said. 'It goes awful fast.' Now and then she gave a little squeal of fright. The driver turned his head and grinned. 'You're O.K. wit' me, lady,' he said. Feely growled at him. Emma waited until he had turned away again, and then she leaned over to my wife and whispered. 'They all take cocaine,' she said. Feely began to make a new sound – a kind of high, agonized yelp. 'He's singing,' said Emma. She gave a strange little giggle, but the expression of her face didn't change. 'I wish you had put the Scotch where we could get at it,' said my wife.

If Emma Inch had been afraid of the taxicab, she was terrified by the *Priscilla* of the Fall River Line. 'I don't think I can go,' said Emma. 'I don't think I could get on a boat. I didn't know they were so big.' She stood rooted to the pier, clasping Feely. She must have squeezed him too hard, for he screamed – he screamed like a woman. We all jumped. 'It's his ears,' said Emma. 'His ears hurt.' We finally got her on the boat, and once aboard, in the saloon, her terror abated somewhat. Then the three parting blasts of the boat whistle rocked lower Manhattan. Emma Inch leaped to her feet and began to run, letting go of her suitcase (which she had refused to give up to a porter) but holding on to Feely. I caught her just as she reached the gangplank. The ship was on its way when I let go of her arm.

It was a long time before I could get Emma to go to her state-room, but she went at last. It was an inside stateroom, and she

141

didn't seem to mind it. I think she was surprised to find that it was like a room, and had a bed and a chair and a wash-bowl. She put Feely down on the floor. 'I think you'll have to do something about the dog,' I said. 'I think they put them somewhere and you get them when you get off.' 'No they don't,' said Emma. I guess, in this case, they didn't. I don't know. I shut the door on Emma Inch and Feely, and went away. My wife was drinking straight Scotch when I got to our stateroom.

The next morning, cold and early, we got Emma and Feely off the *Priscilla* at Fall River and over to New Bedford in a taxi and on to the little boat for Martha's Vineyard. Each move was as difficult as getting a combative drunken man out of the night club in which he fancies he has been insulted. Emma sat in a chair on the Vineyard boat, as far away from sight of the water as she could get, and closed her eyes and held on to Feely. She had thrown a coat over Feely, not only to keep him warm but to prevent any of the ship's officers from taking him away from her. I went in from the deck at intervals to see how she was. She was all right, or at least all right for her, until five minutes before the boat reached the dock at Woods Hole, the only stop between New Bedford and the Vineyard. Then Feely got sick. Or at any rate Emma said he was sick. He didn't seem to me any different from what he always was – his breathing was just as abnormal and irregular. But Emma said he was sick. There were tears in her eyes. 'He's a very sick dog, Mr Thurman,' she said. 'I'll have to take him home.' I knew by the way she said 'home' what she meant. She meant Seventy-eighth Street.

The boat tied up at Woods Hole and was motionless and we could hear the racket of the deckhands on the dock loading freight. 'I'll get off here,' said Emma, firmly, or with more firmness, anyway, than she had shown yet. I explained to her that we would be home in half an hour, that everything would be fine then, everything would be wonderful. I said Feely would be a new dog. I told her people sent sick dogs to Martha's Vineyard to be cured. But it was no good. 'I'll have to take him off here,' said Emma. 'I always have to take him home when he is sick.' I talked to her eloquently about the loveliness of Martha's Vineyard and the nice houses and

142

the nice people and the wonderful accommodations for dogs. But I knew it was useless. I could tell by looking at her. She was going to get off the boat at Woods Hole.

'You really can't do this,' I said, grimly, shaking her arm. Feely snarled weakly. 'You haven't any money and you don't know where you are. You're a long way from New York. Nobody ever got from Woods Hole to New York alone.' She didn't seem to hear me. She began walking toward the stairs leading to the gangplank, crooning to Feely. 'You'll have to go all the way back on boats,' I said, 'or else take a train, and you haven't any money. If you are going to be so stupid and leave us now, I can't give you any money.' 'I don't want any money, Mr Thurman,' she said. 'I haven't earned any money.' I walked along in irritable silence for a moment; then I gave her some money. I made her take it. We got to the gangplank. Feely snaffled and gurgled. I saw now that his eyes were a little red and moist. I know it would do no good to summon my wife – not when Feely's health was at stake. 'How do you expect to get home from here?' I almost shouted at Emma Inch as she moved down the gangplank. 'You're way out on the end of Massachusetts.' She stopped and turned around. 'We'll walk,' she said. 'We like to walk, Feely and me.' I just stood still and watched her go.

When I went up on deck, the boat was clearing for the Vineyard. 'How's everything?' asked my wife. I waved a hand in the direction of the dock. Emma Inch was standing there, her suitcase at her feet, her dog under one arm, waving good-bye to us with her free hand. I had never seen her smile before, but she was smiling now.

There's an Owl in My Room

I saw Gertrude Stein on the screen of a newsreel theatre one afternoon and I heard her read that famous passage of hers about pigeons on the grass, alas (the sorrow is, as you know, Miss Stein's). After reading about the pigeons on the grass alas, Miss Stein said, 'This is a simple description of a landscape I have seen many times.' I don't really believe that that is true. Pigeons on the grass alas may be a simple description of Miss Stein's own consciousness, but it is not a simple description of a plot of grass on which pigeons have alighted, are alighting, or are going to alight. A truly simple description of the pigeons alighting on the grass of the Luxembourg Gardens (which, I believe, is where the pigeons alighted) would say of the pigeons alighting there only that they were pigeons alighting. Pigeons that alight anywhere are neither sad pigeons nor gay pigeons, they are simply pigeons.

It is neither just nor accurate to connect the word alas with pigeons. Pigeons are definitely not alas. They have nothing to do with alas and they have nothing to do with hooray (not even when you tie red, white and blue ribbons on them and let them loose at band concerts); they have nothing to do with mercy me or isn't that fine, either. White rabbits, yes, and Scotch terriers, and blue-jays, and even hippopotamuses, but not pigeons. I happen to have studied pigeons very closely and carefully, and I have studied the effect, or rather the lack of effect, of pigeons very carefully. A number of pigeons alight from time to time on the sill of my hotel window when I am eating breakfast and staring out the window. They never alas me, they never make me feel alas; they never make me feel anything.

Nobody and no animal and no other bird can play a scene so far down as a pigeon can. For instance, when a pigeon on my window ledge becomes aware of me sitting there in a chair in my blue polka-dot dressing-gown, worrying, he pokes his head far out from his shoulders and peers sideways at me, for all the world (Miss Stein might surmise) like a timid man peering around the corner of a

144

building trying to ascertain whether he is being followed by some hoofed fiend or only by the echo of his own footsteps. And yet it is *not* for all the world like a timid man peering around the corner of a building trying to ascertain whether he is being followed by a hoofed fiend or only by the echo of his own footsteps, at all. And that is because there is no emotion in the pigeon and no power to arouse emotion. A pigeon looking is just a pigeon looking. When it comes to emotion, a fish, compared to a pigeon, is practically beside himself.

A pigeon peering at me doesn't make me sad or glad or apprehensive or hopeful. With a horse or a cow or a dog it would be different. It would be especially different with a dog. Some dogs peer at me as if I had just gone completely crazy or as if they had just gone completely crazy. I can go so far as to say that most dogs peer at me that way. This creates in the consciousness of both me and the dog a feeling of alarm or downright terror and legitimately permits me to work into a description of the landscape, in which the dog and myself are figures, a note of emotion. Thus I should not have minded if Miss Stein had written: dogs on the grass, look out, dogs on the grass, look out, look out, dogs on the grass, look out Alice. That would be a simple description of dogs on the grass. But when any writer pretends that a pigeon makes him sad, or makes him anything else, I must instantly protest that this is a highly specialized fantastic impression created in an individual consciousness and that therefore it cannot fairly be presented as a simple description of what actually was to be seen.

People who do not understand pigeons – and pigeons can be understood only when you understand that there is nothing to understand about them – should not go around describing pigeons or the effect of pigeons. Pigeons come closer to a zero of impingement than any other birds. Hens embarrass me the way my old Aunt Hattie used to when I was twelve and she still insisted I wasn't big enough to bathe myself; owls disturb me; if I am with an eagle I always pretend that I am not with an eagle; and so on down to swallows at twilight who scare the hell out of me. But pigeons have absolutely no effect on me. They have absolutely no effect on anybody. They couldn't even startle a child. That is why they are selected from among all birds to be let loose, with coloured ribbons attached to them, at band concerts, library dedications, and christenings of new dirigibles. If anybody let loose a lot of owls on such an occasion there would be rioting and catcalls and whistling and fainting spells and throwing of chairs and the Lord only knows what else.

From where I am sitting now I can look out the window and see a pigeon being a pigeon on the roof of the Harvard Club. No other thing can be less what it is not than a pigeon can, and Miss Stein, of all people, should understand that simple fact. Behind the pigeon I am looking at, a blank wall of tired grey bricks is stolidly trying to sleep off oblivion; underneath the pigeon the cloistered windows of the Harvard Club are staring in horrified bewilderment at something they have seen across the street. The pigeon is just there on the roof being a pigeon, having been, and being, a pigeon and, what is more, always going to be, too. Nothing could be simpler than that. If you read that sentence aloud you will instantly see what I mean. It is a simple description of a pigeon on a roof. It is only with an effort that I am conscious of the pigeon, but I am acutely aware of a great sulky red iron pipe that is creeping up the side of the building intent on sneaking up on a slightly tipsy chimney which is shouting its head off.

There is nothing a pigeon can do or be that would make me feel sorry for it or for myself or for the people in the world, just as there is nothing I could do or be that would make a pigeon feel sorry for itself. Even if I plucked his feathers out it would not make him feel sorry for himself and it would not make me feel sorry for myself or for him. But try plucking the quills out of a porcupine or even plucking the fur out of a jackrabbit. There is nothing a pigeon could be, or can be, rather, which could get into my consciousness like a fumbling hand in a bureau drawer and disarrange my mind or pull anything out of it. I bar nothing at all. You could dress up a pigeon in a tiny suit of evening clothes and put a tiny silk hat on his head and a tiny gold-headed cane under his wing and send him walking into my room at night. It would make no impression on me. I would not shout, 'Good god almighty, the birds are in charge!' But you could send an owl into my room, dressed only in the feathers it was born with, and no monkey

146

business, and I would pull the covers over my head and scream.

No other thing in the world falls so far short of being able to do what it cannot do as a pigeon does. Of being *unable* to do what it *can* do, too, as far as that goes.

The Topaz Cufflinks Mystery

When the motor-cycle cop came roaring up, unexpectedly, out of Never-Never-Land (the way motor-cycle cops do), the man was on his hands and knees in the long grass beside the road, barking like a dog. The woman was driving slowly along in a car that stopped about eighty feet away; its headlights shone on the man: middle-aged, bewildered, sedentary. He got to his feet.

'What's goin' on here?' asked the cop. The woman giggled. 'Cock-eyed,' thought the cop. He did not glance at her.

'I guess it's gone,' said the man. 'I – ah – could not find it.'

'What was it?'

'What I lost?' The man squinted, unhappily. 'Some – some cufflinks; topazes set in gold.' He hesitated: the cop didn't seem to believe him. 'They were the colour of a fine Moselle,' said the man. He put on a pair of spectacles which he had been holding in his hand. The woman giggled.

'Hunt things better with ya glasses off?' asked the cop. He pulled his motor-cycle to the side of the road to let a car pass. 'Better pull over off the concrete, lady,' he said. She drove the car off the roadway.

'I'm near-sighted,' said the man. 'I can hunt things at a distance with my glasses on, but I do better with them off if I am close to something.' The cop kicked his heavy boots through the grass where the man had been crouching.

'He was barking,' ventured the lady in the car, 'so that I could see where he was.' The cop pulled his machine up on its standard; he and the man walked over to the automobile.

'What I don't get,' said the officer, 'is how you lose ya cufflinks a hundred feet in front of where ya car is; a person usually stops his car *past* the place he loses somethin', not a hundred feet before he gits *to* the place.'

The lady laughed again; her husband got slowly into the car, as if he were afraid the officer would stop him any moment. The officer studied them.

148

'Been to a party?' he asked. It was after midnight.

'We're not drunk, if that's what you mean,' said the woman, smiling. The cop tapped his fingers on the door of the car.

'You people didn't lose no topazes,' he said.

'Is it against the law for a man to be down on all fours beside a road, barking in a perfectly civil manner?' demanded the lady.

'No, ma'am,' said the cop. He made no move to get on his motor-cycle, however, and go on about his business. There was just the quiet chugging of the cycle engine and the auto engine, for a time.

'I'll tell you how it was, Officer,' said the man, in a crisp new tone. 'We were settling a bet. O.K.?'

'O.K.,' said the cop. 'Who won?' There was another pulsing silence.

'The lady bet,' said her husband, with dignity, as though he were explaining some important phase of industry to a newly hired clerk, 'the lady bet that my eyes would shine like a cat's do at night, if she came upon me suddenly close to the ground alongside the road. We had passed a cat, whose eyes gleamed. We had passed several persons, whose eyes did *not* gleam –'

'Simply because they were above the light and not under it,' said the lady. 'A man's eyes would gleam like a cat's if people were ordinarily caught by headlights at the same angle as cats are.' The cop walked over to where he had left his motor-cycle, picked it up, kicked the standard out, and wheeled it back.

'A cat's eyes,' he said, 'are different than yours and mine. Dogs, cats, skunks, it's all the same. They can see in a dark room.'

'Not in a *totally* dark room,' said the lady.

'Yes, they can,' said the cop.

'No, they can't; not if there is no light at all in the room, not if it's absolutely *black*,' said the lady. 'The question came up the other night; there was a professor there and he said there must be at least a ray of light, no matter how faint.'

'That may be,' said the cop, after a solemn pause, pulling at his gloves. 'But people's eyes don't shine – I go along these roads every night an' pass hundreds of cats and hundreds of people.'

'The people are never close to the ground,' said the lady.

'*I* was close to the ground,' said her husband.

'Look at it this way,' said the cop. 'I've seen wildcats in *trees* at night and *their* eyes shine.'

'There you are!' said the lady's husband. 'That proves it.'

'I don't see how,' said the lady. There was another silence.

'Because a wildcat in a tree's eyes are higher than the level of a man's,' said her husband. The cop may possibly have followed this, the lady obviously did not; neither one said anything. The cop got on his machine, raced his engine, seemed to be thinking about something, and throttled down. He turned to the man.

'Took ya glasses off so the headlights wouldn't make ya glasses shine, huh?' he asked.

'That's right,' said the man. The cop waved his hand triumphantly, and roared away. 'Smart guy,' said the man to his wife, irritably.

'I still don't see where the wildcat proves anything,' said his wife. He drove off slowly.

'Look,' he said. 'You claim that the whole thing depends on how *low* a *cat's* eyes are; I – '

'I didn't say that; I said it all depends on how *high* a *man's* eyes . . .'

Snapshot of a Dog

I ran across a dim photograph of him the other day, going through some old thing. He's been dead twenty-five years. His name was Rex (my two brothers and I named him when we were in our early teens) and he was a bull terrier. 'An American bull terrier,' we used to say, proudly; none of your English bulls. He had one brindle eye that sometimes made him look like a clown and sometimes reminded you of a politician with derby hat and cigar. The rest of him was white except for a brindle saddle that always seemed to be slipping off and a brindle stocking on a hind leg. Nevertheless, there was a nobility about him. He was big and muscular and beautifully made. He never lost his dignity even when trying to accomplish the extravagant tasks my brothers and myself used to set for him. One of these was the bringing of a ten-foot wooden rail into the yard through the back gate. We would throw it out into the alley and tell him to go get it. Rex was as powerful as a wrestler, and there were not many things that he couldn't manage somehow to get hold of with his great jaws and lift or drag to wherever he wanted to put them, or wherever we wanted them put. He could catch the rail at the balance and lift it clear of the ground and trot with great confidence toward the gate. Of course, since the gate was only four feet wide or so, he couldn't bring the rail in broadside. He found that out when he got a few terrific jolts, but he wouldn't give up. He finally figured out how to do it, by dragging the rail, holding on to one end, growling. He got a great, wagging satisfaction out of his work. We used to bet kids who had never seen Rex in action that he could catch a baseball thrown as high as they could throw it. He almost never let us down. Rex could hold a baseball with ease in his mouth, in one cheek, as if it were a chew of tobacco.

He was a tremendous fighter, but he never started fights. I don't believe he liked to get into them, despite the fact that he came from a line of fighters. He never went for another dog's throat but for one of its ears (that teaches a dog a lesson), and he would get his grip, close his eyes, and hold on. He could hold on for hours. His longest fight lasted from dusk until almost pitch-dark, one Sunday. It was fought in East Main Street in Columbus with a large, snarly nondescript that belonged to a big coloured man. When Rex finally got his ear grip, the brief whirlwind of snarling turned to screeching. It was frightening to listen to and to watch. The Negro boldly picked the dogs up somehow and began swinging them around his head, and finally let them fly like a hammer in a hammer throw, but although they landed ten feet away with a great plump, Rex still held on.

The two dogs eventually worked their way to the middle of the car tracks, and after a while two or three streetcars were held up by the fight. A motorman tried to pry Rex's jaws open with a switch rod; somebody lighted a fire and made a torch of a stick and held that to Rex's tail, but he paid no attention. In the end, all the residents and storekeepers in the neighbourhood were on hand, shouting this, suggesting that. Rex's joy of battle, when battle was joined, was almost tranquil. He had a kind of pleasant expression during fights, not a vicious one, his eyes closed in what would have seemed to be sleep had it not been for the turmoil of the struggle. The Oak Street Fire Department finally had to be sent for – I don't know why nobody thought of it sooner. Five or six pieces of apparatus arrived, followed by a battalion chief. A hose was attached and a powerful stream of water was turned on the dogs. Rex held on for several moments more while the torrent buffeted him about like a log in a freshet. He was a hundred yards away from where the fight started when he finally let go.

The story of that Homeric fight got all around town, and some of our relatives looked upon the incident as a blot on the family name. They insisted that we get rid of Rex, but we were very happy with him, and nobody could have made us give him up. We would have left town with him first, along any road there was to go. It would have been different, perhaps if he'd ever started fights, or looked for trouble. But he had a gentle disposition. He never bit a person in the ten strenuous years that he lived, nor ever growled at anyone except prowlers. He killed cats, that is true, but quickly and neatly and without especial malice, the way men kill certain animals. It was the only thing he did that we could never cure him

152

of doing. He never killed, or even chased, a squirrel. I don't know why. He had his own philosophy about such things. He never ran barking after wagons or automobiles. He didn't seem to see the idea in pursuing something you couldn't catch, or something you couldn't do anything with, even if you did catch it. A wagon was one of the things he couldn't tug along with his mighty jaws, and he knew it. Wagons, therefore, were not a part of his world.

Swimming was his favourite recreation. The first time he ever saw a body of water (Alum Creek), he trotted nervously along the steep bank for a while, fell to barking wildly, and finally plunged in from a height of eight feet or more. I shall always remember that shining, virgin dive. Then he swam upstream and back just for the pleasure of it, like a man. It was fun to see him battle upstream against a stiff current, struggling and growling every foot of the way. He had as much fun in the water as any person I have known. You didn't have to throw a stick in the water to get him to go in. Of course, he would bring back a stick to you if you did throw one in. He would even have brought back a piano if you had thrown one in.

That reminds me of the night, way after midnight, when he went a-roving in the light of the moon and brought back a small chest of drawers that he found somewhere – how far from the house nobody ever knew; since it was Rex, it could easily have been half a mile. There were no drawers in the chest when he got it home, and it wasn't a good one – he hadn't taken it out of anybody's house; it was just an old cheap piece that somebody had abandoned on a trash heap. Still, it was something he wanted, probably because it presented a nice problem in transportation. It tested his mettle. We first knew about his achievement when, deep in the night, we heard him trying to get the chest up on to the porch. It sounded as if two or three people were trying to tear the house down. We came downstairs and turned on the porch light. Rex was on the top step trying to pull the thing up, but it had caught somehow and he was just holding his own. I suppose he would have held his own till dawn if we hadn't helped him. The next day we carted the chest miles away and threw it out. If we had thrown it out in a nearby alley, he would have brought it home again, as a small token of his integrity in such matters. After all, he had been taught to carry

153

heavy wooden objects about, and he was proud of his prowess.

I am glad Rex never saw a trained police dog jump. He was just an amateur jumper himself, but the most daring and tenacious I have ever seen. He would take on any fence we pointed out to him. Six feet was easy for him, and he could do eight by making a tremendous leap and hauling himself over finally by his paws, grunting and straining; but he lived and died without knowing that twelve- and sixteen-feet walls were too much for him. Frequently, after letting him try to go over one for a while, we would have to carry him home. He would never have given up trying.

There was in his world no such thing as the impossible. Even death couldn't beat him down. He died, it is true, but only, as one of his admirers said, after 'straight-arming the death angel' for more than an hour. Late one afternoon he wandered home, too slowly and too uncertainly to be the Rex that had trotted briskly homeward up our avenue for ten years. I think we all knew when he came through the gate that he was dying. He had apparently taken a terrible beating, probably from the owner of some dog that he had got into a fight with. His head and body were scarred. His heavy collar with the teeth marks of many a battle on it was awry; some of the big brass studs in it were sprung loose from the leather. He licked at our hands and, staggering, fell, but got up again. We could see that he was looking for someone. One of his three masters was not home. He did not get home for an hour. During that hour the bull terrier fought against death as he had fought against the cold, strong current of Alum Creek, as he had fought to climb twelve-foot walls. When the person he was waiting for did come through the gate, whistling, ceasing to whistle, Rex walked a few wobbly paces toward him, touched his hand with his muzzle, and fell down again. This time he didn't get up.

Something to Say

Hugh Kingsmill and I stimulated each other to such a pitch that after the first meeting he had a brain storm and I lay sleepless all night and in the morning was on the brink of a nervous breakdown. – William Gerhardi's *Memoirs of a Polyglot*.

Elliot Vereker was always coming into and going out of my life. He was the only man who ever continuously stimulated me to the brink of a nervous breakdown. I met him first at a party in Amawalk, New York, on the Fourth of July, 1927. He arrived about noon in an old-fashioned horse cab, accompanied by a lady in black velvet whom he introduced as 'my niece, Olga Nethersole'. She was, it turned out, neither his niece nor Olga Nethersole. Vereker was a writer; he was gaunt and emaciated from sitting up all night talking; he wore an admiral's hat which he had stolen from an admiral. Usually he carried with him an old Gladstone bag filled with burned-out electric-light bulbs which it was his pleasure to throw, unexpectedly, against the sides of houses and the walls of rooms. He loved the popping sound they made and the tinkling sprinkle of fine glass that followed. He had an inordinate fondness for echoes. 'Halloooo!' he would bawl, wherever he was, in a terrific booming voice that could have conjured up an echo on a prairie. At the most inopportune and inappropriate moments he would snap out frank four-letter words, such as when he was talking to a little child or the sister of a vicar. He had no reverence and no solicitude. He would litter up your house, burn bedspreads and carpets with lighted cigarette stubs, and as likely as not depart with your girl and three or four of your most prized books and neckties. He was enamoured of breaking phonograph records and phonographs; he liked to tear sheets and pillowcases in two; he would unscrew the doorknobs from your doors so that if you were in you couldn't get out and if you were out you couldn't get in. He was the true artistic fire, the rare gesture of genius. When I first met him, he was working on a novel entitled *Sue You Have Seen*.

155

He had worked it out, for some obscure reason, from the familiar expression 'See you soon.' He never finished it, nor did he ever finish, or indeed get very far with, any writing, but he was nevertheless, we all felt, one of the great original minds of our generation. That he had 'something to say' was obvious in everything he did.

Vereker could converse brilliantly on literary subjects: Proust, Goethe, Voltaire, Whitman. Basically he felt for them a certain respect, but sometimes, and always when he was drunk, he would belittle their powers and their achievements in strong and pungent language. Proust, I later discovered, he had never read, but he made him seem more clear to me, and less important, than anybody else ever has. Vereker always liked to have an electric fan going while he talked and he would stick a folded newspaper into the fan so that the revolving blades scuttered against it, making a noise like the rattle of machine-gun fire. This exhilarated him and exhilarated me, too, but I suppose that it exhilarated him more than it did me. He seemed, at any rate, to get something out of it that I missed. He would raise his voice so that I could hear him above the racket. Sometimes, even then, I couldn't make out what he was saying. 'What?' I would shout. 'You heard me!!' he would yell, his good humour disappearing in an instant.

I had, of course, not heard him at all. There was no reasoning with him, no convincing him. I can still hear the musketry of those fans in my ears. They have done, I think, something to me. But for Vereker, and his great promise, one could endure a great deal. He would talk about the interests implicated in life, the coincidence of desire and realization, the symbols behind art and reality. He was fond of quoting Santayana when he was sober.

'Santayana,' he would say when he was drinking, 'has weight; he's a ton of feathers.' Then he would laugh roaringly; if he was at Tony's, he would flounder out into the kitchen, insulting some movie critic on the way, and repeat his line to whoever was there, and come roaring back.

Vereker had a way of flinging himself at a sofa, kicking one end out of it; or he would drop into a fragile chair like a tired bird dog and something would crack. He never seemed to notice. You would invite him to dinner, or, what happened oftener, he would drop in for dinner uninvited, and while you were shaking up a cocktail in

156

the kitchen he would disappear. He might go upstairs to wrench the bathtub away from the wall ('Breaking lead pipe is one of the truly enchanting adventures in life,' he said once), or he might simply leave for good in one of those inexplicable huffs of his which were a sign of his peculiar genius. He was likely, of course, to come back around two in the morning bringing some awful woman with him, stirring up the fire, talking all night long, knocking things off tables, singing, or counting. I have known him to lie back on a sofa, his eyes closed, and count up to as high as twenty-four thousand by ones, in a bitter, snarling voice. It was his protest against the regularization of the mechanized age. 'Achievement,' he used to say, 'is the fool's gold of idiots.' He never believed in doing anything or in having anything done, either for the benefit of mankind or for individuals. He would have written, but for his philosophical indolence, very great novels indeed. We all knew that, and we treated him with a deference for which, now that he is gone, we are sincerely glad.

Once Vereker invited me to a house which a lady had turned over to him when she went to Paris for a divorce. (She expected to marry Vereker afterward but he would not marry her, nor would he move out of her house until she took legal action. 'American women,' Vereker would say, 'are like American colleges: they have dull, half-dead faculties.') When I arrived at the house, Vereker chose to pretend that he did not remember me. It was rather difficult to carry the situation off, for he was in one of his black moods. It was then that he should have written, but never did; instead he would gabble brilliantly about other authors. 'Goethe,' he would say, 'was a wax figure stuffed with hay. When you say that Proust was sick, you have said everything. Shakespeare was a dolt. If there had been no Voltaire, it would not have been necessary to create one.' Etc. I had been invited for the week-end and I intended to stay; none of us ever left Vereker alone when we came upon him in one of his moods. He frequently threatened suicide and six or seven times attempted it but, in every case, there was someone on hand to prevent him. Once, I remember, he got me out of bed late at night at my apartment. 'I'm going through with it this time,' he said, and darted into the bathroom. He was fumbling around for some poison in the medicine chest, which fortunately contained none when I ran in and pleaded with him. 'You have so many things yet to do,' I said to him. 'Yes,' he said, 'and so many people yet to insult.' He talked brilliantly all night long, and drank up a bottle of cognac that I had got to send to my father.

I had gone to the bathroom for a shower, the time he invited me to his lady's house, when he stalked into the room. 'Get out of that tub, you common housebreaker,' he said, 'or I shall summon the police!' I laughed, of course, and went on bathing. I was rubbing myself with a towel when the police arrived – he had sent for them! Vereker would have made an excellent actor; he convinced the police that he had never seen me before in his life. I was arrested, taken away, and locked up for the night. A few days later I got a note from Vereker. 'I shall never ask you to my house again,' he wrote, 'after the way I acted last Saturday.' His repentances, while whimsical, were always as complete as the erratic charades which called them forth. He was unpredictable and, at times, difficult, but he was always stimulating. Sometimes he keyed you up to a point beyond which, you felt, you could not go.

Vereker had a close escape from death once which I shall never forget. A famous American industrialist had invited a number of American writers and some visiting English men of letters out to his Long Island place. We were to make the trip in a huge bus that had been chartered for the purpose. Vereker came along and insisted, when we reached Long Island, on driving the bus. It was an icy night and he would put on the brakes at a curve, causing the heavy vehicle to skid ponderously. Several times we surged perilously near to a ditch and once the bus snapped off a big tree like a match. I remember that H. G. Bennett was along, and Arnold Wells, the three Sitwells, and four or five Waughs. One of them finally shut off the ignition and another struck Vereker over the head with a crank. His friends were furious. When the car stopped, we carried him outside and put him down on the hard, cold ground. Marvin Deane, the critic, held Vereker's head, which was bleeding profusely, in his lap, looked up at the busload of writers, and said: 'You might have killed him! And he is a greater genius than any of you!' It was superb. Then the amazing Vereker opened his eyes. 'That goes for me, too,' he said, and closed them again.

We hurried him to a hospital, where, in two days, he was on his feet again; he left the hospital without a word to anybody, and we all chipped in to pay the bill. Vereker had some money at the time which his mother had given him but, as he said, he needed it. 'I am glad he is up and out,' I said to the nurse who had taken care of him. 'So am I,' she said. Vereker affected everybody the same way.

Some time after this we all decided to make up a fund and send Vereker to Europe to write. His entire output, I had discovered, consisted of only twenty or thirty pages, most of them bearing the round stain of liquor glasses; one page was the beginning of a play done more or less in the style of Gertrude Stein. It seemed to me as brilliant as anything of its kind.

We got together about fifteen hundred dollars and I was delegated to approach Vereker, as tactfully as possible. We knew that it was folly for him to go on the way he was, dissipating his talent; for weeks he had been in one of his blackest moods: he would call on people, drink up their rye, wrench light-brackets off the walls, hurl scintillating gibes at his friends and at the accepted literary masters of all time, through whose superficiality Vereker saw more clearly, I think, than anybody else I have ever known. He would end up by bursting into tears. 'Here, but for the gracelessness of God,' he would shout, 'stands the greatest writer in the history of the world!' We felt that, despite Vereker's drunken exaggeration, there was more than a grain of truth in what he said: certainly nobody else we ever met had, so utterly, the fire of genius that blazed in Vereker, if outward manifestations meant anything.

He would never try for a Guggenheim fellowship. 'Guggenheim follow-sheep!' he would snarl. 'Fall in line, all you little men! Don't talk to me about Good-in-time fellowships!' He would go on that way, sparklingly, for an hour, his tirade finally culminating in one of those remarkable fits of temper in which he could rip up any apartment at all, no matter whose, in less than fifteen minutes.

Vereker, much to my surprise and gratification, took the fifteen hundred dollars without making a scene. I had suspected that he might denounce us all, that he might go into one of his brilliant philippics against Money, that he might even threaten again to take his life, for it had been several months since he had attempted suicide. But no; he snarled a bit, it is true, but he accepted the money. 'I'm cheap at twice the price,' he said.

It was the most money Vereker had ever had in his life and of course we should have known better than to let him have it all at once. The night of the day I gave it to him he cut a wide swath in the cheaper West Side night clubs and in Harlem, spent three hundred dollars, insulted several women, and figured in fist fights with a policeman, two taxi-drivers, and two husbands, all of whom won. We instantly decided to arrange his passage on a ship that was sailing for Cherbourg three nights later. Somehow or other we kept him out of trouble until the night of the sailing, when we gave a going-away party for him at Marvin Deane's house. Everybody was there: Gene Tunney, Sir Hubert Wilkins, Count von Luckner, Edward Bernays, and the literary and artistic crowd generally. Vereker got frightfully drunk. He denounced everybody at the party and also Hugh Walpole, Joseph Conrad, Crane, Henry James, Hardy and Meredith. He dwelt on the subject of *Jude the Obscure*. 'Jude the Obscure,' he would shout, 'Jude the Obscene, June the Obscude, Obs the June Moon.' He combined with his penetrating critical evaluations and his rare creative powers a certain unique fantasy not unlike that of Lewis Carroll. I once told him so. 'Not unlike your goddam grandmother!' he screamed. He was sensitive; he hated to be praised to his face; and then of course he held the works of Carroll in a certain disesteem.

Thus the party went on. Everybody was speechless, spell-bound, listening to Elliot Vereker. You could not miss his force. He was always the one person in a room. When it got to be eleven o'clock, I felt that we had better round up Vereker and start for the docks, for the boat sailed at midnight. He was nowhere to be found. We were alarmed. We searched every room, looked under beds, and into closets, but he was gone. Some of us ran downstairs and out into the street, asking cab-drivers and passers-by if they had seen him, a gaunt, tall, wild man with his hair in his eyes. Nobody had. It was almost eleven-thirty when somebody thought to look on the roof, to which there was access by a ladder through a trapdoor. Vereker was there. He lay sprawled on his face, the back of his head crushed in by a blow from some heavy instrument, probably a bottle. He was quite dead. 'The world's loss,' murmured Deane, as he looked down at the pitiful dust so lately the most burning genius we had ever been privileged to know, 'is Hell's gain.'

I think we all felt that way.

The Kerb in the Sky

When Charlie Deshler announced that he was going to marry Dorothy, someone said he would lose his mind posthaste. 'No,' said a wit who knew them both, 'post hoc.' Dorothy had begun, when she was quite young, to finish sentences for people. Sometimes she finished them wrongly, which annoyed the person who was speaking, and sometimes she finished them correctly, which annoyed the speaker even more.

'When William Howard Taft was – ' some guest in Dorothy's family's home would begin.

'President!' Dorothy would pipe up. The speaker may have meant to say 'President' or he may have meant to say 'young', or 'Chief Justice of the Supreme Court of the United States'. In any case, he would shortly put on his hat and go home. Like most parents, Dorothy's parents did not seem to be conscious that her mannerism was a nuisance. Very likely they thought that it was cute, or even bright. It is even probable that when Dorothy's mother first said 'Come, Dorothy, eat your – ' and Dorothy said 'Spinach, dear,' the former telephoned Dorothy's father at the office and told him about it, and he told everybody he met that day about it – and the next day and the day after.

When Dorothy grew up she became quite pretty and so even more of a menace. Gentlemen became attracted to her and then attached to her. Emotionally she stirred them, but mentally she soon began to wear them down. Even in her late teens she began correcting their English. 'Not "was", Arthur,' she would say, '"were". "Were prepared." See?' Most of her admirers tolerated this habit because of their interest in her lovely person, but as time went on and her interest in them remained more instructive than sentimental, they slowly drifted away to less captious, if dumber, girls.

Charlie Deshler, however, was an impetuous man, of the sweep-them-off-their-feet persuasion, and he became engaged to Dorothy so quickly and married her in so short a time that, being deaf to

162

the warnings of friends, whose concern he regarded as mere jealousy, he really didn't know anything about Dorothy except that she was pretty and bright-eyed and (to him) desirable.

Dorothy as a wife came, of course, into her great flowering: she took to correcting Charlie's stories. He had travelled widely and experienced greatly and was a truly excellent *raconteur*. Dorothy was, during their courtship, genuinely interested in him and in his stories, and since she had never shared any of the adventures he told about, she could not know when he made mistakes in time or in place or in identities. Beyond suggesting a change here and there in the number of a verb, she more or less let him alone. Charlie spoke rather good English, anyway – he knew when to say 'were' and when to say 'was' after 'if' – and this was another reason he didn't find Dorothy out.

I didn't call on them for quite a while after they were married, because I liked Charlie and I knew I would feel low if I saw him coming out of the anaesthetic of her charms and beginning to feel the first pains of reality. When I did finally call, conditions were, of course, all that I had feared. Charlie began to tell, at dinner, about a motor trip the two had made to this town and that – I never found out for sure what towns, because Dorothy denied almost everything that Charlie said. 'The next day,' he would say, 'we got an early start and drove two hundred miles to Fairview –' 'Well,' Dorothy would say, 'I wouldn't call it *early*. It wasn't as early as the first day we set out, when we got up about *seven*. And we only drove a hundred and eighty miles, because I remember looking at that mileage thing when we started.'

'Anyway, when we got to Fairview –' Charlie would go on. But Dorothy would stop him. 'Was it Fairview that day, darling?' she would ask. Dorothy often interrupted Charlie by asking him if he were right, instead of telling him that he was wrong, but it amounted to the same thing, for if he would reply: 'Yes, I'm sure it was Fairview,' she would say: 'But it *wasn't*, darling,' and then go on with the story herself. (She called everybody that she differed from 'darling'.)

Once or twice, when I called on them or they called on me, Dorothy would let Charlie get almost to the climax of some interesting account of a happening and then, like a tackler from behind, throw him just as he was about to cross the goal-line. There is nothing in life more shocking to the nerves and to the mind than this. Some husbands will sit back amiably – almost it seems, proudly – when their wives interrupt, and let them go on with the story, but these are beaten husbands. Charlie did not become beaten. But his wife's tackles knocked the wind out of him, and he began to realize that he would have to do something. What he did was rather ingenious. At the end of the second year of their marriage, when you visited the Deshlers, Charlie would begin some outlandish story about a dream he had had, knowing that Dorothy could not correct him on his own dreams. They became the only life he had that was his own.

'I thought I was running an airplane,' he would say, 'made out of telephone wires and pieces of old leather. I was trying to make it fly to the moon, taking off from my bedroom. About half-way up to the moon, however, a man who looked like Santa Claus, only he was dressed in the uniform of a customs officer, waved at me to stop – he was in a plane made of telephone wires, too. So I pulled over to a cloud. "Here," he said to me, "You can't go to the moon, if you are the man who invented these wedding cookies." Then he showed me a cookie made in the shape of a man and woman being married – little images of a man and a woman and a minister, made of dough and fastened firmly to a round, crisp cookie base.' So he would go on.

Any psychiatrist will tell you that at the end of the way Charlie was going lies madness in the form of monomania. You can't live in a fantastic dream world, night in and night out and then day in and day out, and remain sane. The substance began to die slowly out of Charlie's life, and he began to live entirely in shadow. And since monomania of this sort is likely to lead in the end to the reiteration of one particular story, Charlie's invention began to grow thin and he eventually took to telling, over and over again, the first dream he had ever described – the story of his curious flight toward the moon in an airplane made of telephone wires. It was extremely painful. It saddened us all.

After a month or two, Charlie finally had to be sent to an asylum. I was out of town when they took him away, but Joe Fultz, who went with him, wrote me about it. 'He seemed to like it up here right away,' Joe wrote. 'He's calmer and his eyes look better.' (Charlie had developed a wild, hunted look.) 'Of course,' concluded Joe, 'he's finally got away from that woman.'

It was a couple of weeks later that I drove up to the asylum to see Charlie. He was lying on a cot on a big screened-in porch, looking wan and thin. Dorothy was sitting on a chair beside his bed, bright-eyed and eager. I was somehow surprised to see her there, having figured that Charlie had, at least, won sanctuary from his wife. He looked quite mad. He began at once to tell me the story of his trip to the moon. He got to the part where the man who looked like Santa Claus waved at him to stop. 'He was in a plane made of telephone wires, too,' said Charlie. 'So I pulled over to a kerb – '

'No. You pulled over to a *cloud*,' said Dorothy. 'There aren't any kerbs in the *sky*. There *couldn't* be. You pulled over to a cloud.'

Charlie sighed and turned slightly in his bed and looked at me. Dorothy looked at me, too, with her pretty smile.

'He always gets that story wrong,' she said.

The Black Magic of Barney Haller

It was one of those hot days on which the earth is uninhabitable; even as early as ten o'clock in the morning, even on the hill where I live under the dark maples. The long porch was hot and the wicker chair I sat in complained hotly. My coffee was beginning to wear off and with it the momentary illusion it gives that things are Right and life is Good. There were sultry mutterings of thunder. I had a quick feeling that if I looked up from my book I would see Barney Haller. I looked up, and there he was, coming along the road, lightning playing about his shoulders, thunder following him like a dog.

Barney is (or was) my hired man. He is strong and amiable, sweaty and dependable, slowly and heavily competent. But he is also eerie: he trafficks with the devil. His ears twitch when he talks, but it isn't so much that as the things he says. Once in late June, when all of a moment sabres began to flash brightly in the heavens and bowling balls rumbled, I took refuge in the barn. I always have a feeling that I am going to be struck by lightning and either riven like an old apple tree or left with a foot that aches in rainy weather and a habit of fainting. Those things happen. Barney came in, not to escape the storm to which he is, or pretends to be, indifferent, but to put the scythe away. Suddenly he said the first of those things that made me, when I was with him, faintly creepy. He pointed at the house. 'Once I see dis boat come down de rock,' he said. It is phenomena like that of which I stand in constant dread: boats coming down rocks, people being teleported, statues dripping blood, old regrets and dreams in the form of Luna moths fluttering against the windows at midnight.

Of course I finally figured out what Barney meant – or what I comforted myself with believing he meant; something about a bolt coming down the lightning rod on the house; a common-place, an utterly natural thing. I should have dismissed it, but it had its effect on me. Here was a stolid man, smelling of hay and leather, who talked like somebody out of Charles Fort's books, or like a traveller back from Oz. And all the time the lightning was zigging and zagging around him.

On this hot morning when I saw Barney coming along with his faithful storm trudging behind him, I went back frowningly to my copy of *Swann's Way*. I hoped that Barney, seeing me absorbed in a book, would pass by without saying anything. I read: '. . . I myself seemed actually to have become the subject of my book: a church, a quartet, the rivalry between Francis I and Charles V . . .' I could feel Barney standing looking at me, but I didn't look at him.

'Dis morning bime by,' said Barney, 'I go hunt grotches in de voods.'

'That's fine,' I said, and turned a page and pretended to be engrossed in what I was reading. Barney walked on; he had wanted to talk some more, but he walked on. After a paragraph or two, his words began to come between me and the words in the book. 'Bime by I go hunt grotches in de voods.' If you are susceptible to such things, it is not difficult to visualize grotches. They fluttered into my mind: ugly little creatures, about the size of whippoor-wills, only covered with blood and honey and the scrapings of church bells. Grotches . . . Who and what, I wondered, really was this thing in the form of a hired man that kept anointing me omin-ously, in passing, with abracadabra?

Barney didn't go toward the woods at once; he weeded the corn, he picked apple boughs up off the lawn, he knocked a yellow jacket's nest down out of a plum tree. It was raining now, but he didn't seem to notice it. He kept looking at me out of the corner of his eye, and I kept looking at him out of the corner of my eye. 'Vot dime is it, blease?' he called to me finally. I put down my book and sauntered out to him. 'When you go for those grotches,' I said, firmly, 'I'll go with you.' I was sure he wouldn't want me to go. I was right; he protested that he could get the grotches himself. 'I'll go with you,' I said stubbornly. We stood looking at each other. And then, abruptly, just to give him something to ponder over, I quoted:

> 'I'm going out to clean the pasture spring;
> I'll only stop to rake the leaves away
> (And wait to watch the water clear, I may):
> I shan't be gone long.—You come too.'

It wasn't, I realized, very good abracadabra, but it served: Barney looked at me in a puzzled way. 'Yes,' he said, vaguely.

'It's five minutes of twelve,' I said, remembering he had asked.

'Den we go,' he said, and we trudged through the rain over to the orchard fence and climbed that, and opened a gate and went out into the meadow that slopes up to the woods. I had a prefiguring of Barney, at some proper spot deep in the woods, prancing around like a goat, casting off his false nature, shedding his hired man's garments, dropping his Teutonic accent, repeating diabolical phrases, conjuring up grotches.

There was a great slash of lightning and a long bumping of thunder as we reached the edge of the woods.

I turned and fled. Glancing over my shoulder, I saw Barney standing and staring after me. . . .

It turned out (on the face of it) to be as simple as the boat that came down the rock. Grotches were 'crotches'; crotched saplings which he cut down to use as supports under the peach boughs, because in bearing time they became so heavy with fruit that there was danger of the branches snapping off. I saw Barney later, putting the crotches in place. We didn't have much to say to each other. I can see now that he was beginning to suspect me too.

About six o'clock next evening, I was alone in the house and sleeping upstairs. Barney rapped on the door of the front porch. I knew it was Barney because he called to me. I woke up slowly. It was dark for six o'clock. I heard rumblings and saw flickerings. Barney was standing at the front door with his storm at heel! I had the conviction that it wasn't storming anywhere except around my house. There couldn't, without the intervention of the devil or one of his agents, be so many lightning storms in one neighbourhood.

I had been dreaming of Proust and the church at Combray and *madeleines* dipped in tea, and the rivalry between Francis I and Charles V. My head whirled and I didn't get up. Barney kept on rapping. He called out again. There was a flash, followed by a sharp splitting sound. I leaped up. This time, I thought, he is here to get me. I had a notion that he was standing at the door barefooted, with a wreath of grape leaves around his head, and a wild

168

animal's skin slung over his shoulder. I didn't want to go down, but I did.

He was as usual, solid, amiable, dressed like a hired man. I went out on the porch and looked at the improbable storm, now on in all its fury. 'This is getting pretty bad,' I said, meaningly. Barney looked at the rain placidly. 'Well,' I said, irritably, 'what's up?' Barney turned his little squinty blue eyes on me.

'We go to the garrick now and become warbs,' he said.

'The hell we do!' I thought to myself, quickly. I was uneasy – I was, you might even say, terrified – but I determined not to show it. If he began to chant incantations or to make obscene signs or if he attempted to sling me over his shoulder, I resolved to plunge right out into the storm, lightning and all, and run to the nearest house. I didn't know what they would think at the nearest house when I burst in upon them, or what I would tell them. But I didn't intend to accompany this amiable-looking fiend to any garrick and become a warb. I tried to persuade myself that there was some simple explanation, that warbs would turn out to be as innocuous as boats on rocks and grotches in the woods, but the conviction gripped me in the growling of the thunder that here at last was the Moment when Barney Haller, or whoever he was, had chosen to get me. I walked toward the steps that lead to the lawn, and turned and faced him, grimly.

'Listen!' I barked, suddenly. 'Did you know that even when it isn't brillig I can produce slithy toves? Did you happen to know that the mome rath never lived that could outgrabe me? Yeah and furthermore I can become anything I want to; even if I were a warb, I wouldn't have to keep on being one if I didn't want to. I can become a playing card at will, too; once I was the jack of clubs, only I forgot to take my glasses off and some guy recognized me. I . . .'

Barney was backing slowly away, toward the petunia box at one end of the porch. His little blue eyes were wide. He saw that I had him. 'I think I go now,' he said. And he walked out into the rain. The rain followed him down the road.

I have a new hired man now. Barney never came back to work for me after that day. Of course I figured out finally what he meant about the garrick and the warbs: he had simply got horribly mixed up in trying to tell me that he was going up to the garret and clear out the wasps, of which I have thousands. The new hired man is afraid of them. Barney could have scooped them up in his hands and thrown them out a window without getting stung. I am sure he trafficked with the devil. But I am sorry I let him go.

If Grant had been Drinking at Appomattox

(*Scribner's Magazine* published a series of three articles: 'If Booth Had Missed Lincoln', 'If Lee Had Not Won The Battle of Gettysburg', and 'If Napoleon Had Escaped to America'. This is the fourth.)

The morning of the ninth of April, 1865, dawned beautifully. General Meade was up with the first streaks of crimson in the eastern sky. General Hooker and General Burnside were up, and had breakfasted, by a quarter after eight. The day continued beautiful. It drew on toward eleven o'clock. General Ulysses S. Grant was still not up. He was asleep in his famous old navy hammock, swung high above the floor of his headquarters' bedroom. Headquarters was distressingly disarranged: papers were strewn on the floor; confidential notes from spies scurried here and there in the breeze from an open window; the dregs of an overturned bottle of wine flowed pinkly across an important military map.

Corporal Shultz, of the Sixty-fifth Ohio Volunteer Infantry, aide to General Grant, came into the outer room, looked around him, and sighed. He entered the bedroom and shook the General's hammock roughly. General Ulysses S. Grant opened one eye.

'Pardon, sir,' said Corporal Shultz, 'but this is the day of surrender. You ought to be up, sir.'

'Don't swing me,' said Grant, sharply, for his aide was making the hammock sway gently. 'I feel terrible,' he added, and he turned over and closed his eye again.

'General Lee will be here any minute now,' said the Corporal firmly, swinging the hammock again.

'Will you cut that out?' roared Grant. 'D'ya want to make me sick, or what?' Shultz clicked his heels and saluted. 'What's he coming here for?' asked the General.

'This is the day of surrender, sir,' said Shultz. Grant grunted bitterly.

'Three hundred and fifty generals in the Northern armies,' said

171

Grant, 'and he has to come to *me* about this. What time it is?'

'You're the Commander-in-Chief, that's why,' said Corporal Shultz. 'It's eleven twenty-five, sir.'

'Don't be crazy,' said Grant. 'Lincoln is the Commander-in-Chief. Nobody in the history of the world ever surrendered before lunch. Doesn't he know that an army surrenders on its stomach?' He pulled a blanket up over his head and settled himself again.

'The generals of the Confederacy will be here any minute now,' said the Corporal. 'You really ought to be up, sir.'

Grant stretched his arms above his head and yawned.

'All right, all right,' he said. He rose to a sitting position and stared about the room. 'This place looks awful,' he growled.

'You must have had quite a time of it last night, sir,' ventured Shultz.

'Yeh,' said General Grant, looking around for his clothes. 'I was wrassling some general. Some general with a beard.'

Shultz helped the commander of the Northern armies in the field to find his clothes.

'Where's my other sock?' demanded Grant. Shultz began to look around for it. The General walked uncertainly to a table and poured a drink from a bottle.

'I don't think it wise to drink, sir,' said Shultz.

'Nev' mind about me,' said Grant, helping himself to a second, 'I can take it or let it alone. Didn' ya ever hear the story about the fella went to Lincoln to complain about me drinking too much? "So-and-So says Grant drinks too much," this fella said. "So-and-So is a fool," said Lincoln. So this fella went to What's-His-Name and told him what Lincoln said and he came roarin' to Lincoln about it. "Did you tell So-and-So I was a fool?" he said. "No," said Lincoln, "I thought he knew it."' The General smiled, reminiscently, and had another drink. '*That's* how I stand with Lincoln,' he said, proudly.

The soft thudding sound of horses' hooves came through the open window. Shultz hurriedly walked over and looked out.

'Hoof steps,' said Grant, with a curious chortle.

'It is General Lee and his staff,' said Shultz.

'Show him in,' said the General, taking another drink. 'And see what the boys in the back room will have.'

Shultz walked smartly over to the door, opened it, saluted, and stood aside. General Lee, dignified against the blue of the April sky, magnificent in his dress uniform, stood for a moment framed in the doorway. He walked in, followed by his staff. They bowed, and stood silent. General Grant stared at them. He only had one boot on and his jacket was unbuttoned.

'I know who you are,' said Grant. 'You're Robert Browning, the poet.'

'This is General Robert E. Lee,' said one of his staff, coldly.

'Oh,' said Grant. 'I thought he was Robert Browning. He certainly looks like Robert Browning. There was a poet for you, Lee: Browning. Did ja ever read "How They Brought the Good News from Ghent to Aix"? "Up Derek, to saddle, up Derek, away; up Dunder, up Blitzen, up Prancer, up Dancer, up Bouncer, up Vixen, up – "'

'Shall we proceed at once to the matter in hand?' asked General Lee, his eyes disdainfully taking in the disordered room.

'Some of the boys was wrassling here last night,' explained Grant. 'I threw Sherman, or some general a whole lot like Sherman. It was pretty dark.' He handed a bottle of Scotch to the commanding officer of the Southern armies, who stood holding it, in amazement and discomfiture. 'Get a glass, somebody,' said Grant, looking straight at General Longstreet. 'Didn't I meet you at Cold Harbour?' he asked. General Longstreet did not answer.

'I should like to have this over with as soon as possible,' said Lee. Grant looked vaguely at Shultz, who walked up close to him, frowning.

'The surrender, sir, the surrender,' said Corporal Shultz in a whisper.

'Oh sure, sure,' said Grant. He took another drink. 'All right,' he said 'Here we go.' Slowly, sadly, he unbuckled his sword. Then he handed it to the astonished Lee. 'There you are, General,' said Grant. 'We dam' near licked you. If I'd been feeling better we *would* of licked you.'

The Remarkable Case of Mr Bruhl

Samuel O. Bruhl was just an ordinary-looking citizen, like you and me, except for a curious, shoe-shaped scar on his left cheek, which he got when he fell against a wagon-tongue in his youth. He had a good job as treasurer for a syrup-and-fondant concern, a large, devout wife, two tractable daughters, and a nice home in Brooklyn. He worked from nine to five, took in a show occasionally, played a bad, complacent game of golf, and was usually in bed by eleven o'clock. The Bruhls had a dog named Bert, a small circle of friends, and an old sedan. They had made a comfortable, if unexciting, adjustment to life.

There was no reason in the world why Samuel Bruhl shouldn't have lived along quietly until he died of some commonplace malady. He was a man designed by Nature for an uneventful life, an inexpensive but respectable funeral, and a modest stone marker. All this you would have predicted had you observed his colourless comings and goings, in mild manner, the small stature of his dreams. He was, in brief, the sort of average citizen that observers of Judd Gray thought Judd Gray was. And precisely as that mild little family man was abruptly hurled into an incongruous tragedy, so was Samuel Bruhl suddenly picked out of the hundreds of men just like him and marked for an extravagant and unpredictable end. Oddly enough it was the shoe-shaped scar on his left cheek which brought to his heels a Nemesis he had never dreamed of. A blemish on his heart, a tic in his soul would have been different; one would have blamed Bruhl for whatever anguish an emotional or spiritual flaw laid him open to, but it is ironical indeed when the Furies ride down a man who has been guilty of nothing worse than an accident in his childhood.

Samuel O. Bruhl looked very much like George ('Shoescar') Clinigan. Clinigan had that same singular shoe-shaped scar on his left cheek. There was also a general resemblance in height, weight, and complexion. A careful study would have revealed very soon that Clinigan's eyes were shifty and Bruhl's eyes were clear, and that the syrup-and-fondant company's treasurer had a more pleasant mouth and a higher forehead than the gangster and racketeer, but at a glance the similarity was remarkable.

Had Clinigan not become notorious, this prank of Nature would never have been detected, but Clinigan did become notorious and dozens of persons observed that he looked like Bruhl. They saw Clinigan's picture in the papers the day he was shot, and the day after, and the day after that. Presently someone in the syrup-and-fondant concern mentioned to someone else that Clinigan looked like Mr Bruhl, remarkably like Mr Bruhl. Soon everybody in the place had commented on it, among themselves, and to Mr Bruhl.

Mr Bruhl rather laughed it off at first, but one day when Clinigan had been in the hospital a week, a cop peered closely at Mr Bruhl when he was on his way home from work. After that, the little treasurer noticed a number of other strangers staring at him with mingled surprise and alarm. One small, dark man hastily thrust a hand into his coat pocket and paled slightly.

Mr Bruhl began to worry. He began to imagine things. 'I hope this fellow Clinigan doesn't pull through,' he said one morning at breakfast. 'He's a bad actor. He's better off dead.'

'Oh, he'll pull through,' said Mrs Bruhl, who had been reading the morning paper. 'It says here he'll pull through. But it says they'll shoot him again. It says they're sure to shoot him again.'

The morning after the night that Clinigan left the hospital, secretly, by a side door, and disappeared into the town, Bruhl decided not to go to work. 'I don't feel so good today,' he said to his wife. 'Would you call up the office and tell them I'm sick?'

'You don't look well,' said his wife. 'You really don't look well. Get down, Bert,' she added, for the dog had jumped upon her lap and whined. The animal knew that something was wrong.

That evening Bruhl, who had mooned about the house all day, read in the papers that Clinigan had vanished, but was believed to be somewhere in the city. His various rackets required his presence, at least until he made enough money to skip out with; he had left the hospital penniless. Rival gangsters, the papers said, were sure to seek him out, to hunt him down, to give it to him again. 'Give him what again?' asked Mrs Bruhl when she read this. 'Let's talk about something else,' said her husband.

It was little Joey, the office boy at the syrup-and-fondant company, who first discovered that Mr Bruhl was afraid. Joey, who went about with tennis shoes on, entered the treasurer's office suddenly – flung open the door and started to say something. 'Good God!' cried Mr Bruhl, rising from his chair. 'Why, what's the matter, Mr Bruhl?' asked Joey. Other little things happened. The switchboard girl phoned Mr Bruhl's desk one afternoon and said there was a man waiting to see him, a Mr Globe. 'What's he look like?' asked Bruhl, who didn't know anybody named Globe. 'He's small and dark,' said the girl. 'A small, dark man?' said Bruhl. 'Tell him I'm out. Tell him I've gone to California.' The personnel, comparing notes, decided at length that the treasurer was afraid of being mistaken for Shoescar and put on the spot. They said nothing to Mr Bruhl about this, because they were forbidden to by Ollie Breithofter, a fattish clerk who was a tireless and inventive practical joker and who had an idea.

As the hunt went on for Clinigan and he still wasn't found and killed, Mr Bruhl lost weight and grew extremely fidgety. He began to figure out new ways of getting to work, one requiring the use of two different ferry lines; he ate his lunch in, he wouldn't answer bells, he cried out when anyone dropped anything, and he ran into stores or banks when cruising taxi-drivers shouted at him. One morning, in setting the house to rights, Mrs Bruhl found a revolver under his pillow. 'I found a revolver under your pillow,' she told him that night. 'Burglars are bad in this neighbourhood,' he said. 'You oughtn't to have a revolver,' she said. They argued about it, he irritably, she uneasily, until time for bed. As Bruhl was undressing, after locking and bolting all the doors, the telephone rang. 'It's for you, Sam,' said Mrs Bruhl. Her husband went slowly to the phone, passing Bert on the way. 'I wish I was you,' he said to the dog, and took up the receiver. 'Get this, Shoescar,' said a husky voice. 'We trailed you where you are, see? You're cooked.' The receiver at the other end was hung up. Bruhl shouted. His wife came running. 'What is it, Sam, what is it?' she cried. Bruhl, pale, sick-looking, had fallen into a chair. 'They got me,' he moaned. 'They got me.' Slowly, deviously, Minnie Bruhl got it out of her husband that he had been mistaken for Clinigan and that he was cooked. Mrs Bruhl was not very quick mentally, but she had a certain intuition and this intuition told her, as she trembled there in her nightgown above her broken husband, that this was the work of Ollie Breithofter. She instantly phoned Ollie Breithofter's wife and, before she hung up, had got the truth out of Mrs Breithofter. It was Ollie who had called.

The treasurer of the Maskonsett Syrup & Fondant Company, Inc., was so relieved to know that the gangs weren't after him that he admitted frankly at the office next day that Ollie had fooled him for a minute. Mr Bruhl even joined in the laughter and wise-cracking, which went on all day. After that, for almost a week, the mild little man had comparative peace of mind. The papers said very little about Clinigan now. He had completely disappeared. Gang warfare had died down for the time being.

One Sunday morning Mr Bruhl went for an automobile ride with his wife and daughters. They had driven about a mile through Brooklyn streets when, glancing in the mirror above his head, Mr Bruhl observed a blue sedan just behind him. He turned off into the next side street, and the sedan turned off too. Bruhl made another turn, and the sedan followed him. 'Where are you going, dear?' asked Mrs Bruhl. Mr Bruhl didn't answer her, he speeded up, he drove terrifically fast, he turned corners so wildly that the rear wheels swung around. A traffic cop shrilled at him. The younger daughter screamed. Bruhl drove right on, weaving in and out. Mrs Bruhl began to berate him wildly. 'Have you lost your mind, Sam?' she shouted. Mr Bruhl looked behind him. The sedan was no longer to be seen. He slowed up. 'Let's go home,' he said. 'I've had enough of this.'

A month went by without incident (thanks largely to Mrs Breithofter) and Samuel Bruhl began to be himself again. On the day that he was practically normal once more, Sluggy Pensiotta, alias Killer Lewis, alias Strangler Koetschke, was shot. Sluggy was the leader of the gang that had sworn to get Shoescar Clinigan. The papers instantly took up the gang-war story where they had left off. Pictures of Clinigan were published again. The slaying of Pensiotta, said the papers, meant but one thing: it meant that

177

Shoescar Clinigan was cooked. Mr Bruhl, reading this, went gradually to pieces once more.

After another week of skulking about, starting at every noise, and once almost fainting when an automobile backfired near him, Samuel Bruhl began to take on a remarkable new appearance. He talked out of the corner of his mouth, his eyes grew shifty. He looked more and more like Shoescar Clinigan. He snarled at his wife. Once he called her 'Babe', and he had never called her anything but Minnie. He kissed her in a strange, new way, acting rough, almost brutal. At the office he was mean and overbearing. He used peculiar language. One night when the Bruhls had friends in for bridge – old Mr Creegan and his wife – Bruhl suddenly appeared from upstairs with a pair of scarlet pyjamas on, smoking a cigarette, and gripping his revolver. After a few loud and incoherent remarks of a boastful nature, he let fly at a clock on the mantel, and hit it squarely in the middle. Mrs Bruhl screamed. Mr Creegan fainted. Bert, who was in the kitchen, howled. 'What's the matta you?' snarled Bruhl. 'Ya bunch of softies.'

Quite by accident, Mrs Bruhl discovered, hidden away in a closet, eight or ten books on gangs and gangsters, which Bruhl had put there. They included *Al Capone, You Can't Win, 10,000 Public Enemies*, and a lot of others; and they were all well thumbed. Mrs Bruhl realized that it was high time something was done, and she determined to have a doctor for her husband. For two or three days Bruhl had not gone to work. He lay around in his bedroom, in his red pyjamas, smoking cigarettes. The office phoned once or twice. When Mrs Bruhl urged him to get up and dress and go to work, he laughed and patted her roughly on the head. 'It's a knockover, kid,' he said. 'We'll be sitting pretty. To hell with it.'

The doctor who finally came and slipped into Bruhl's bedroom was very grave when he emerged. 'This is a psychosis,' he said, 'a definite psychosis. Your husband is living in a world of fantasy. He has built up a curious defence mechanism against something or other.' The Doctor suggested that a psychiatrist be called in, but after he had gone Mrs Bruhl decided to take her husband out of town on a trip. The Maskonsett Syrup & Fondant Company, Inc., was very fine about it. Mr Scully said of course. 'Sam is very valuable to us, Mrs Bruhl,' said Mr Scully, 'and we all hope he'll be all right.' Just the same he had Mr Bruhl's accounts examined, when Mrs Bruhl had gone.

Oddly enough, Samuel Bruhl was amenable to the idea of going away. 'I need a rest,' he said. 'You're right. Let's get the hell out of here.' He seemed normal up to the time they set out for the Grand Central and then he insisted on leaving from the 125th Street station. Mrs Bruhl took exception to this, as being ridiculous, whereupon her doting husband snarled at her. 'God, what a dumb moll *I* picked,' he said to Minnie Bruhl, and he added bitterly that if the heat was put on him it would be his own babe who was to blame. 'And what do you think of *that*?' he said, pushing her to the floor of the cab.

They went to a little inn in the mountains. It wasn't a very nice place, but the rooms were clean and the meals were good. There was no form of entertainment, except a Tom Thumb golf course and an uneven tennis court, but Mr Bruhl didn't mind. He said it was too cold outdoors, anyway. He stayed indoors, reading and smoking. In the evening he played the mechanical piano in the dining-room. He liked to play 'More Than You Know' over and over again. One night, about nine o'clock, he was putting in his seventh or eighth nickel when four men walked into the dining-room. They were silent men, wearing overcoats, and carrying what appeared to be cases for musical instruments. They took out various kinds of guns from their cases, quickly, expertly, and walked over toward Bruhl, keeping step. He turned just in time to see them line up four abreast and aim at him. Nobody else was in the room. There was a cumulative roar and a series of flashes. Mr Bruhl fell and the men walked out in single file, rapidly, nobody having said a word.

Mrs Bruhl, state police, and the hotel manager tried to get the wounded man to talk. Chief Witznitz of the nearest town's police force tried it. It was no good. Bruhl only snarled and told them to go away and let him alone. Finally, Commissioner O'Donnell of the New York City Police Department arrived at the hospital. He asked Bruhl what the men looked like. 'I don't know what they looked like,' snarled Bruhl, 'and if I did know I wouldn't tell you.'

179

He was silent for a moment, then: 'Cop!' he added, bitterly. The Commissioner sighed and turned away. 'They're all like that,' he said to the others in the room. 'They never talk.' Hearing this, Mr Bruhl smiled, a pleased smile, and closed his eyes.

The Luck of Jad Peters

Aunt Emma Peters, at eighty-three – the year she died – still kept in her unused front parlour, on the table with Jad Peters' collection of lucky souvenirs, a large rough fragment of rock weighing perhaps twenty pounds. The rock stood in the centre of a curious array of odds and ends: a piece of tent canvas, a chip of pine wood, a yellowed telegram, some old newspaper clippings, the cork from a bottle, a bill from a surgeon. Aunt Emma never talked about the strange collection except once, during her last days, when somebody asked her if she wouldn't feel better if the rock were thrown away. 'Let it stay where Lisbeth put it,' she said. All that I know about the souvenirs I have got from other members of the family. A few of them didn't think it was 'decent' that the rock should have been part of the collection, but Aunt Lisbeth, Emma's sister, had insisted that it should be. In fact, it was Aunt Lisbeth Banks who hired a man to lug it to the house and put it on the table with the rest of the things. 'It's as much God's doing as that other clutter-trap,' she would say. And she would rock back and forth in her rocking chair with a grim look. 'You can't taunt the Lord,' she would add. She was a very religious woman. I used to see her now and again at funerals, tall, gaunt, grim, but I never talked to her if I could help it. She liked funerals and she liked to look at corpses, and that made me afraid of her.

Just back of the souvenir table at Aunt Emma's, on the wall, hung a heavy-framed, full-length photograph of Aunt Emma's husband, Jad Peters. It showed him wearing a hat and overcoat and carrying a suitcase. When I was a little boy in the early nineteen-hundreds and was taken to Aunt Emma's house near Sugar Grove, Ohio, I used to wonder about that photograph (I didn't wonder about the rock and the other objects, because they weren't put there till much later). It seemed so funny for anyone to be photographed in a hat and overcoat and carrying a suitcase, and even funnier to have the photograph enlarged to almost life size and put inside so elaborate a frame. When we children would sneak

181

into the front parlour to look at the picture, Aunt Emma would hurry us out again. When we asked her about the picture, she would say, 'Never you mind.' But when I grew up, I learned the story of the big photograph and of how Jad Peters came to be known as Lucky Jad. As a matter of fact, it was Jad who began calling himself that; once when he ran for a county office (and lost) he had 'Lucky Jad Peters' printed on his campaign cards. Nobody else took the name up except in a scoffing way.

It seems that back in 1888, when Jad Peters was about thirty-five, he had a pretty good business of some kind or other which caused him to travel around quite a lot. One week he went to New York with the intention of going on to Newport, later, by ship. Something turned up back home, however, and one of his employees sent him a telegram reading 'Don't go to Newport. Urgent you return here.' Jad's story was that he was on the ship, ready to sail, when the telegram was delivered; it had been sent to his hotel, he said, a few minutes after he had checked out, and an obliging clerk had hustled the messenger boy on down to the dock. That was Jad's story. Most people believed, when they heard the story, that Jad had got the wire at his hotel, probably hours before the ship sailed, for he was a great one at adorning a tale. At any rate, whether or not he rushed off the ship just before the gangplank was hauled up, it sailed without him and some eight or nine hours out of the harbour sank in a storm with the loss of everybody on board. That's why he had the photograph taken and enlarged: it showed him just as he was when he got off the ship, he said. And that is how he came to start his collection of lucky souvenirs. For a few years he kept the telegram, and newspaper clippings of the ship disaster, tucked away in the family Bible, but one day he got them out and put them on the parlour table under a big glass bell.

From 1888 up until 1920, when Jad died, nothing much happened to him. He is remembered in his later years as a garrulous, boring old fellow whose business slowly went to pieces because of his lack of industry and who finally settled down on a small farm near Sugar Grove and barely scraped out an existence. He took to drinking in his sixties, and from then on made Aunt Emma's life miserable. I don't know how she managed to keep up the payments on his life-insurance policy, but some way or other she did. Some of her relatives said among themselves that it would be a blessing if Jad died in one of his frequent fits of nausea. It was pretty well known that Aunt Emma had never liked him very much – she married him because he asked her to twice a week for seven years and because there had been nobody else she cared about; she stayed married to him on account of their children and because her people always stayed married. She grew, in spite of Jad, to be a quiet, kindly old lady as the years went on, although her mouth would take on a strained, tight look when Jad showed up at dinner time from wherever he had been during the day – usually from down at Prentice's store in the village, where he liked to sit around telling about the time he just barely got off the doomed boat in New York harbour in '88 and adding tales, more or less fantastic, of more recent close escapes he had had. There was his appendicitis operation, for one thing: he had come out of the ether, he would say, just when they had given him up. Dr Benham, who had performed the operation, was annoyed when he heard this, and once met Jad in the street and asked him to quit repeating the preposterous story, but Jad added the doctor's bill to his collection of talismans, anyway. And there was the time when he had got up in the night to take a swig of stomach bitters for a bad case of heartburn and had got hold of the carbolic-acid bottle by mistake. Something told him, he would say, to take a look at the bottle before he uncorked it, so he carried it to a lamp, lighted the lamp, and he'd be god-dam if it wasn't carbolic acid! It was then that he added the cork to his collection.

Old Jad got so that he could figure out lucky escapes for himself in almost every disaster and calamity that happened in and around Sugar Grove. Once, for example, a tent blew down during a wind storm at the Fairfield County Fair, killing two people and injuring a dozen others. Jad hadn't gone to the fair that year for the first time in nine or ten years. Something told him, he would say, to stay away from the fair that year. The fact that he always went to the fair, when he did go, on a Thursday and that the tent blew down on a Saturday didn't make any difference to Jad. He hadn't been there and the tent blew down and two people were killed. After the accident, he went to the fair grounds and cut a piece of canvas from the tent and put it on the parlour table next to the cork from the carbolic-acid bottle. Lucky Jad Peters!

I think Aunt Emma got so that she didn't hear Jad when he was talking, except on evenings when neighbours dropped in, and then she would have to take hold of the conversation and steer it away from any opening that might give Jad a chance to tell of some close escape he had had. But he always got his licks in. He would bide his time, creaking back and forth in his chair, clicking his teeth, and not listening much to the talk about crops and begonias and the latest reports on the Spencers' feeble-minded child, and then, when there was a long pause, he would clear his throat and say that that reminded him of the time he had had a mind to go down to Pullen's lumber yard to fetch home a couple of two-by-fours to shore up the chicken house. Well, sir, he had pottered around the house a little while and was about to set out for Pullen's when something told him not to go a step. And it was that very day that a pile of lumber in the lumber yard let go and crushed Grant Pullen's leg so's it had to be amputated. Well, sir, he would say – but Aunt Emma would cut in on him at this point. 'Everybody's heard that old chestnut,' she would say, with a forced little laugh, fanning herself in quick strokes with an old palm-leaf fan. Jad would go sullen and rock back and forth in his chair, clicking his teeth. He wouldn't get up when the guests rose to go – which they always did at this juncture. The memento of his close escape from the Pullen lumbar-yard disaster was, of course, the chip of pine wood.

I think I have accounted for all of Jad's souvenirs that I remember except the big rough fragment of rock. The story of the rock is a strange one. In August 1920, county engineers were widening the channel of the Hocking River just outside of Sugar Grove and had occasion to do considerable blasting out of river-bed rock. I have never heard Clem Warden tell the story himself, but it has been told to me by people who have. It seems that Clem was walking along the main street of Sugar Grove at about a quarter to four when he saw Jad coming along toward him. Clem was an old crony of Jad's – one of the few men of his own generation who could tolerate Jad – and the two stopped on the sidewalk and talked.

184

Clem figured later that they had talked for about five minutes, and then either he or Jad said something about getting on, so they separated, Jad going on toward Prentice's store, slowly, on account of his rheumatic left hip, and Clem going in the other direction. Clem had taken about a dozen steps when suddenly he heard Jad call to him. 'Say, Clem!' Jad said. Clem stopped and turned around, and here was Jad walking back toward him. Jad had taken about six steps when suddenly he was flung up against the front of Matheny's harness store 'like a sack o' salt', as Clem put it. By the time Clem could reach him, he was gone. He never knew what hit him, Clem said, and for quite a few minutes nobody else knew what hit him, either. Then somebody in the crowd that gathered found the big muddy rock lying in the road by the gutter. A particularly big shot of dynamite, set off in the river bed, had hurtled the fragment through the air with terrific force. It had come flying over the four-storey Jackson Building like a cannon ball and had struck Jad Peters squarely in the chest.

I suppose old Jad hadn't been in his grave two days before the boys at Prentice's quit shaking their heads solemnly over the accident and began making funny remarks about it. Cal Gregg's was the funniest. 'Well, sir,' said Cal, 'I don't suppose none of us will ever know what it was now, but somethin' must of told Jad to turn around.'

The Greatest Man in the World

Looking back on it now, from the vantage point of 1950, one can only marvel that it hadn't happened long before it did. The United States of America had been, ever since Kitty Hawk, blindly constructing the elaborate petard by which, sooner or later, it must be hoist. It was inevitable that some day there would come roaring out of the skies a national hero of insufficient intelligence, background, and character successfully to endure the mounting orgies of glory prepared for aviators who stayed up a long time or flew a great distance. Both Lindbergh and Byrd, fortunately for national decorum and international amity, had been gentlemen; so had our other famous aviators. They wore their laurels gracefully, withstood the awful weather of publicity, married excellent women, usually of fine family, and quietly retired to private life and the enjoyment of their varying fortunes. No untoward incidents, on a worldwide scale, marred the perfection of their conduct on the perilous heights of fame. The exception to the rule was, however, bound to occur and it did, in July 1937, when Jack ('Pal') Smurch, erstwhile mechanic's helper in a small garage in Westfield, Iowa, flew a second-hand, single-motored Bresthaven Dragon-Fly III monoplane all the way around the world, without stopping.

Never before in the history of aviation had such a flight as Smurch's ever been dreamed of. No one had ever taken seriously the weird floating auxiliary gas tanks, invention of the mad New Hampshire professor of astronomy, Dr Charles Lewis Gresham, upon which Smurch placed full reliance. When the garage worker, a slightly built, surly, unprepossessing young man of twenty-two, appeared at Roosevelt Field in early July 1937, slowly chewing a great quid of scrap tobacco, and announced 'Nobody ain't seen no flyin' yet,' the newspapers touched briefly and satirically upon his projected twenty-five-thousand-mile flight. Aeronautical and automotive experts dismissed the idea curtly, implying that it was a hoax, a publicity stunt. The rusty, battered, second-hand plane wouldn't go. The Gresham auxiliary tanks wouldn't work. It was simply a cheap joke.

Smurch, however, after calling on a girl in Brooklyn who worked in the flap-folding department of a large paper-box factory, a girl whom he later described as his 'sweet patootie', climbed nonchalantly into his ridiculous plane at dawn of the memorable seventh of July 1937, spat a curve of tobacco juice into the still air, and took off, carrying with him only a gallon of bootleg gin and six pounds of salami.

When the garage boy thundered out over the ocean the papers were forced to record, in all seriousness, that a mad, unknown young man – his name was variously misspelled – had actually set out upon a preposterous attempt to span the world in a rickety, one-engined contraption, trusting to the long-distance refuelling device of a crazy schoolmaster. When, nine days later, without having stopped once, the tiny plane appeared above San Francisco Bay, headed for New York, spluttering and choking, to be sure, but still magnificently and miraculously aloft, the headlines, which long since had crowded everything else off the front page – even the shooting of the Governor of Illinois by the Vileti gang – swelled to unprecedented size, and the news stories began to run to twenty-five and thirty columns. It was noticeable, however, that the accounts of the epoch-making flight touched rather lightly upon the aviator himself. This was not because facts about the hero as a man were too meagre, but because they were too complete.

Reporters, who had been rushed out to Iowa when Smurch's plane was first sighted over the little French coast town of Serly-e-Mer, to dig up the story of the great man's life, had promptly discovered that the story of his life could not be printed. His mother, a sullen short-order cook in a shack restaurant on the edge of a tourists' camping ground near Westfield, met all inquiries as to her son with an angry 'Ah, the hell with him; I hope he drowns.' His father appeared to be in jail somewhere for stealing spotlights and laprobes from tourists' automobiles; his young brother, a weak-minded lad, had but recently escaped from the Preston, Iowa, Reformatory and was already wanted in several Western towns for the theft of money-order blanks from post offices. These

187

alarming discoveries were still piling up at the very time that Pa
Smurch, the greatest hero of the twentieth century, blear-eyed
dead for sleep, half-starved, was piloting his crazy junk-heap high
above the region in which the lamentable story of his private life
was being unearthed, headed for New York and a greater glory
than any man of his time had ever known.

The necessity for printing some account in the papers of the
young man's career and personality had led to a remarkable predicament. It was of course impossible to reveal the facts, for a
tremendous popular feeling in favour of the young hero had
sprung up, like a grass fire, when he was half-way across Europe
on his flight around the globe. He was, therefore, described as a
modest chap, taciturn, blond, popular with his friends, popular
with girls. The only available snapshot of Smurch, taken at the
wheel of a phoney automobile in a cheap photo studio at an amusement park, was touched up so that the little vulgarian looked quite
handsome. His twisted leer was smoothed into a pleasant smile.
The truth was, in this way, kept from the youth's ecstatic com-
patriots; they did not dream that the Smurch family was despised
and feared by its neighbours in the obscure Iowa town, nor that
the hero himself, because of numerous unsavoury exploits, had
come to be regarded in Westfield as a nuisance and a menace. He
had, the reporters discovered, once knifed the principal of his high
school – not mortally, to be sure, but he had knifed him; and on
another occasion, surprised in the act of stealing an altar-cloth
from a church, he had bashed the sacristan over the head with a
pot of Easter lilies; for each of these offences he had served a
sentence in the reformatory.

Inwardly, the authorities, both in New York and in Washington,
prayed that an understanding Providence might, however awful
such a thing seemed, bring disaster to the rusty, battered plane and
its illustrious pilot, whose unheard-of flight had aroused the
civilized world to hosannas of hysterical praise. The authorities
were convinced that the character of the renowned aviator was
such that the limelight of adulation was bound to reveal him to all
the world, as a congenital hooligan mentally and morally un-
equipped to cope with his own prodigious fame. 'I trust,' said the
Secretary of State, at one of many secret Cabinet meetings called
188

to consider the national dilemma, 'I trust that his mother's prayer will be answered,' by which he referred to Mrs Emma Smurch's wish that her son might be drowned. It was, however, too late for that – Smurch had leaped the Atlantic and then the Pacific as if they were millponds. At three minutes after two o'clock on the afternoon of 17 July 1937, the garage boy brought his idiotic plane into Roosevelt Field for a perfect three-point landing.

It had, of course, been out of the question to arrange a modest little reception for the greatest flier in the history of the world. He was received at Roosevelt Field with such elaborate and pretentious ceremonies as rocked the world. Fortunately, however, the worn and spent hero promptly swooned, had to be removed bodily from his plane, and was spirited from the field without having opened his mouth once. Thus he did not jeopardize the dignity of this first reception, a reception illumined by the presence of the Secretaries of War and the Navy, Mayor Michael J. Moriarity of New York, the Premier of Canada, Governors Fanniman, Groves, McFeely and Critchfield, and a brilliant array of European diplomats. Smurch did not, in fact, come to in time to take part in the gigantic hullabaloo arranged at City Hall for the next day. He was rushed to a secluded nursing home and confined to bed. It was nine days before he was able to get up, or to be more exact, before he was permitted to get up. Meanwhile the greatest minds in the country, in solemn assembly, had arranged a secret conference of city, state, and government officials, which Smurch was to attend for the purpose of being instructed in the ethics and behaviour of heroism.

On the day that the little mechanic was finally allowed to get up and dress and, for the first time in two weeks, took a great chew of tobacco, he was permitted to receive the newspapermen – this by way of testing him out. Smurch did not wait for questions. 'Youse guys,' he said – and the *Times* man winced – 'youse guys can tell the cock-eyed world dat I put it over on Lindbergh, see? Yeh – an' made an ass o' them two frogs.' The 'two frogs' was a reference to a pair of gallant French fliers who, in attempting a flight only half-way round the world, had, two weeks before, unhappily been lost at sea. The *Times* man was bold enough, at this point, to sketch out for Smurch the accepted formula for interviews in cases of this kind; he explained that there should be no arrogant statements belittling the achievements of other heroes, particularly heroes of foreign nations. 'Ah, the hell with that,' said Smurch. 'I did it, see? I did it, an' I'm talkin' about it.' And he did talk about it.

None of this extraordinary interview was, of course, printed. On the contrary, the newspapers, already under the disciplined direction of a secret directorate created for the occasion and composed of statesmen and editors, gave out to a panting and restless world that 'Jacky', as he had been arbitrarily nicknamed, would consent to say only that he was very happy and that anyone could have done what he did. 'My achievement has been, I fear, slightly exaggerated,' the *Times* man's article had him protest, with a modest smile. These newspaper stories were kept from the hero, a restriction which did not serve to abate the rising malevolence of his temper. The situation was, indeed, extremely grave, for Pal Smurch was, as he kept insisting, 'rarin' to go'. He could not much longer be kept from a nation clamorous to lionize him. It was the most desperate crisis the United States of America had faced since the sinking of the *Lusitania*.

On the afternoon of the twenty-seventh of July, Smurch was spirited away to a conference-room in which were gathered mayors, governors, government officials, behaviourist psychologists, and editors. He gave them each a limp, moist paw and a brief unlovely grin. 'Hah ya?' he said. When Smurch was seated, the Mayor of New York arose and, with obvious pessimism, attempted to explain what he must say and how he must act when presented to the world, ending his talk with a high tribute to the hero's courage and integrity. The Mayor was followed by Governor Fanniman of New York, who, after a touching declaration of faith, introduced Cameron Spottiswood, Second Secretary of the American Embassy in Paris, the gentleman selected to coach Smurch in the amenities of public ceremonies. Sitting in a chair, with a soiled yellow tie in his hand and his shirt open at the throat, unshaved, smoking a rolled cigarette, Jack Smurch listened with a leer on his lips. 'I get ya, I get ya,' he cut in, nastily. 'Ya want me to ack like a softy, huh? Ya want me to ack like that — — baby-faced Lindbergh, huh? Well, nuts to that, see?' Everyone took in his breath

190

sharply; it was a sigh and a hiss. 'Mr Lindbergh,' began a United States Senator, purple with rage, 'and Mr Byrd— ' Smurch, who was paring his nails with a jackknife, cut in again. 'Byrd!' he exclaimed. 'Aw fa God's sake, dat big – ' Somebody shut off his blasphemies with a sharp word. A newcomer had entered the room. Everyone stood up, except Smurch, who, still busy with his nails, did not even glance up. 'Mr Smurch,' said someone sternly, 'the President of the United States!' It had been thought that the presence of the Chief Executive might have a chastening effect upon the young hero, and the former had been, thanks to the remarkable cooperation of the press, secretly brought to the obscure conference-room.

A great, painful silence fell. Smurch looked up, waved a hand at the President. 'How ya comin'?' he asked, and began rolling a fresh cigarette. The silence deepened. Someone coughed in a strained way. 'Geez, it's hot, ain't it?' said Smurch. He loosened two more shirt buttons, revealing a hairy chest and the tattooed word 'Sadie' enclosed in a stencilled heart. The great and important men in the room, faced by the most serious crisis in recent American history, exchanged worried frowns. Nobody seemed to know how to proceed. 'Come awn, come awn,' said Smurch. 'Let's get the hell out of here! When do I start cuttin' in on de parties, huh? And what's they goin' to be *in* it?' He rubbed a thumb and forefinger together meaningly. 'Money!' exclaimed a state senator, shocked, pale. 'Yeh, money,' said Pal, flipping his cigarette out of a window. 'An' big money.' He began rolling a fresh cigarette. 'Big money,' he repeated, frowning over the rice paper. He tilted back in his chair, and leered at each gentleman, separately, the leer of an animal that knows its power, the leer of a leopard loose in a bird-and-dog shop. 'Aw fa God's sake, let's get some place where it's cooler,' he said. 'I been cooped up plenty for three weeks!'

Smurch stood up and walked over to an open window, where he stood staring down into the street, nine floors below. The faint shouting of newsboys floated up to him. He made out his name. 'Hot dog!' he cried, grinning, ecstatic. He leaned out over the sill. 'You tell 'em, babies!' he shouted down. 'Hot diggity dog!' In the tense little knot of men standing behind him, a quick, mad impulse flared up. An unspoken word of appeal, of command, seemed to ring through the room. Yet it was deadly silent. Charles K. L. Brand, secretary to the Mayor of New York City, happened to be standing nearest Smurch; he looked inquiringly at the President of the United States. The President, pale, grim, nodded shortly. Brand, a tall, powerfully built man, once a tackle at Rutgers, stepped forward, seized the greatest man in the world by his left shoulder and the seat of his pants, and pushed him out the window.

'My God, he's fallen out the window!' cried a quick-witted editor.

'Get me out of here!' cried the President. Several men sprang to his side and he walked hurriedly escorted out of a door toward a side-entrance of the building. The editor of the Associated Press took charge, being used to such things. Crisply he ordered certain men to leave, others to stay; quickly he outlined a story which all the papers were to agree on, sent two men to the street to handle that end of the tragedy, commanded a Senator to sob and two Congressmen to go to pieces nervously. In a word, he skilfully set the stage for the gigantic task that was to follow, the task of breaking to a grief-stricken world the sad story of the untimely, accidental death of its most illustrious and spectacular figure.

The funeral was, as you know, the most elaborate, the finest, the solemnest, and the saddest ever held in the United States of America. The monument in Arlington Cemetery, with its clean white shaft of marble and the simple device of a tiny plane carved on its base, is a place for pilgrims, in deep reverence, to visit. The nations of the world paid lofty tributes to little Jacky Smurch, America's greatest hero. At a given hour there were two minutes of silence throughout the nation. Even the inhabitants of the small, bewildered town of Westfield, Iowa, observed the touching ceremony; agents of the Department of Justice saw to that. One of them was especially assigned to stand grimly in the doorway of a little shack restaurant on the edge of the tourists' camping ground just outside the town. There, under his stern scrutiny, Mrs Emma Smurch bowed her head above two hamburger steaks sizzling on her grill – bowed her head and turned away, so that the Secret Service man could not see the twisted, strangely familiar, leer on her lips.

The Evening's at Seven

He hadn't lighted the upper light in his office all afternoon and now he turned out the desk lamp. It was a quarter of seven in the evening and it was dark and raining. He could hear the rattle of taxicabs and trucks and the sound of horns. Very far off a siren screamed its frenzied scream and he thought: it's a little like an anguish dying with the years. When it gets to Third Avenue, or Ninety-fifth Street, he thought, I won't hear it any more.

I'll be home, he said to himself, as he got up slowly and slowly put on his hat and overcoat (the overcoat was damp), by seven o'clock, if I take a taxicab, I'll say hello, my dear, and the two yellow lamps will be lighted and my papers will be on my desk, and I'll say I guess I'll lie down a few minutes before dinner, and she will say all right and ask two or three small questions about the day and I'll answer them.

When he got outside of his office, in the street, it was dark and raining and he lighted a cigarette. A young man went by whistling loudly. Two girls went by talking gaily, as if it were not raining, as if this were not a time for silence and for remembering. He called to a taxicab and it stopped and he got in, and sat there, on the edge of the seat, and the driver finally said where to? He gave a number he was thinking about.

She was surprised to see him and, he believed, pleased. It was very nice to be in her apartment again. He faced her, quickly, and it seemed to him as if he were facing somebody in a tennis game. She would want to know (but wouldn't ask) why he was, so suddenly, there, and he couldn't exactly say: I gave a number to a taxi-driver and it was your number. He couldn't say that; and besides, it wasn't that simple.

It was dark in the room and still raining outside. He lighted a cigarette (not wanting one) and looked at her. He watched her lovely gestures as of old and she said he looked tired and he said he wasn't tired and he asked her what she had been doing and she said oh, nothing much. He talked, sitting awkwardly on the edge of a chair, and she talked, lying gracefully on a chaise-longue, about people they had known and hadn't cared about. He was mainly conscious of the rain outside and of the soft darkness in the room and of other rains and other darknesses. He got up and walked around the room looking at pictures but not seeing what they were, and realizing that some old familiar things gleamed darkly, and he came abruptly face to face with something he had given her, a trivial and comic thing, and it didn't seem trivial or comic now, but very large and important and embarrassing, and he turned away from it and asked after somebody else he didn't care about. Oh, she said, and this and that and so and such (words he wasn't listening to). Yes, he said, absently, I suppose so. Very much, he said (in answer to something else), very much. Oh, she said, laughing at him, not *that* much! He didn't have any idea what they were talking about.

She asked him for a cigarette and he walked over and gave her one, not touching her fingers but very conscious of her fingers. He was remembering a twilight when it had been raining and dark, and he thought of April and kissing and laughter. He noticed a clock on the mantel and it was ten after seven. She said you never used to believe in clocks. He laughed and looked at her for a time and said I have to be at the hotel by seven-thirty, or I don't get anything to eat; it's that sort of hotel. Oh, she said.

He walked to a table and picked up a figurine and set it down again with extreme care, looking out of the corner of his eye at the trivial and comic and gigantic present he had given her. He wondered if he would kiss her and when he would kiss her and if she wanted to be kissed and if she were thinking of it, but she asked him what he would have to eat tonight at his hotel. He said clam chowder. Thursday, he said, they always have clam chowder. Is that the way you know it's Thursday, she said, or is that the way you know it's clam chowder?

He picked up the figurine and put it down again, so that he could look (without her seeing him look) at the clock. It was eighteen minutes after seven and he had the mingled thoughts clocks gave him. You mustn't, she said, miss your meal. (She

194

emembered he hated the word meal.) He turned around quickly
and went over quickly and sat beside her and took hold of one of
her fingers and she looked at the finger and not at him and he
ooked at the finger and not at her, both of them as if it were a new
and rather remarkable thing.

He got up suddenly and picked up his hat and coat and as suddenly put them down again and took two rapid determined steps
toward her, and her eyes seemed a little wider. A bell rang. Oh that,
he said, will be Clarice. And they relaxed. He looked a question
and she said: my sister; and he said oh, of course. In a minute it
was Clarice like a small explosion in the dark and rainy day talking
rapidly of this and that: my dear he and this awful and then of all
people so nothing loth and I said and he said, if you can imagine
that! He picked up his hat and coat and Clarice said hello to him
and he said hello and looked at the clock and it was almost twenty-
ive after seven.

She went to the door with him looking lovely, and it was lovely
and dark and raining outside and he laughed and she laughed and
he was going to say something but he went out into the rain and
waved back at her (not wanting to wave back at her) and she closed
the door and was gone. He lighted a cigarette and let his hand get
wet in the rain and the cigarette get wet and rain dripped from his
hat. A taxicab drove up and the driver spoke to him and he said:
what? and: oh, sure. And now he was going home.

He was home by seven-thirty, almost exactly, and he said good
evening to old Mrs Spencer (who had the sick husband), and good
evening to old Mrs Holmes (who had the sick Pomeranian), and
he nodded and smiled and presently he was sitting at his table and
the waitress spoke to him. She said: the Mrs will be down, won't
she? and he said yes, she will. And the waitress said clam chowder
tonight, and consommé: you always take the clam chowder, ain't
I right? No, he said, I'll have the consommé.

One is a Wanderer

The walk up Fifth Avenue through the slush of the sidewalks and the dankness of the air had tired him. The dark was coming quickly down, the dark of a February Sunday evening, and that vaguely perturbed him. He didn't want to go 'home', though, and get out of it. It would be gloomy and close in his hotel room, and his soiled shirts would be piled on the floor of the closet where he had been flinging them for weeks, where he had been flinging them for months, and his papers would be disarranged on the tops of the tables and on the desk, and his pipes would be lying around, the pipes he had smoked determinedly for a while only to give them up, as he always did, to go back to cigarettes. He turned into the street leading to his hotel, walking slowly, trying to decide what to do with the night. He had had too many nights alone. Once he had enjoyed being alone. Now it was hard to be alone. He couldn't read any more, or write, at night. Books he tossed aside after nervously flipping through them; the writing he tried to do turned into spirals and circles and squares and empty faces.

I'll just stop in, he thought, and see if there are any messages; I'll see if there have been any phone calls. He hadn't been back to the hotel, after all, for – let's see – for almost five hours; just wandering around. There might be some messages. I'll just stop in, he thought, and see; and maybe I'll have one brandy. I don't want to sit there in the lobby again and drink brandy; I don't want to do that.

He didn't go through the revolving doors of the hotel, though. He went on past the hotel and over to Broadway. A man asked him for some money. A shabbily dressed woman walked by, muttering. She had what he called the New York Mouth, a grim, set mouth, a strained, querulous mouth, a mouth that told of suffering and discontent. He looked in the window of a cane-and-umbrella shop and in the window of a cheap restaurant, a window holding artificial pie and cake, a cup of cold coffee, a plate of artificial vegetables. He got into the shoving and pushing and halting and

196

slow flowing of Broadway. A big cop with a red face was striking his hands together and kidding with a couple of girls whom he had kept from crossing the street against a red light. A thin man in a thin overcoat watched them out of thin, emotionless eyes.

It was a momentary diversion to stand in front of the book counter in the drugstore at Forty-fifth Street and Broadway and look at the books, cheap editions of ancient favourites, movie editions of fairly recent best-sellers. He picked up some of the books and opened them and put them down again, but there was nothing he wanted to read. He walked over to the soda counter and sat down and asked for hot chocolate. It warmed him up a little and he thought about going to the movie at the Paramount; it was a movie with action and guns and aeroplanes, and Myrna Loy, the kind of movie that didn't bother you. He walked down to the theatre and stood there a minute, but he didn't buy a ticket. After all, he had been to one movie that day. He thought about going to the office. It would be quiet there, nobody would be there; maybe he could get some work done; maybe he could answer some of the letters he had been putting off for so long.

It was too gloomy, it was too lonely. He looked around the office for a while, sat down at his typewriter, tapped out the alphabet on a sheet of paper, took a paper-clip, straightened it, cleaned the 'e' and the 'o' on the typewriter, and put the cover over it. He never remembered to put the cover over the typewriter when he left in the evening. I never, as a matter of fact, remember anything, he thought. It is because I keep trying not to; I keep trying not to remember anything. It is an empty and cowardly thing, not to remember. It might lead you anywhere; no, it might stop you, it might stop you from getting anywhere. Out of remembrance comes everything; out of remembrance comes a great deal, anyway. You can't do anything if you don't let yourself remember things. He began to whistle a song because he found himself about to remember things, and he knew what things they would be, things that would bring a grimace to his mouth and to his eyes, disturbing fragments of old sentences, old scenes and gestures, hours, and rooms, and tones of voice, and the sound of a voice crying. All voices cry differently; there are no two voices

197

in the whole world that cry alike; they're like footsteps and finger-prints and the faces of friends . . .

He became conscious of the song he was whistling. He got up from the chair in front of his covered typewriter, turned out the light, and walked out of the room to the elevator, and there he began to sing the last part of the song, waiting for the elevator. 'Make my bed and light the light, for I'll be home late tonight, blackbird, bye bye.' He walked over to his hotel through the slush and the damp gloom and sat down in a chair in the lobby, without taking off his overcoat. He didn't want to sit there long.

'Good evening, sir,' said the waiter who looked after the guests in the lobby. 'How are you?'

'I'm fine, thank you,' he said. 'I'm fine. I'll have a brandy, with water on the side.'

He had several brandies. Nobody came into the lobby that he knew. People were gone to all kinds of places Sunday night. He hadn't looked at his letter box back of the clerk's desk when he came in, to see if there were any messages there. That was a kind of game he played, or something. He never looked for messages until after he had had a brandy. He'd look now after he had another brandy. He had another brandy and looked. 'Nothing,' said the clerk at the desk, looking too.

He went back to his chair in the lobby and began to think about calling up people. He thought of the Graysons. He saw the Gray-sons, not as they would be, sitting in their apartment, close to-gether and warmly, but as he and Lydia had seen them in another place and another year. The four had shared a bright vacation once. He remembered various attitudes and angles and lights and colours of that vacation. There is something about four people, two couples, that like each other and get along; that have a swell time; that grow in intimacy and understanding. One's life is made up of twos, and of fours. The Graysons understood the nice little ar-rangements of living, the twos and fours. Two is company, four is a party, three is a crowd. One is a wanderer.

No, not the Graysons. Somebody would be there on Sunday night, some couple, some two; somebody he knew, somebody they had known. That is the way life is arranged. One arranges one's life – no, two arrange their life – in terms of twos, and fours,

198

and sixes. Marriage does not make two people one, it makes two people two. It's sweeter that way, and simpler. All this, he thought, summoning the waiter, is probably very silly and sentimental. I must look out that I don't get to that state of tipsiness where all silly and lugubrious things seem brilliant divinations of mine, sound and original ideas and theories. What I must remember is that such things are sentimental and tiresome and grow out of not working enough and out of too much brandy. That's what I must remember. It is no good remembering that it takes four to make a party, two to make a house.

People living alone, after all, have made a great many things. Let's see, what have people living alone made? Not love, of course, but a great many other things: money, for example, and black marks on white paper. 'Make this one a double-brandy,' he told the waiter. Let's see, who that I *know* has made something alone, who that I know *of* has made something alone? Robert Browning? No, not Robert Browning. Odd, that Robert Browning would be the first person he thought of. 'And had you only heard me play one tune, or viewed me from a window, not so soon with you would such things fade as with the rest.' He had written that line of Browning's in a book once for Lydia, or Lydia had written it in a book for him; or they had both written it in a book for each other. 'Not so soon with you would such things fade as with the rest.' Maybe he didn't have it exactly right; it was hard to remember now, after so long a time. It didn't matter. 'Not so soon with you would such things fade as with the rest.' The fact is that all things do fade; with twos, and with fours; all bright things, all attitudes and angles and lights and colours, all growing in intimacy and understanding.

I think maybe I'll call the Bradleys, he thought, getting up out of his chair. And don't, he said to himself, standing still a moment, don't tell me you're not cockeyed now, because you are cockeyed now, just as you said you wouldn't be when you got up this morning and had orange juice and coffee and determined to get some work done, a whole lot of work done; just as you said you wouldn't be but you knew you would be, all right. You knew you would be, all right.

The Bradleys, he thought, as he walked slowly around the lobby, avoiding the phone booths, glancing at the headlines of the papers on the newsstand, the Bradleys have that four-square thing, that two-square thing – that two-square thing, God damn them! Somebody described it once in a short story that he had read: an intimacy that you could feel, that you could almost take hold of, when you went into such a house, when you went into where such people were, a warming thing, a nice thing to be in, like being in warm sea water, a little embarrassing, too, yes, damned embarrassing, too. He would only take a damp blanket into that warmth. That's what I'd take into that warmth, he told himself, a damp blanket. They know it, too. Here comes old Kirk again with his damp blanket. It isn't because I'm so damned unhappy – I'm not so damned unhappy – it's because they're so damned happy, damn them. Why don't they know that? Why don't they do something about it? What right have they got to flaunt it at me, for God's sake? . . . Look here now, he told himself, you're getting too cockeyed now; you're getting into one of those states, you're getting into one of those states that Marianne keeps telling you about, one of those states when people don't like to have you around . . . Marianne, he thought. He went back to his chair, ordered another brandy, and thought about Marianne.

She doesn't know how I start my days, he thought, she only knows how I end them. She doesn't even know how I started my life. She only knows me when night gets me. If I could only be the person she wants me to be, why, then I would be fine, I would be fine, I would be the person she wants me to be. Like ordering a new dress from a shop, a new dress that nobody ever wore, a new dress that nobody's ever going to wear but you. I wouldn't get mad suddenly, about nothing. I wouldn't walk out of places suddenly, about nothing. I wouldn't snarl at nice people. About what she says is nothing. I wouldn't be 'unbearable'. Her word 'unbearable'. A female word, female as a cat. Well, she's right, too. I am unbearable. 'George,' he said to the waiter, 'I am unbearable, did you know that?' 'No, sir, I did not, sir,' said the waiter. 'I would not call you unbearable, Mr Kirk.' 'Well, you don't know, George,' he said. 'It just happens that I am unbearable. It just happened that way. It's a long story.' 'Yes, sir,' said the waiter.

I could call up the Mortons, he thought. They'll have twos and fours there, too, but they're not so damned happy that they're unbearable. The Mortons are all right. Now look, the Mortons had said to him, if you and Marianne would only stop fighting and arguing and forever analysing yourselves and forever analysing everything, you'd be fine. You'd be fine if you got married and just shut up, just shut up and got married. That would be fine. Yes, sir, that would be fine. Everything would work out all right. You just shut up and get married, you just get married and shut up. Everybody knows that. It is practically the simplest thing in the world. . . . Well, it would be, too, if you were twenty-five maybe, it would be if you were twenty-five, and not forty.

'George,' he said, when the waiter walked over for his empty glass, 'I will be forty-one next November.' 'But that's not old, sir, and that's a long way off,' said George. 'No, it isn't,' he said. 'It's almost here. So is forty-two and forty-three and fifty, and here I am trying to be – do you know what I'm trying to be, George? I'm trying to be happy.' 'We all want to be happy, sir,' said George. 'I would like to see you happy, sir.' 'Oh, you will,' he said. 'You will, George. There's a simple trick to it. You just shut up and get married. But you see, George, I am an analyser. I am also a rememberer. I have a pocketful of old used years. You put all those things together and they sit in a lobby getting silly and old.' 'I'm very sorry, sir ' said George.

'And I'll have one more drink, George,' he called after the waiter.

He had one more drink. When he looked up at the clock in the lobby it was only 9.30. He went up to his room and, feeling sleepy, he lay down on his bed without turning out the overhead light. When he woke up it was 12.30 by his wristwatch. He got up and washed his face and brushed his teeth and put on a clean shirt and another suit and went back down into the lobby, without looking at the disarranged papers on the tables and on the desk. He went into the dining-room and had some soup and a lamb chop and a glass of milk. There was nobody there he knew. He began to realize that he had to see somebody he knew. He paid his check and went out and got into a cab and gave the driver an address on Fifty-third Street.

There were several people in Dick and Joe's that he knew. There were Dick and Joe, for two – or, rather, for one, because he always thought of them as one; he could never tell them apart. There were Bill Vardon and Mary Wells. Bill Vardon and Mary Wells were a little drunk and gay. He didn't know them very well, but he could sit down with them. . . .

It was after three o'clock when he left the place and got into a cab. 'How are you tonight, Mr Kirk?' asked the driver. The driver's name was Willie. 'I'm fine tonight, Willie,' he said. 'You want to go on somewheres else?' asked Willie. 'Not tonight, Willie,' he said. 'I'm going home.' 'Well,' said Willie, 'I guess you're right there, Mr Kirk. I guess you're right about that. These places is all right for what they are – you know what I mean – it's O.K. to kick around in 'em for a while and maybe have a few drinks with your friends, but when you come right down to it, home is the best place there is. Now, you take me, I'm hackin' for ten years, mostly up around here – because why? Because all these places know me; you know that, Mr Kirk. I can get into 'em you might say the same way you do, Mr Kirk – I have me a couple drinks in Dick and Joe's maybe or in Tony's or anywheres else I want to go into – hell, I've had drinks in 'em with you, Mr Kirk – like on Christmas night, remember? But I got a home over in Brooklyn and a wife and a couple kids and, boy, I'm tellin' you that's the best place, you know what I mean?'

'You're right, Willie,' he said. 'You're absolutely right, there.'

'You're darn tootin' I am,' said Willie. 'These joints is all right when a man wants a couple drinks or maybe even get a little tight with his friends, that's O.K. with me – '

'Getting tight with friends is O.K. with me, too,' he said to Willie.

'But when a man gets fed up on that kind of stuff, a man wants to go home. Am I right, Mr Kirk?'

'You're absolutely right, Willie,' he said. 'A man wants to go home.'

'Well, here we are, Mr Kirk. Home it is.'

He got out of the cab and gave the driver a dollar and told

him to keep the change and went into the lobby of the hotel. The night clerk gave him his key and then put two fingers into the recesses of the letter box. 'Nothing,' said the night clerk.

When he got to his room, he lay down on the bed a while and smoked a cigarette. He found himself feeling drowsy and he got up. He began to take his clothes off, feeling drowsily contented, mistily contented. He began to sing, not loudly, because the man in 711 would complain. The man in 711 was a grey-haired man, living alone . . . an analyser . . . a rememberer . . .

'Make my bed and light the light, for I'll be home late tonight . . .'

5 | *My Life and Hard Times*

Preface to a Life

Benvenuto Cellini said that a man should be at least forty years old before he undertakes so fine an enterprise as that of setting down the story of his life. He said also that an autobiographer should have accomplished something of excellence. Nowadays nobody who has a typewriter pays any attention to the old master's quaint rules. I myself have accomplished nothing of excellence except a remarkable and, to some of my friends, unaccountable expertness in hitting empty ginger ale bottles with small rocks at a distance of thirty paces. Moreover, I am not yet forty years old. But the grim date moves toward me apace; my legs are beginning to go, things blur before my eyes, and the faces of the rose-lipped maids I knew in my twenties are misty as dreams.

At forty my faculties may have closed up like flowers at evening, leaving me unable to write my memoirs with a fitting and discreet inaccuracy or, having written them, unable to carry them to the publisher's. A writer verging into the middle years lives in dread of losing his way to the publishing house and wandering down to the Bowery or the Battery, there to disappear like Ambrose Bierce. He has sometimes also the kindred dread of turning a sudden corner and meeting himself sauntering along in the opposite direction. I have known writers at this dangerous and tricky age to phone their homes from their offices, or their offices from their homes, ask for themselves in a low tone, and then, having fortunately discovered that they were 'out', to collapse in hard-breathing relief. This is particularly true of writers of light pieces running from a thousand to two thousand words.

The notion that such persons are gay of heart and carefree is curiously untrue. They lead, as a matter of fact, an existence of jumpiness and apprehension. They sit on the edge of the chair of Literature. In the house of Life they have the feeling that they have never taken off their overcoats. Afraid of losing themselves in the larger flight of the two-volume novel, or even the one-volume novel, they stick to short accounts of their misadventures

207

because they never get so deep into them but that they feel they can get out. This type of writing is not a joyous form of self-expression but the manifestation of a twitchiness at once cosmic and mundane. Authors of such pieces have, nobody knows why, a genius for getting into minor difficulties: they walk into the wrong apartments, they drink furniture polish for stomach bitters, they drive their cars into the prize tulip beds of haughty neighbours, they playfully slap gangsters, mistaking them for old school friends. To call such persons 'humourists', a loose-fitting and ugly word, is to miss the nature of their dilemma and the dilemma of their nature. The little wheels of their invention are set in motion by the damp hand of melancholy.

Such a writer moves about restlessly wherever he goes, ready to get the hell out at the drop of a pie-pan or the lift of a skirt. His gestures are the ludicrous reflexes of the maladjusted; his repose is the momentary inertia of the nonplussed. He pulls the blinds against the morning and creeps into smokey corners at night. He talks largely about small matters and smally about great affairs. His ears are shut to the ominous rumblings of the dynasties of the world moving toward a cloudier chaos than ever before, but he hears with an acute perception the startling sounds that rabbits make twisting in the bushes along a country road at night and a cold chill comes upon him when the comic supplement of a Sunday newspaper blows unexpectedly out of an areaway and envelopes his knees. He can sleep while the commonwealth crumbles but a strange sound in the pantry at three in the morning will strike terror into his stomach. He is not afraid, or much aware, of the menaces of empire but he keeps looking behind him as he walks along darkening streets out of the fear that he is being softly followed by little men padding along in single file, about a foot and a half high, large-eyed, and whiskered.

It is difficult for such a person to conform to what Ford Madox Ford in his book of recollections has called the sole reason for writing one's memoirs: namely, to paint a picture of one's time. Your short-piece writer's time is not Walter Lippmann's time, or Stuart Chase's time, or Professor Einstein's time. It is his own personal time, circumscribed by the short boundaries of his pain and his embarrassment, in which what happens to his digestion, the rear axle of his car, and the confused flow of his relationships with six or eight persons and two or three buildings is of greater importance than what goes on in the nation or in the universe. He knows vaguely that the nation is not much good any more; he has read that the crust of the earth is shrinking alarmingly and that the universe is growing steadily colder, but he does not believe that any of the three is in half as bad a shape as he is.

Enormous strides are made in star-measurement, theoretical economics, and the manufacture of bombing planes, but he usually doesn't find out about them until he picks up an old copy of *Time* on a picnic grounds or in the summer house of a friend. He is aware that billions of dollars are stolen every year by bankers and politicians, and that thousands of people are out of work, but these conditions do not worry him a tenth as much as the conviction that he has wasted three months on a stupid psychoanalyst or the suspicion that a piece he has been working on for two long days was done much better and probably more quickly by Robert Benchley in 1924.

The 'time' of such a writer, then, is hardly worth reading about if the reader wishes to find out what was going on in the world while the writer in question was alive and at what might be laughingly called 'his best'. All that the reader is going to find out is what happened to the writer. The compensation, I suppose, must lie in the comforting feeling that one has had, after all, a pretty sensible and peaceful life, by comparison. It is unfortunate, however, that even a well-ordered life cannot lead anybody safely around the inevitable doom that waits in the skies. As F. Hopkinson Smith long ago pointed out, the claw of the sea-puss gets us all in the end.

J. T.

Sandy Hook,
Connecticut,
25 *September* 1933.

The Night the Bed Fell

I suppose that the high-water mark of my youth in Columbus, Ohio, was the night the bed fell on my father. It makes a better recitation (unless, as some friends of mine have said, one has heard it five or six times) than it does a piece of writing, for it is almost necessary to throw furniture around, shake doors, and bark like a dog, to lend the proper atmosphere and verisimilitude to what is admittedly a somewhat incredible tale. Still, it did take place.

It happened, then, that my father had decided to sleep in the attic one night, to be away where he could think. My mother opposed the notion strongly because, she said, the old wooden bed up there was unsafe; it was wobbly and the heavy headboard would crash down on father's head in case the bed fell, and kill him. There was no dissuading him, however, and at a quarter past ten he closed the attic door behind him and went up the narrow twisting stairs. We later heard ominous creakings as he crawled into bed. Grandfather, who usually slept in the attic bed when he was with us, had disappeared some days before. (On these occasions he was usually gone six or eight days and returned growling and out of temper, with the news that the federal Union was run by a passel of blockheads and that the Army of the Potomac didn't have any more chance than a fiddler's bitch.)

We had visiting us at this time a nervous first cousin of mine named Briggs Beall, who believed that he was likely to cease breathing when he was asleep. It was his feeling that if he were not awakened every hour during the night, he might die of suffocation. He had been accustomed to setting an alarm clock to ring at intervals until morning, but I persuaded him to abandon this. He slept in my room and I told him that I was such a light sleeper that if anybody quit breathing in the same room with me, I would wake instantly. He tested me the first night – which I had suspected he would – by holding his breath after my regular breathing had convinced him I was asleep. I was not asleep, however, and called to him. This seemed to allay his fears a little, but he took the precaution of putting a glass of spirits of camphor on a little table at the head of his bed. In case I didn't arouse him until he was almost gone, he said, he would sniff the camphor, a powerful reviver. Briggs was not the only member of his family who had his crotchets. Old Aunt Melissa Beall (who could whistle like a man, with two fingers in her mouth) suffered under the premonition that she was destined to die on South High Street, because she had been born on South High Street and married on South High Street. Then there was Aunt Sarah Shoaf, who never went to bed at night without the fear that a burglar was going to get in and blow chloroform under her door through a tube. To avert this calamity – for she was in greater dread of anaesthetics than of losing her household goods – she always piled her money, silverware, and other valuables in a neat stack just outside her bedroom, with a note reading: 'This is all I have. Please take it and do not use your chloroform, as this is all I have.' Aunt Gracie Shoaf also had a burglar phobia, but she met it with more fortitude. She was confident that burglars had been getting into her house every night for forty years. The fact that she never missed anything was to her no proof to the contrary. She always claimed that she scared them off before they could take anything, by throwing shoes down the hallway. When she went to bed she piled, where she could get at them handily, all the shoes there were about her house. Five minutes after she had turned off the light, she would sit up in bed and say 'Hark!' Her husband, who had learned to ignore the whole situation as long ago as 1903, would either be sound asleep or pretend to be sound asleep. In either case he would not respond to her tugging and pulling, so that presently she would arise, tiptoe to the door, open it slightly and heave a shoe down the hall in one direction, and its mate down the hall in the other direction. Some nights she threw them all, some nights only a couple of pair.

But I am straying from the remarkable incidents that took place during the night that the bed fell on father. By midnight we were all in bed. The layout of the rooms and the disposition of their occupants is important to an understanding of what later occurred. In the front room upstairs (just under father's attic bedroom) were my mother and my brother Herman, who sometimes sang in his sleep, usually 'Marching Through Georgia' or

Some Nights She Threw Them All

'Onward, Christian Soldiers'. Briggs Beall and myself were in a room adjoining this one. My brother Roy was in a room across the hall from ours. Our bull terrier, Rex, slept in the hall.

My bed was an army cot, one of those affairs which are made wide enough to sleep on comfortably only by putting up, flat with the middle section, the two sides which ordinarily hang down like the sideboards of a drop-leaf table. When these sides are up, it is perilous to roll too far toward the edge, for then the cot is likely to tip completely over, bringing the whole bed down on top of one, with a tremendous banging crash. This, in fact, is precisely what happened, about two o'clock in the morning. (It was my mother who, in recalling the scene later, first referred to it as 'the night the bed fell on your father'.)

Always a deep sleeper, slow to arouse (I had lied to Briggs), I was at first unconscious of what had happened when the iron cot rolled me on to the floor and toppled over on me. It left me still warmly bundled up and unhurt, for the bed rested above me like a canopy. Hence I did not wake up, only reached the edge of consciousness and went back. The racket, however, instantly awakened my mother, in the next room, who came to the immediate conclusion that her worst dread was realized: the big wooden bed upstairs had fallen on father. She therefore screamed, 'Let's go to your poor father!' It was this shout, rather than the noise of my cot falling, that awakened Herman, in the same room with her. He thought that mother had become, for no apparent reason, hysterical. 'You're all right, Mamma!' he shouted, trying to calm her. They exchanged shout for shout for perhaps ten seconds: 'Let's go to your poor father!' and 'You're all right!' That woke up Briggs. By this time I was conscious of what was going on, in a vague way, but did not yet realize that I was under my bed instead of on it. Briggs, awakening in the midst of loud shouts of fear and apprehension, came to the quick conclusion that he was suffocating and that we were all trying to 'bring him out'. With a low moan, he grasped the glass of camphor at the head of his bed and instead of sniffing it poured it over himself. The room reeked of camphor. 'Ugf, ahfg,' choked Briggs, like a drowning man, for he had almost succeeded in stopping his breath under the deluge of pungent spirits. He leaped out of bed and groped

213

He Came to the Conclusion That He Was Suffocating

toward the open window, but he came up against one that was closed. With his hand, he beat out the glass, and I could hear it crash and tinkle on the alleyway below. It was at this juncture that I, in trying to get up, had the uncanny sensation of feeling my bed above me! Foggy with sleep, I now suspected, in my turn, that the whole uproar was being made in a frantic endeavour to extricate me from what must be an unheard-of and perilous situation. 'Get me out of this!' I bawled. 'Get me out!' I think I had the nightmarish belief that I was entombed in a mine. 'Gugh,' gasped Briggs, floundering in his camphor.

By this time my mother, still shouting, pursued by Herman, still shouting, was trying to open the door to the attic, in order to go up and get my father's body out of the wreckage. The door was stuck, however, and wouldn't yield. Her frantic pulls on it only added to the general banging and confusion. Roy and the dog were up, the one shouting questions, the other barking.

Father, farthest away and soundest sleeper of all, had by this time awakened by the battering on the attic door. He decided that the house was on fire. 'I'm coming, I'm coming!' he wailed in a slow, sleepy voice – it took him many minutes to regain full consciousness. My mother, still believing he was caught under the bed, detected in his 'I'm coming!' the mournful, resigned note of one who is preparing to meet his Maker. 'He's dying!' she shouted.

'I'm all right!' Briggs yelled to reassure her. 'I'm all right!' He still believed that it was his own closeness to death that was worrying mother. I found at last the light switch in my room, unlocked the door, and Briggs and I joined the others at the attic door. The dog, who never did like Briggs, jumped for him – assuming that he was the culprit in whatever was going on – and Roy had to throw Rex and hold him. We could hear father crawling out of bed upstairs. Roy pulled the attic door open, with a mighty jerk, and father came down the stairs, sleepy and irritable but safe and sound. My mother began to weep when she saw him. Rex began to howl. 'What in the name of God is going on here?' asked father.

The situation was finally put together like a gigantic jig-saw puzzle. Father caught a cold from prowling around in his bare feet but there were no other bad results. 'I'm glad,' said mother, who always looked on the bright side of things, 'that your grandfather wasn't here.'

Roy Had to Throw Rex

The Car We Had To Push

Many autobiographers, among them Lincoln Steffens and Gertrude Atherton, described earthquakes their families have been in. I am unable to do this because my family was never in an earthquake, but we went through a number of things in Columbus that were a great deal like earthquakes. I remember in particular some of the repercussions of an old Reo we had that wouldn't go unless you pushed it for quite a way and suddenly let your clutch out. Once, we had been able to start the engine easily by cranking it, but we had had the car for so many years that finally it wouldn't go unless you pushed it and let your clutch out. Of course, it took more than one person to do this; it took sometimes as many as five or six, depending on the grade of the roadway and conditions

It Took Sometimes as Many as Five or Six

underfoot. The car was unusual in that the clutch and brake were on the same pedal, making it quite easy to stall the engine after it got started, so that the car would have to be pushed again.

216

My father used to get sick at his stomach pushing the car, and very often was unable to go to work. He had never liked the machine, even when it was good, sharing my ignorance and suspicion of all automobiles of twenty years ago and longer. The boys I went to school with used to be able to identify every car as it passed by: Thomas Flyer, Firestone-Columbus, Stevens Duryea, Rambler, Winton, White Steamer, etc. I never could. The only

The Get-Ready Man

car I was really interested in was one that the Get-Ready Man, as we called him, rode around town in: a big Red Devil with a door in the back. The Get-Ready Man was a lank unkempt elderly gentleman with wild eyes and a deep voice who used to go about shouting at people through a megaphone to prepare for the end of the world. 'GET READY! GET READY!' he would bellow. 'THE WORLLLD IS COMING TO AN END!' His startling exhortations would come up, like summer thunder, at the most unexpected times and in the most surprising places. I remember once during Mantell's production of *King Lear* at the Colonial Theatre, that the Get-Ready Man added his bawlings to the squealing of Edgar and the ranting of the King and the mouthing of the Fool, rising from somewhere in the balcony to join in. The theatre was in absolute darkness and there were rumblings of thunder and flashes of lightning offstage. Neither father nor I, who were there,

217

ever completely got over the scene, which went something like
this:

Edgar: Tom's a-cold. – O, do de do de, do de! – Bless thee from
whirlwinds, star-blasting, and taking . . . the foul fiend vexes!

(Thunder off.

Lear: What! Have his daughters brought him to this pass? –
Get-Ready Man: Get ready! Get ready!
Edgar: Pillicock sat on Pillocock-hill –

Halloo, halloo, loo, loo!
(Lightning flashes

Get-Ready Man: The Worllld is com-ing to an End!
Fool: This cold night will turn us all to fools and madmen!
Edgar: Take heed o' the foul fiend: obey thy paren –
Get-Ready Man: Get *Rea*-dy!
Edgar:Tom's a-*cold*!
Get-Ready Man: The *Worr*-uld is coming to an end! . . .

They found him finally, and ejected him, still shouting. The
Theatre, in our time, has known few such moments.

But to get back to the automobile. One of my happiest memories
of it was when, in its eighth year, my brother Roy got together a
great many articles from the kitchen, placed them in a square of
canvas, and swung this under the car with a string attached to it
so that, at a twitch, the canvas would give way and the steel and tin
things would clatter to the street. This was a little scheme of Roy's
to frighten father, who had always expected the car might explode. It worked perfectly. That was twenty-five years ago, but
it is one of the few things in my life I would like to live over again
if I could. I don't suppose that I can, now. Roy twitched the string
in the middle of a lovely afternoon, on Bryden Road near Eigh-
teenth Street. Father had closed his eyes and, with his hat off,
was enjoying a cool breeze. The clatter on the asphalt was
tremendously effective: knives, forks, can-openers, pie pans,
pot lids, biscuit-cutters, ladles, egg-beaters fell, beautifully together, in a lingering, clamant crash. 'Stop the *car*!' shouted father.
'I can't,' Roy said. 'The engine fell out.' 'God Almighty!' said
father, who knew what *that* meant, or knew what it sounded as if
it might mean.

It ended unhappily, of course, because we finally had to drive back and pick up the stuff and even father knew the difference between the works of an automobile and the equipment of a pantry. My mother wouldn't have known, however, nor *her* mother. My mother, for instance, thought – or, rather, knew – that it was dangerous to drive an automobile without gasoline: it fried the valves, or something: 'Now don't you dare drive all over town without gasoline!' she would say to us when we started off. Gasoline, oil, and water were much the same to her, a fact that made her life both confusing and perilous. Her greatest dread, however, was the Victrola – we had a very early one, back in the 'Come Josephine in My Flying Machine' days. She had an idea that the Victrola might blow up. It alarmed her, rather than reassured her, to explain that the phonograph was run neither by gasoline nor by electricity. She could only suppose that it was propelled by some newfangled and untested apparatus which was likely to let go at any minute, making us all the victims and martyrs of the wild-eyed Edison's dangerous experiments. The telephone she was comparatively at peace with, except, of course, during storms, when for some reason or other she always took the receiver off the hook and let it hang. She came naturally by her confused and groundless fears, for her own mother lived the latter years of her life in the horrible suspicion that electricity was dripping invisibly all over the house. It leaked, she contended, out of empty sockets if the wall switch had been left on. She would go around screwing in bulbs, and if they lighted up she would hastily and fearfully turn off the wall switch and go back to her *Pearson's* or *Everybody's*, happy in the satisfaction that she had stopped not only a costly but a dangerous leakage. Nothing could ever clear this up for her.

Our poor old Reo came to a horrible end, finally. We had parked it too far from the curb on a street with a car line. It was late at night and the street was dark. The first streetcar that came along couldn't get by. It picked up the tired old automobile as a terrier might seize a rabbit and drubbed it unmercifully, losing its hold now and then but catching a new grip a second later. Tyres pooped and whooshed, the fenders queeled and graked, the steering wheel rose up like a spectre and disappeared in the direction of

Electricity Was Leaking All Over the House

Franklin Avenue with a melancholy whistling sound, bolts and gadgets flew like sparks from a Catherine wheel. It was a splendid spectacle but, of course, saddening to everybody (except the motorman of the streetcar, who was sore). I think some of us broke down and wept. It must have been the weeping that caused grandfather to take on so terribly. Time was all mixed up in his mind; automobiles and the like he never remembered having seen. He apparently gathered, from the talk and excitement and weeping, that somebody had died. Nor did he let go of this delusion. He insisted, in fact, after almost a week in which we strove mightily to divert him, that it was a sin and a shame and a disgrace on the family to put the funeral off any longer. 'Nobody is dead! The automobile is smashed!' shouted my father, trying for the thirtieth time to explain the situation to the old man. 'Was he drunk?' demanded grandfather, sternly. 'Was who drunk?' asked father. 'Zenas,' said grandfather. He had a name for the corpse now: it was his brother Zenas, who, as it happened, *was* dead, but not from driving an automobile while intoxicated. Zenas had died in 1866. A sensitive, rather poetical boy of twenty-one when the Civil War broke out, Zenas had gone to South America – 'just,' as he wrote back, 'until it blows over'. Returning after the war had blown over, he caught the same disease that was killing off the chestnut trees in those years, and passed away. It was the only case in history where a tree doctor had to be called in to spray a person, and our family had felt it very keenly; nobody else in the United States caught the blight. Some of us have looked upon Zenas's fate as a kind of poetic justice.

Now that grandfather knew, so to speak, who was dead, it became increasingly awkward to go on living in the same house with him as if nothing had happened. He would go into towering rages in which he threatened to write to the Board of Health unless the funeral were held at once. We realized that something had to be done. Eventually, we persuaded a friend of father's, named George Martin, to dress up in the manner and costume of the eighteen-sixties and pretend to be Uncle Zenas, in order to set grandfather's mind at rest. The impostor looked fine and impressive in sideburns and a high beaver hat, and not unlike the daguerreotypes of Zenas in our album. I shall never forget the

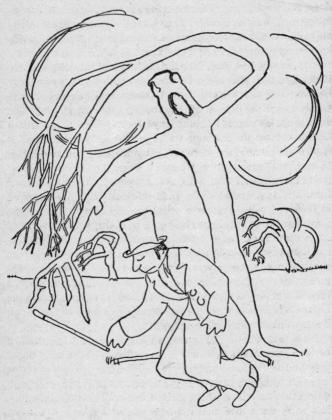

He Caught the Same Disease That Was Killing the Chestnut Trees

night, just after dinner, when this Zenas walked into the living-room. Grandfather was stomping up and down, tall, hawk-nosed, round-oathed. The newcomer held out both his hands. 'Clem!' he cried to grandfather. Grandfather turned slowly, looked at the intruder, and snorted. 'Who air *you*?' he demanded in his deep, resonant voice. 'I'm Zenas!' cried Martin. 'Your brother Zenas, fit as a fiddle and sound as a dollar!' 'Zenas, my foot!' said grand-father. 'Zenas died of the chestnut blight in '66!'

Grandfather was given to these sudden, unexpected, and ex-tremely lucid moments; they were generally more embarrassing than his other moments. He comprehended before he went to bed that night that the old automobile had been destroyed and that its destruction had caused all the turmoil in the house. 'It flew all to pieces, Pa,' my mother told him, in graphically describing the accident, 'I knew 'twould,' growled grandfather. 'I allus told ye to git a Pope-Toledo.'

The Day The Dam Broke

My memories of what my family and I went through during the 1913 flood in Ohio I would gladly forget. And yet neither the hardships we endured nor the turmoil and confusion we experienced can alter my feeling toward my native state and city. I am having a fine time now and wish Columbus were here, but if anyone ever wished a city was in hell it was during that frightful and perilous afternoon in 1913 when the dam broke, or, to be more exact, when everybody in town thought that the dam broke. We were both ennobled and demoralized by the experience. Grandfather especially rose to magnificent heights which can never lose their splendour for me, even though his reactions to the flood were based upon a profound misconception; namely, that Nathan Bedford Forrest's cavalry was the menace we were called upon to face. The only possible means of escape for us was to flee the house, a step which grandfather sternly forbade, brandishing his old army sabre in his hand. 'Let the sons — — come!' he roared. Meanwhile hundreds of people were streaming by our house in wild panic, screaming 'Go east! Go east!' We had to stun grandfather with the ironing board. Impeded as we were by the inert form of the old gentleman – he was taller than six feet and weighed almost a hundred and seventy pounds – we were passed, in the first half-mile, by practically everybody else in the city. Had grandfather not come to, at the corner of Parsons Avenue and Town Street, we would unquestionably have been overtaken and engulfed by the roaring waters – that is, if there had *been* any roaring waters. Later, when the panic had died down and people had gone rather sheepishly back to their homes and their offices, minimizing the distances they had run and offering various reasons for running, city engineers pointed out that even if the dam had broken, the water level would not have risen more than two additional inches in the West Side. The West Side was, at the time of the dam scare, under thirty feet of water – as, indeed, were all Ohio river towns during the great spring floods of twenty years ago. The East Side (where we

224

lived and where all the running occurred) had never been in any danger at all. Only a rise of some ninety-five feet could have caused the flood waters to flow over High Street – the thoroughfare that divided the east side of town from the west – and engulf the East Side.

The fact that we were all as safe as kittens under a cookstove did not, however, assuage in the least the fine despair and the grotesque desperation which seized upon the residents of the East Side when the cry spread like a grass fire that the dam had given way. Some of the most dignified, staid, cynical, and clear-thinking men in town abandoned their wives, stenographers, homes, and offices and ran east. There are few alarms in the world more terrifying than 'The dam has broken!' There are few persons capable of stopping to reason when that clarion cry strikes upon their ears, even persons who live in towns no nearer than five hundred miles to a dam.

The Columbus, Ohio, broken-dam rumour began, as I recall it, about noon of 12 March 1913. High Street, the main canyon of trade, was loud with the placid hum of business and the buzzing of placid businessmen arguing, computing, wheedling, offering, refusing, compromising. Darius Conningway, one of the foremost corporation lawyers in the Middle-West, was telling the Public Utilities Commission in the language of Julius Caesar that they might as well try to move the Northern Star as to move him. Other men were making their little boasts and their gestures. Suddenly somebody began to run. It may be that he had simply remembered, all of a moment, an engagement to meet his wife, for which he was now frightfully late. Whatever it was, he ran east on Broad Street (probably toward the Maramor Restaurant, a favourite place for a man to meet his wife). Somebody else began to run, perhaps a newsboy in high spirits. Another man, a portly gentleman of affairs, broke into a trot. Inside of ten minutes, everybody on High Street, from the Union Depot to the Courthouse was running. A loud mumble gradually crystallized into the dread word 'dam', 'The dam has broke!' The fear was put into words by a little old lady in an electric, or by a traffic cop, or by a small boy: nobody knows who, nor does it now really matter. Two thousand people were abruptly in full flight. 'Go east!' was the cry that arose – east away from the river, east to safety. 'Go east! Go east! Go east!'

Black streams of people flowed eastward down all the streets leading in that direction; these streams, whose headwaters were in the dry-goods stores, office buildings, harness shops, movie

Two Thousand People Were in Full Flight

theatres, were fed by trickles of housewives, children, cripples, servants, dogs, and cats, slipping out of the houses past which the main streams flowed, shouting and screaming. People ran out leaving fires burning and food cooking and doors wide open. I remember, however, that my mother turned out all the fires and that she took with her a dozen eggs and two loaves of bread. It was her plan to make Memorial Hall, just two blocks away, and take refuge somewhere in the top of it, in one of the dusty rooms where war veterans met and where old battle flags and stage scenery were stored. But the seething throngs, shouting 'Go east!' drew her along and the rest of us with her. When grandfather regained full consciousness, at Parsons Avenue, he turned upon the retreating mob like a vengeful prophet and exhorted the men to form ranks and stand off the Rebel dogs, but at length he, too, got the idea that the dam had broken and, roaring 'Go east!' in his powerful voice, he caught up in one arm a small child and in the other a slight clerkish man of perhaps forty-two and we slowly began to gain on those ahead of us.

A scattering of firemen, policemen, and army officers in dress uniforms – there had been a review at Fort Hayes, in the northern part of town – added colour to the surging billows of people. 'Go east!' cried a little child in a piping voice, as she ran past a porch on which drowsed a lieutenant-colonel of infantry. Used to quick decisions, trained to immediate obedience, the officer bounded off the porch and, running at full tilt, soon passed the child, bawling 'Go east!' The two of them emptied rapidly the houses of the little street they were on. 'What is it? What is it?' demanded a fat, waddling man who intercepted the colonel. The officer dropped behind and asked the little child what it was. 'The dam has broke!' gasped the girl. 'The dam has broke!' roared the colonel. 'Go east! Go east! Go east!' He was soon leading, with the exhausted child in his arms, a fleeing company of three hundred persons who had gathered round him from living-rooms, shops, garages, backyards, and basements.

Nobody has ever been able to compute with an exactness how many people took part in the great rout of 1913, for the panic, which extended from the Winslow Bottling Works in the south end to Clintonville, six miles north, ended as abruptly as it began and the bobtail and ragtag and velvet-gowned groups of refugees melted away and slunk home, leaving the streets peaceful and deserted. The shouting, weeping, tangled evacuation of the city lasted not more than two hours in all. Some few people got as far east as Reynoldsburg, twelve miles away; fifty or more reached the Country Club, eight miles away; most of the others gave up, exhausted, or climbed trees in Franklin Park, four miles out. Order was restored and fear dispelled finally by means of militiamen riding about in motor lorries bawling through megaphones: 'The dam has *not* broken!' At first this tended only to add to the confusion and increase the panic, for many stampeders thought the

227

soldiers were bellowing 'The dam has now broken!,' thus setting an official seal of authentication on the calamity.

All the time, the sun shone quietly and there was nowhere any sign of oncoming waters. A visitor in an aeroplane, looking down on the straggling, agitated masses of people below, would have been hard put to it to divine a reason for the phenomenon. It must have inspired, in such an observer, a peculiar kind of terror, like the sight of the *Marie Celeste*, abandoned at sea, its galley fires peacefully burning, its tranquil decks bright in the sunlight.

An aunt of mine, Aunt Edith Taylor, was in a movie theatre on High Street when, over and above the sound of the piano in the pit (a W. S. Hart picture was being shown), there rose the steadily increasing tromp of running feet. Persistent shouts rose above the tromping. An elderly man, sitting near by aunt, mumbled something, got out of his seat, and went up the aisle at a dogtrot. This started everybody. In an instant the audience was jamming the aisles. 'Fire!' shouted a woman who always expected to be burned up in a theatre; but now the shouts outside were louder and coherent. 'The dam has broke!' cried somebody. 'Go east!' screamed a small woman in front of my aunt. And east they went, pushing and shoving and clawing, knocking women and children down, emerging finally into the street, torn and sprawling. Inside the theatre, Bill Hart was calmly calling some desperado's bluff and the brave girl at the piano played 'Row! Row! Row!' loudly and then 'In My Harem'. Outside, men were streaming across the Statehouse yard, others were climbing trees, a woman managed to get up on to the 'These Are My Jewels' statue, whose bronze figures of Sherman, Stanton, Grant, and Sheridan watched with cold unconcern the going to pieces of the capital city.

'I ran south to State Street, east on State to Third, south on Third to Town, and out east on Town,' my Aunt Edith has written me. 'A tall spare woman with grim eyes and a determined chin ran past me down the middle of the street. I was still uncertain as to what was the matter, in spite of all the shouting. I drew up alongside the woman with some effort, for although she was in her late fifties, she had a beautiful easy running form and seemed to be in excellent condition. "What is it?" I puffed. She gave me a quick glance and then looked ahead again, stepping up her pace a trifle. "Don't ask me, ask God!" she said.

'When I reached Grant Avenue, I was so spent that Dr H. R. Mallory – you remember Dr Mallory, the man with the white beard who looks like Robert Browning? – well, Dr Mallory, whom I had drawn away from at the corner of Fifth and Town, passed me. "It's got us!" he shouted, and I felt sure that whatever it was *did* have us, for you know what conviction Dr Mallory's statements always carried. I didn't know at the time what he meant, but I found out later. There was a boy behind him on roller-skates, and

'It's Got Us!' He Shouted

Dr Mallory mistook the swishing of the skates for the sound of rushing water. He eventually reached the Columbus School for Girls, at the corner of Parsons Avenue and Town Street, where he collapsed, expecting the cold frothing waters of the Scioto to sweep him into oblivion. The boy on the skates swirled past him and Dr Mallory realized for the first time what he had been running from. Looking back up the street, he could see no signs of water, but nevertheless, after resting a few minutes, he jogged on east again. He caught up with me at Ohio Avenue, where we rested together. I should say that about seven hundred people passed us. A funny thing was that all of them were on foot. Nobody seemed to have had the courage to stop and start his car; but as I remember it, all cars had to be cranked in those days, which is probably the reason.'

The next day, the city went about its business as if nothing had happened, but there was no joking. It was two years or more before you dared treat the breaking of the dam lightly. And even now, twenty years after, there are a few persons, like Dr Mallory, who will shut up like a clam if you mention the Afternoon of the Great Run.

The Night The Ghost Got In

The ghost that got into our house on the night of 17 November 1915 raised such a hullabaloo of misunderstandings that I am sorry I didn't just let it keep on walking, and go to bed. Its advent caused my mother to throw a shoe through a window of the house next door and ended up with my grandfather shooting a patrolman. I am sorry, therefore, as I have said, that I ever paid any attention to the footsteps.

They began about a quarter past one o'clock in the morning, a rhythmic, quick-cadenced walking around the dining-room table. My mother was asleep in one room upstairs, my brother Herman in another; grandfather was in the attic, in the old walnut bed which, as you will remember, once fell on my father. I had just stepped out of the bathtub and was busily rubbing myself with a towel when I heard the steps. They were the steps of a man walking rapidly around the dining-room table downstairs. The light from the bathroom shone down the back steps, which dropped directly into the dining-room; I could see the faint shine of plates on the plate-rail; I couldn't see the table. The steps kept going round and round the table; at regular intervals a board creaked, when it was trod upon. I supposed at first that it was my father or my brother Roy, who had gone to Indianapolis but were expected home at any time. I suspected next that it was a burglar. It did not enter my mind until later that it was a ghost.

After the walking had gone on for perhaps three minutes, I tiptoed to Herman's room. 'Psst!' I hissed, in the dark, shaking him. 'Awp,' he said, in the low, hopeless tone of a despondent beagle – he always half suspected that something would 'get him' in the night. I told him who I was. 'There's something downstairs!' I said. He got up and followed me to the head of the back staircase. We listened together. There was no sound. The steps had ceased. Herman looked at me in some alarm: I had only the bath towel around my waist. He wanted to go back to bed, but I gripped his arm. 'There's something down there!' I said.

231

Instantly the steps began again, circled the dining-room table like a man running, and started up the stairs toward us, heavily, two at a time. The light still shone palely down the stairs; we saw nothing coming; we only heard the steps. Herman rushed to his room and slammed the door. I slammed shut the door at the stairs top and held my knee against it. After a long minute, I slowly opened it again. There was nothing there. There was no sound. None of us ever heard the ghost again.

He Always Half Suspected That Something Would Get Him

The slamming of the doors had aroused mother: she peered out of her room. 'What on earth are you boys doing?' she demanded. Herman ventured out of his room. 'Nothing,' he said, gruffly, but he was, in colour, a light green. 'What was all that running around downstairs?' said mother. So she had heard the steps, too! We just looked at her. 'Burglars!' she shouted intuitively. I tried to quiet her by starting lightly downstairs.

'Come on, Herman,' I said.

'I'll stay with mother,' he said. 'She's all excited.'

I stepped back on to the landing.

'Don't either of you go a step,' said mother. 'We'll call the police.' Since the phone was downstairs, I didn't see how we were going to call the police – nor did I want the police – but mother made one of her quick, incomparable decisions. She flung up a window of her bedroom, which faced the bedroom windows of the house of a neighbour, picked up a shoe, and whammed it through a pane of glass across the narrow space that separated the two houses. Glass tinkled into the bedroom occupied by a retired engraver named Bodwell and his wife. Bodwell had been for some years in rather a bad way and was subject to mild 'attacks'. Most everybody we knew or lived near had *some* kind of attacks.

It was now about two o'clock of a moonless night; clouds hung black and low. Bodwell was at the window in a minute, shouting, frothing a little, shaking his fist. 'We'll sell the house and go back to Peoria,' we could hear Mrs Bodwell saying. It was some time before mother 'got through' to Bodwell. 'Burglars!' she shouted. 'Burglars in the house!' Herman and I hadn't dared to tell her that it was not burglars but ghosts, for she was even more afraid of ghosts than of burglars. Bodwell at first thought that she meant there were burglars in his house, but finally he quieted down and called the police for us over an extension phone by his bed. After he had disappeared from the window, mother suddenly made as if to throw another shoe, not because there was further need of it but, as she later explained, because the thrill of heaving a shoe through a window glass had enormously taken her fancy. I prevented her.

The police were on hand in a commendably short time: a Ford sedan full of them, two on motor-cycles, and a patrol wagon with about eight in it and a few reporters. They began banging at our front door. Flashlights shot streaks of gleam up and down the walls, across the yard, down the walk between our house and Bodwell's. 'Open up!' cried a hoarse voice. 'We're men from Headquarters!' I wanted to go down and let them in, since there they were, but mother wouldn't hear of it. 'You haven't a stitch on,' she pointed out. 'You'd catch your death.' I wound the towel around me again. Finally the cops put their shoulders to our big heavy front door with its thick bevelled glass and broke it in: I could hear a rending of wood and a splash of glass on the floor of the hall. Their lights played all over the living-room and criss-crossed nervously in the dining-room, stabbed into hallways, shot up the front stairs and finally up the back. They caught me standing in my towel at the top. A heavy policeman bounded up the steps. 'Who are you?' he demanded. 'I live here,' I said. 'Well, whattsa matta, ya hot?' he asked. It was, as a matter of fact, cold; I went to my room and pulled on some trousers. On my way out, a cop stuck a gun into my ribs. 'Whatta you doin' here?' he demanded.

Police Were All Over the Place

'I live here,' I said.

The officer in charge reported to mother. 'No sign of nobody, lady,' he said. 'Musta got away – whatt'd he look like?' 'There were two or three of them,' mother said, 'whooping and carrying on and slamming doors.' 'Funny,' said the cop. 'All ya windows and doors was locked on the inside tight as a tick.'

Downstairs, we could hear the tromping of the other police. Police were all over the place; doors were yanked open, drawers were yanked open, windows were shot up and pulled down, furniture fell with dull thumps. A half-dozen policemen emerged out of the darkness of the front hallway upstairs. They began to ransack the floor: pulled beds away from walls, tore clothes off hooks in the closets, pulled suitcases and boxes off shelves. One of them found an old zither that Roy had won in a pool tournament. 'Looky here, Joe,' he said strumming it with a big paw. The cop named Joe took it and turned it over. 'What is it?' he asked me. 'It's an old zither our guinea pig used to sleep on,' I said. It was true that a pet guinea pig we once had would never sleep anywhere except on the zither, but I should never have said so. Joe and the other cop looked at me a long time. They put the zither back on a shelf.

'No sign o' nuthin',' said the cop who had first spoken to mother. 'This guy,' he explained to the others, jerking a thumb at me, 'was nekked. The lady seems historical.' They all nodded, but said nothing; just looked at me. In the small silence we all heard a creaking in the attic. Grandfather was turning over in bed. 'What's 'at?' snapped Joe. Five or six cops sprang for the attic door before I could intervene or explain. I realized that it would be bad if they burst in on grandfather unannounced or even announced. He was going through a phase in which he believed that General Meade's men, under steady hammering by Stonewall Jackson, were beginning to retreat and even desert.

When I got to the attic, things were pretty confused. Grandfather had evidently jumped to the conclusion that the police were deserters from Meade's army, trying to hide away in his attic. He bounded out of bed wearing a long flannel nightgown over long woollen underwear, a night-cap, and a leather jacket around his chest. The cops must have realized at once that the indignant white-haired old man belonged in the house, but they had no chance to say so. 'Back, ye cowardly dogs!' roared grandfather. 'Back t' the lines, ye goddam lily-livered cattle!' With that, he fetched the officer who found the zither a flat-handed smack alongside his head that sent him sprawling. The others beat a retreat, but not fast enough; grandfather grabbed Zither's gun from its holster and let fly. The report seemed to crack the rafters; smoke filled the attic. A cop cursed and shot his hand to his shoulder. Somehow, we all finally got downstairs again and locked the door

235

against the old gentleman. He fired once or twice more in the darkness and then went back to bed. 'That was grandfather,' I explained to Joe, out of breath. 'He thinks you're deserters,' 'I'll say he does,' said Joe.

The cops were reluctant to leave without getting their hands on somebody besides grandfather; the night had been distinctly a defeat for them. Furthermore, they obviously didn't like the 'layout', something looked – and I can see their viewpoint – phony. They began to poke into things again. A reporter, a thin-faced, wispy man, came up to me. I had put on one of mother's blouses, not being able to find anything else. The reporter looked at me with mingled suspicion and interest. 'Just what the hell is the real lowdown here, Bud?' he asked. I decided to be frank with him. 'We had ghosts,' I said. He gazed at me a long time as if I were a slot machine into which he had, without results, dropped a nickel. Then he walked away. The cops followed him, the one grandfather shot holding his now-bandaged arm, cursing and blaspheming. 'I'm gonna get my gun back from that old bird,' said the zither-cop. 'Yeh,' said Joe. 'You – and who else?' I told them I would bring it to the station house the next day.

'What was the matter with that one policeman?' mother asked, after they had gone. 'Grandfather shot him,' I said. 'What for?' she demanded. I told her he was a deserter. 'Of all things!' said mother. 'He was such a nice-looking young man.'

Grandfather was fresh as a daisy and full of jokes at breakfast next morning. We thought at first he had forgotten all about what had happened, but he hadn't. Over his third cup of coffee, he glared at Herman and me. 'What was the idee of all them cops tarryhootin' round the house last night?' he demanded. He had us there.

One of the incidents that I always think of first when I cast back over my youth is what happened the night that my father 'threatened to get Buck'. This, as you will see, is not precisely a fair or accurate description of what actually occurred, but it is the way in which I and the other members of my family invariably allude to the occasion. We were living at the time in an old house at 77 Lexington Avenue, in Columbus, Ohio. In the early years of the nineteenth century, Columbus won out, as state capital, by only one vote over Lancaster, and ever since then has had the hallucination that it is being followed, a curious municipal state of mind which affects, in some way or other, all those who live there. Columbus is a town in which almost anything is likely to happen and in which almost everything has.

My father was sleeping in the front room on the second floor next to that of my brother Roy, who was then about sixteen. Father was usually in bed by nine-thirty and up again by ten-thirty to protest bitterly against a Victrola record we three boys were in the habit of playing over and over, namely 'No News, or What Killed the Dog', a recitation by Nat Wills. The record had been played so many times that its grooves were deeply cut and the needle often kept revolving in the same groove, repeating over and over the same words. Thus: 'ate some burnt hoss flesh, ate some burnt hoss flesh, ate some burnt hoss flesh'. It was this reiteration that generally got father out of bed.

On the night in question, however, we had all gone to bed at about the same time, without much fuss. Roy, as a matter of fact, had been in bed all day with a kind of mild fever. It wasn't severe enough to cause delirium and my brother was the last person in the world to give way to delirium. Nevertheless, he had warned father when father went to bed, that he *might* become delirious.

About three o'clock in the morning, Roy, who was wakeful, decided to pretend that delirium was on him, in order to have, as he later explained it, some 'fun'. He got out of bed and, going to my father's room, shook him and said, 'Buck your time has come!' My father's name was not Buck but Charles, nor had he ever been called Buck. He was a tall, mildly nervous, peaceable gentleman, given to quiet pleasures, and eager that everything should run smoothly. 'Hmm?' he said, with drowsy bewilderment. 'Get up, Buck,' said my brother, coldly, but with a certain gleam in his eyes. My father leaped out of bed, on the side away from his son, rushed from the room, locked the door behind him, and shouted us all up.

We were naturally reluctant to believe that Roy, who was quiet and self-contained, had threatened his father with any such abracadabra as father said he had. My older brother, Herman, went back to bed without any comment. 'You've had a bad dream,' my mother said. This vexed my father. 'I tell you he called me Buck and told me my time had come,' he said. We went to the door of his room, unlocked it, and tiptoed through it to Roy's room. He lay in his bed, breathing easily, as if he were fast asleep. It was apparent at a glance that he did not have a high fever. My mother gave my father a look. 'I tell you he did,' whispered father.

Our presence in the room finally seemed to awaken Roy and he was (or rather, as we found out long afterward, pretended to be) astonished and bewildered. 'What's the matter?' he asked. 'Nothing,' said my mother. 'Just your father had a nightmare.' 'I did not have a nightmare,' said father, slowly and firmly. He wore an old-fashioned, 'side-slit' nightgown which looked rather odd on his tall, spare figure. The situation, before we let it drop and everybody went back to bed again, became, as such situations in our family usually did, rather more complicated than ironed out. Roy demanded to know what had happened, and my mother told him, in considerably garbled fashion, what father had told her. At this a light dawned in Roy's eyes. 'Dad's got it backward,' he said. He then explained that he had heard father get out of bed and had called to him. 'I'll handle this,' his father had answered. 'Buck is downstairs.' 'Who is this Buck?' my mother demanded of father. 'I don't know any Buck and I never said that,' father contended, irritably. None of us (except Roy, of course) believed him. 'You had a dream,' said mother. 'People have these dreams.' 'I did not have a dream,' father said. He was pretty well nettled by this time, and he stood in front of a bureau mirror, brushing his hair with a pair of military brushes; it always seemed to calm father to brush his hair. My mother declared that it was 'a sin and a shame' for a grown man to wake up a sick boy simply because he (the grown man: father) had got on his back and had a bad dream. My father, as a matter of fact, *had* been known to have nightmares, usually about Lillian Russell and President Cleveland, who chased him.

We argued the thing for perhaps another half-hour, after which mother made father sleep in her room. 'You're all safe now, boys,' she said, firmly, as she shut her door I could hear father grumbling for a long time, with an occasional monosyllable of doubt from mother.

It was some six months after this that father went through a similar experience with me. He was at that time sleeping in the room next to mine. I had been trying all afternoon, in vain, to think of the name Perth Amboy. It seems now like a very simple name to recall and yet on the day in question I thought of every other town in the country, as well as such words and names and phrases as terra cotta, Walla-Walla, bill of lading, vice versa, hoity-toity, Pall Mall, Bodley Head, Schumann-Heink, etc., without even coming close to Perth Amboy. I suppose terra cotta was the closest I came, although it was not very close.

Long after I had gone to bed, I was struggling with the problem. I began to indulge in the wildest fancies as I lay there in the dark, such as that there was no such town, and even that there was no such state as New Jersey. I fell to repeating the word 'Jersey' over and over again, until it became idiotic and meaningless. If you have ever lain awake at night and repeated one word over and over, thousands and millions and hundreds of thousands of millions of times, you know the disturbing mental state you can get into. I got to thinking that there was nobody else in the world but me, and various other wild imaginings of that nature. Eventually, lying there thinking these outlandish thoughts, I grew slightly alarmed. I began to suspect that one might lose one's mind over some such trivial mental tic as a futile search for terra firma Piggly Wiggly Gorgonzola Prester John Arc de Triomphe Holy Moses Lares

239

and Penates. I began to feel the imperative necessity of human contact. This silly and alarming tangle of thought and fancy had gone far enough. I might get into some kind of mental aberrancy unless I found out the name of that Jersey town and could go to sleep. Therefore, I got out of bed, walked into the room where father was sleeping, and shook him. 'Um!' he mumbled. I shook him more fiercely and he finally woke up, with a glaze of dream and apprehension in his eyes. 'What's matter?' he asked, thickly. I must, indeed, have been rather wild of eye, and my hair, which is unruly, becomes monstrously tousled and snarled at night. 'Wha's it?' said my father, sitting up, in readiness to spring out of bed on the far side. The thought must have been going through his mind that all his sons were crazy, or on the verge of going crazy. I see that now, but I didn't then, for I had forgotten the Buck incident and did not realize how similar my appearance must have been to Roy's the night he called father Buck and told him his time had come. 'Listen,' I said. 'Name some towns in New Jersey quick!' It must have been around three in the morning. Father got up, keeping the bed between him and me, and started to pull his trousers on. 'Don't bother about dressing,' I said. 'Just name some towns in New Jersey.' While he hastily pulled on his clothes – I remember he left his socks off and put his shoes on his bare feet – father began to name, in a shaky voice various New Jersey cities. I can still see him reaching for his coat without taking his eyes off me. 'Newark,' he said, 'Jersey City, Atlantic City, Elizabeth, Paterson, Passaic, Trenton, Jersey City, Trenton, Paterson –' 'It has two names,' I snapped. 'Elizabeth and Paterson,' he said. 'No, no!' I told him, irritably. 'This is one town with one name, but there are two words in it, like helter-skelter.' 'Helter-skelter,' said my father, moving slowly toward the bedroom door and smiling in a faint, strained way which I understand now – but didn't then – was meant to humour me. When he was within a few paces of the door, he fairly leaped for it and ran out into the hall, his coattails and shoelaces flying. The exit stunned me. I had no notion that he thought I had gone out of my senses; I could only believe that he had gone out of *his* or that, only partially awake, he was engaged in some form of running in his sleep. I ran after him and I caught him at the door of mother's room and grabbed him, in order to

240

reason with him. I shook him a little, thinking to wake him completely. 'Mary! Roy! Herman!' he shouted. I, too, began to shout for my brothers and my mother. My mother opened her door instantly, and there we were at 3.30 in the morning grappling and shouting, father partly dressed, but without socks or shirt, and I in pyjamas.

'*Now*, what?' demanded my mother, grimly, pulling us apart. She was capable, fortunately, of handling any two of us and she never in her life was alarmed by the words or actions of any one of us.

'Look out for Jamie!' said father. (He always called me Jamie when excited.) My mother looked at me.

'What's the matter with your father?' she demanded. I said I didn't know; I said he had got up suddenly and dressed and ran out of the room.

'Where did you think you were going?' mother asked him, coolly. He looked at me. We looked at each other, breathing hard, but somewhat calmer.

'He was babbling about New Jersey at this infernal hour of the night,' said father. 'He came to my room and asked me to name towns in New Jersey.' Mother looked at me.

'I just asked him,' I said. 'I was trying to think of one and couldn't sleep.'

'You see?' said father, triumphantly. Mother didn't look at him.

'Get to bed, both of you,' she said. 'I don't want to hear any more out of you tonight. Dressing and tearing up and down the hall at this hour in the morning!' She went back into the room and shut her door. Father and I went back to bed. 'Are you all right?' he called to me. 'Are you?' I asked. 'Well, good night,' he said. 'Good night,' I said.

Mother would not let the rest of us discuss the affair next morning at breakfast. Herman asked what the hell had been the matter. 'We'll go on to something more elevating,' said mother.

When I look back on the long line of servants my mother hired during the years I lived at home, I remember clearly ten or twelve of them (we had about a hundred and sixty-two, all told, but few of them were memorable). There was, among the immortals, Dora Gedd, a quiet, mousy girl of thirty-two who one night shot at a man in her room, throwing our household into an uproar that was equalled perhaps only by the goings-on the night the ghost got in. Nobody knew how her lover, a morose garage man, got into the house, but everybody for two blocks knew how he got out. Dora had dressed up in a lavender evening gown for the occasion and she wore a mass of jewellery, some of which was my mother's. She kept shouting something from Shakespeare after the shooting – I forget just what – and pursued the gentleman downstairs from her attic room. When he got to the second floor he rushed into my father's room. It was this entrance, and not the shot or the shouting, that aroused father, a deep sleeper always. 'Get me out of here!' shouted the victim. This situation rapidly developed, from then on, into one of those bewildering involvements for which my family had, I am afraid, a kind of unhappy genius. When the cops arrived Dora was shooting out the Welsbach gas mantles in the living-room, and her gentleman friend had fled. By dawn everything was quiet once more.

There were others. Gertie Straub: big, genial, and ruddy, a collector of pints of eye (we learned after she was gone), who came in after two o'clock one night from a dancing party at Buckeye Lake and awakened us by bumping into and knocking over furniture. 'Who's down there?' called mother from upstairs. 'It's me, dearie,' said Gertie, 'Gertie Straub.' 'What are you *doing*?' demanded mother. 'Dusting,' said Gertie.

Juanemma Kramer was one of my favourites. Her mother loved the name Juanita so dearly that she had worked the first part of it into the names of all her daughters – they were (in addition to Juanita) Juanemma, Juanhelen, and Juangrace. Juanemma was a

242

'Dusting,' Said Gertie

thin, nervous maid who lived in constant dread of being hypnotized. Nor were her fears unfounded, for she was so extremely susceptible to hypnotic suggestion that one evening at B. F. Keith's theatre when a man on the stage was hypnotized, Juanemma, in audience, was hypnotized too and floundered out into the aisle making the same cheeping sound that the subject on the stage, who had been told he was a chicken, was making. The act was abandoned and some xylophone players were brought on to restore order. One night, when our house was deep in quiet slumber, Juanemma became hypnotized in her sleep. She dreamed that a man 'put her under' and then disappeared without 'bringing her out'. This was explained when, at last, a police surgeon whom we called in – he was the only doctor we could persuade to come out at three in the morning – slapped her into consciousness. It got so finally that any buzzing or whirling sound or any flashing object would put Juanemma under, and we had to let her go. I was reminded of her recently when, at a performance of the movie *Rasputin and the Empress*, there came the scene in which Lionel Barrymore as the unholy priest hypnotizes the Czarevitch by spinning before his eyes a glittering watch. If Juanemma sat in any theatre and witnessed that scene she must, I am sure, have gone under instantly. Happily, she seems to have missed the picture, for otherwise Mr Barrymore might have had to dress up again as Rasputin (which God forbid) and journey across the country to get her out of it – excellent publicity but a great bother.

Before I go on to Vashti, whose last name I forget, I will look in passing at another of our white maids (Vashti was coloured). Belle Giddin distinguished herself by one gesture which fortunately did not result in the bedlam occasioned by Juanemma's hypnotic states or Dora Gedd's shooting spree. Bella burned her finger grievously, and purposely, one afternoon in the steam of a boiling kettle so that she could find out whether the pain-killer she had bought one night at a tent-show for fifty cents was any good. It was only fair.

Vashti turned out, in the end, to be partly legendary. She was a comely and sombre negress who was always able to find things my mother lost. 'I don't know what's become of my garnet brooch,' my mother said one day. 'Yassum,' said Vashti. In half

244

an hour she had found it. 'Where in the world was it?' asked mother. 'In de yahd,' said Vashti. 'De dog mussa drug it out.'

Vashti was in love with a young coloured chauffeur named Charley, but she was also desired by her stepfather, whom none of us had ever seen but who was, she said, a handsome but messin' round gentleman from Georgia who had come north and married Vashti's mother just so he could be near Vashti. Charley, her fiancé, was for killing the stepfather but we counselled flight to another city. Vashti, however, would burst into tears and hymns and vow she'd never leave us; she got a certain pleasure out of bearing her cross. Thus we all lived in jeopardy, for the possibility that Vashti, Charley, and her stepfather might fight it out some night in our kitchen did not, at times, seem remote. Once I went into the kitchen at midnight to make some coffee. Charley was standing at a window looking out into the backyard; Vashti was rolling her eyes. 'Heah he come! Heah he come!' she moaned. The stepfather didn't show up, however.

Charley finally saved up twenty-seven dollars toward taking Vashti away but one day he impulsively bought a ·22 revolver with a mother-of-pearl handle and demanded that Vashti tell him where her mother and stepfather lived. 'Doan go up dere, doan go *up* dere!' said Vashti. 'Mah mothah is just as rarin' as he is!' Charley, however, insisted. It came out then that Vashti didn't have any stepfather; there was no such person. Charley threw her over for a yellow gal named Nancy: he never forgave Vashti for the vanishing from his life of a menace that had come to mean more to him than Vashti herself. Afterwards, if you asked Vashti about her stepfather or about Charley she would say, proudly, and with a woman-of-the-world air, 'Neither one ob 'em is messin' round *me* any mo'.'

Mrs. Doody, a huge, middle-aged woman with a religious taint, came into and went out of our house like a comet. The second night she was there she went berserk while doing the dishes and, under the impression that father was the Antichrist, pursued him several times up the backstairs and down the front. He had been sitting quietly over his coffee in the living-room when she burst in from the kitchen waving a bread knife. My brother Herman finally felled her with a piece of Libby's cut-glass that had been

'One Night While Doing the Dishes . . .'

a wedding present of mother's. Mother, I remember, was in the attic at the time, trying to find some old things, and, appearing on the scene in the midst of it all, got the quick and mistaken impression that father was chasing Mrs Doody.

Mrs Robertson, a fat and mumbly old coloured woman, who might have been sixty and who might have been a hundred, gave us more than one turn during the many years that she did our washing. She had been a slave down South and she remembered 'having seen the troops marching – a mess o' blue, den a mess o' grey'. 'What,' my mother asked her once, 'were they fighting about?' 'Dat,' said Mrs Robertson, 'Ah don't know.' She had a feeling, at all times, that something was going to happen. I can see her now, staggering up from the basement with a basketful of clothes and coming abruptly to a halt in the middle of the kitchen. 'Hahk!' she would say, in a deep, guttural voice. We would all hark; there was never anything to be heard. Neither, when she shouted 'Look yondah!' and pointed a trembling hand at a window, was there ever anything to be seen. Father protested time and again that he couldn't stand Mrs Robertson around, but mother always refused to let her go. It seems that she was a jewel. Once she walked unbidden, a dishpan full of wrung-out clothes under her arm, into father's study, where he was engrossed in some figures. Father looked up. She regarded him for a moment in silence. Then – 'Look out!' she said, and withdrew. Another time, a murky winter afternoon, she came flubbering up the cellar stairs and bounced, out of breath, into the kitchen. Father was in the kitchen sipping some black coffee; he was in a jittery state of nerves from the effects of having had a tooth out, and had been in bed most of the day. 'Dey is a death watch downstaihs!' rumbled the old coloured lady. It developed that she had heard a strange 'chipping' noise back of the furnace. 'That was a cricket,' said father. 'Um-*hm*,' said Mrs Robertson. 'Dat was uh death watch!' With that she put on her hat and went home, poising just long enough at the back door to observe darkly to father. '*Dey ain't no way!*' It upset him for days.

Mrs Robertson had only one great hour that I can think of – Jack Johnson's victory over Mistah Jeffries on the Fourth of July, 1910. She took a prominent part in the coloured parade through the South End that night, playing a Spanish fandango on a banjo. The procession was led by the pastor of her church who, Mrs Robertson later told us, had 'splained that the victory of Jack over Mistah Jeffries proved 'de 'speriority ob de race'.

'What,' asked my mother, 'did he mean by that?' 'Dat,' said Mrs Robertson, 'Ah don't know.'

Our other servants I don't remember so clearly, except the one who set the house on fire (her name eludes me), and Edda Millmoss. Edda was always slightly morose but she had gone along for months, all the time she was with us, quietly and efficiently attending to her work, until the night we had Carson Blair and F. R. Gardiner to dinner – both men of importance to my father's ambitions. Then, suddenly, while serving the entrée, Edda dropped everything and, pointing a quivering finger at father, accused him in a long rigamarole of having done her out of her rights to the land on which Trinity Church in New York stands. Mr Gardiner had one of his 'attacks' and the whole evening turned out miserably.

The Dog That Bit People

Probably no one man should have as many dogs in his life as I have had, but there was more pleasure than distress in them for me except in the case of an Airedale named Muggs. He gave me more trouble than all the other fifty-four or -five put together, although my moment of keenest embarrassment was the time a Scotch terrier named Jeannie, who had just had six puppies in the clothes closet of a fourth floor apartment in New York, had the unexpected seventh and last at the corner of Eleventh Street and Fifth Avenue during a walk she had insisted on taking. Then, too, there was the prize-winning French poodle, a great big black poodle – none of your little, untroublesome white miniatures – who got sick riding in the rumble seat of a car with me on her way to the Greenwich Dog Show. She had a red rubber bib tucked around her throat and, since a rain storm came up when we were half way through the Bronx, I had to hold over her a small green umbrella, really more of a parasol. The rain beat down fearfully and suddenly the driver of the car drove into a big garage, filled with mechanics. It happened so quickly that I forgot to put the umbrella down and I will always remember, with sickening distress, the look of incredulity mixed with hatred that came over the face of the particular hardened garage man that came over to see what we wanted, when he took a look at me and the poodle. All garage men, and people of that intolerant stripe, hate poodles with their curious haircut, especially the pom-poms that you got to leave on their hips if you expect the dogs to win a prize.

But the Airedale, as I have said, was the worst of all my dogs. He really wasn't my dog, as a matter of fact: I came home from a vacation one summer to find that my brother Roy had bought him while I was away. A big, burly, choleric dog, he always acted as if he thought I wasn't one of the family. There was a slight advantage in being one of the family, for he didn't bite the family as often as he bit strangers. Still, in the years that we had him he bit everybody but mother, and he made a pass at her once but missed.

249

That was during the month when we suddenly had mice, and Muggs refused to do anything about them. Nobody ever had mice exactly like the mice we had that month. They acted like pet mice, almost like mice somebody had trained. They were so friendly that one night when mother entertained at dinner the Friraliras, a club she and my father had belonged to for twenty years, she put down a lot of little dishes with food in them on the pantry floor so that the mice would be satisfied with that and wouldn't come into the dining-room. Muggs stayed out in the pantry with the mice, lying on the floor, growling to himself – not at the mice, but about all the people in the next room that he would have liked to get at. Mother slipped out into the pantry once to see how everything was going. Everything was going fine. It made her so mad to see Muggs lying there, oblivious of the mice – they came running up to her – that she slapped him and he slashed at her, but didn't make it. He was sorry immediately, mother said. He was always sorry, she said, after he bit someone, but we could not understand how she figured this out. He didn't act sorry.

Mother used to send a box of candy every Christmas to the people the Airedale bit. The list finally contained forty or more names. Nobody could understand why we didn't get rid of the dog. I didn't understand it very well myself, but we didn't get rid of him. I think that one or two people tried to poison Muggs – he acted poisoned once in a while – and old Major Moberly fired at him once with his service revolver near the Seneca Hotel in East Broad Street – but Muggs lived to be almost eleven years old and even when he could hardly get around he bit a Congressman who had called to see my father on business. My mother had never liked the Congressman – she said the signs of his horoscope showed he couldn't be trusted (he was Saturn with the moon in Virgo) – but she sent him a box of candy that Christmas. He sent it right back, probably because he suspected it was trick candy. Mother persuaded herself it was all for the best that the dog had bitten him, even though father lost an important business association because of it. 'I wouldn't be associated with such a man,' mother said, 'Muggs could read him like a book.'

We used to take turns feeding Muggs to be on his good side, but that didn't always work. He was never in a very good humour, even after a meal. Nobody knew exactly what was the matter with him, but whatever it was it made him irascible, especially in the mornings. Roy never felt very well in the morning, either, especially before breakfast, and once when he came downstairs and found that Muggs had moodily chewed up the morning paper he hit him in the face with a grapefruit and then jumped up on the dining-room table, scattering dishes and silverware and spilling the coffee. Muggs' first free leap carried him all the way across the

Nobody Knew Exactly What Was the Matter with Him

table and into a brass fire screen in front of the gas grate but he was back on his feet in a moment and in the end he got Roy and gave him a pretty vicious bite in the leg. Then he was all over it; he never bit anyone more than once at a time. Mother always mentioned that as an argument in his favour; she said he had a quick temper but that he didn't hold a grudge. She was forever defending him. I think she liked him because he wasn't well. 'He's not strong,' she would say, pityingly, but that was inaccurate; he may not have been well but he was terribly strong.

One time my mother went to the Chittenden Hotel to call on a woman mental healer who was lecturing in Columbus on the subject of 'Harmonious Vibrations'. She wanted to find out if if was possible to get harmonious vibrations into a dog. 'He's a large tan-coloured Airedale,' mother explained. The woman said that she had never treated a dog but she advised my mother to hold the thought that he did not bite and would not bite. Mother was holding the thought the very next morning when Muggs got the iceman but she blamed that slip-up on the iceman. 'If you didn't think he would bite you, he wouldn't,' mother told him. He stomped out of the house in a terrible jangle of vibrations.

One morning when Muggs bit me slightly, more or less in passing, I reached down and grabbed his short stumpy tail and hoisted him into the air. It was a foolhardy thing to do and the last time I saw my mother, about six months ago, she said she didn't know what possessed me. I don't either, except that I was pretty mad. As long as I held the dog off the floor by his tail he couldn't get at me, but he twisted and jerked so, snarling all the time, that I realized I couldn't hold him that way very long. I carried him to the kitchen and flung him on to the floor and shut the door on him just as he crashed against it. But I forgot about the backstairs. Muggs went up the backstairs and down the frontstairs and had me cornered in the living-room. I managed to get up on to the mantel-piece above the fireplace, but it gave way and came down with a tremendous crash throwing a large marble clock, several vases, and myself heavily to the floor. Muggs was so alarmed by the racket that when I picked myself up he had disappeared. We couldn't find him anywhere, although we whistled and shouted, until old Mrs Detweiler called after dinner that night. Muggs had bitten her once, in the leg, and she came into the living-room only after we assured her that Muggs had run away. She had just seated herself when, with a great growling and scratching of claws, Muggs emerged from under a davenport where he had been quietly hiding all the time, and bit her again. Mother examined the bite and put arnica on it and told Mrs Detweiler that it was only a bruise. 'He just bumped you,' she said. But Mrs Detweiler left the house in a nasty state of mind.

Lots of people reported our Airedale to the police but my father held a municipal office at the time and was on friendly terms with the police. Even so, the cops, had been out a couple of times –

252

nce when Muggs bit Mrs Rufus Sturtevant and again when he bit Lieutenant-Governor Malloy – but mother told them that it hadn't been Muggs' fault but the fault of the people who were bitten. 'When he starts for them, they scream,' she explained, 'and that excites him.' The cops suggested that it might be a good idea to tie the dog up, but mother said that it mortified him to be tied up and that he wouldn't eat when he was tied up.

Lots of People Reported Our Dog to the Police

Muggs at his meals was an unusual sight. Because of the fact that if you reached toward the floor he would bite you, we usually put his food plate on top of an old kitchen table with a bench alongside the table. Muggs would stand on the bench and eat. I remember that my mother's Uncle Horatio, who boasted that he was the third man up Missionary Ridge, was splutteringly indignant when he found out that we fed the dog on a table because we were afraid to put his plate on the floor. He said he wasn't afraid of any dog that ever lived and that he would put the dog's plate on the floor if we would give it to him. Roy said that if Uncle Horatio had fed Muggs on the ground just before the battle he would have been the first man up Missionary Ridge. Uncle Horatio was furious. 'Bring him in! Bring him in now!' he shouted. 'I'll feed the — on the floor!' Roy was all for giving him a chance, but my father wouldn't hear of it. He said that Muggs had already been fed. 'I'll feed him again!' bawled Uncle Horatio. We had quite a time quieting him.

Muggs at His Meals Was an Unusual Sight

In his last year Muggs used to spend practically all of his time outdoors. He didn't like to stay in the house for some reason or other – perhaps it held too many unpleasant memories for him. Anyway, it was hard to get him to come in and as a result the garbage man, the iceman, and the laundryman wouldn't come near the house. We had to haul the garbage down to the corner, take

254

the laundry out and bring it back, and meet the iceman a block from home. After this had gone on for some time we hit on an ingenious arrangement for getting the dog in the house so that we could lock him up while the gas meter was read, and so on. Muggs was afraid of only one thing, an electrical storm. Thunder and lightning frightened him out of his senses (I think he thought a storm had broken the day the mantelpiece fell). He would rush into the house and hide under a bed or in a clothes closet. So we fixed up a thunder machine out of a long narrow piece of sheet iron with a wooden handle on one end. Mother would shake this vigorously when she wanted to get Muggs into the house. It made an excellent imitation of thunder, but I suppose it was the most roundabout system for running a household that was ever devised. It took a lot out of mother.

A few months before Muggs died, he got to 'seeing things'. He would rise slowly from the floor, growling low, and stalk stiff-legged and menacing toward nothing at all. Sometimes the Thing would be just a little to the right or left of a visitor. Once a Fuller Brush salesman got hysterics. Muggs came wandering into the room like Hamlet following his father's ghost. His eyes were fixed on a spot just to the left of the Fuller Brush man, who stood it until Muggs was about three slow, creeping paces from him. Then he shouted. Muggs wavered on past him into the hallway grumbling to himself but the Fuller man went on shouting. I think mother had to throw a pan of cold water on him before he stopped. That was the way she used to stop us boys when we got into fights.

Muggs died quite suddenly one night. Mother wanted to bury him in the family lot under a marble stone with some such inscription as 'Flights of angels sing thee to thy rest' but we persuaded her it was against the law. In the end we just put up a smooth board above his grave along a lonely road. On the board I wrote with an indelible pencil 'Cave Canem'. Mother was quite pleased with the simple classic dignity of the old Latin epitaph.

I passed all the other courses that I took at my University, but I could never pass botany. This was because all botany students had to spend several hours a week in a laboratory looking through a microscope at plant cells, and I could never see through a microscope. I never once saw a cell through a microscope. This used to enrage my instructor. He would wander around the laboratory pleased with the progress all the students were making in drawing the involved and, so I am told, interesting structure of flower cells, until he came to me. I would just be standing there. 'I can't see anything,' I would say. He would begin patiently enough, explaining how anybody can see through a microscope, but he would always end up in a fury, claiming that I could *too* see through a microscope but just pretended that I couldn't. 'It takes away from the beauty of flowers anyway,' I used to tell him. 'We are not concerned with beauty in this course,' he would say. 'We are concerned solely with what I may call the *mechanics* of flars.' 'Well,' I'd say, 'I can't see anything.' 'Try it just once again,' he'd say, and I would put my eye to the microscope and see nothing at all, except now and again a nebulous milky substance – a phenomenon of maladjustment. You were supposed to see a vivid, restless clockwork of sharply defined plant cells. 'I see what looks like a lot of milk,' I would tell him. This, he claimed, was the result of my not having adjusted the microscope properly, so he would readjust it for me, or rather, for himself. And I would look again and see milk.

I finally took a deferred pass, as they called it, and waited a year and tried again. (You had to pass one of the biological sciences or you couldn't graduate.) The professor had come back from vacation brown as a berry, bright-eyed, and eager to explain cell-structure again to his classes. 'Well,' he said to me, cheerily, when we met in the first laboratory hour of the semester, 'we're going to see cells this time, aren't we?' 'Yes, sir,' I said. Students to right of me and to left of me and in front of me were seeing cells; what's more, they were quietly drawing pictures of them in their note-books. Of course, I didn't see anything.

'We'll try it,' the professor said to me, grimly, 'with every adjustment of the microscope known to man. As God is my witness, I'll arrange this glass so that you see cells through it or I'll give up teaching. In twenty-two years of botany, I – ' He cut off abruptly for he was beginning to quiver all over, like Lionel Barrymore, and he genuinely wished to hold on to his temper; his scenes with me had taken a great deal out of him.

So we tried it with every adjustment of the microscope known to man. With only one of them did I see anything but blackness or the familiar lacteal opacity, and that time I saw, to my pleasure and amazement, a variegated constellation of flecks, specks and dots. These I hastily drew. The instructor, noting my activity, came back from an adjoining desk, a smile on his lips and his eyebrows high in hope. He looked at my cell drawing. 'What's that?' he deman-ded, with a hint of a squeal in his voice. 'That's what I saw,' I said. 'You didn't, you didn't, you *did*n't!' he screamed, losing control of his temper instantly, and he bent over and squinted into the microscope. His head snapped up. 'That's your eye!' he shouted. 'You've fixed the lens so that it reflects! You've drawn your eye!'

Another course that I didn't like, but somehow managed to pass, was economics. I went to that class straight from the botany class, which didn't help me any in understanding either subject. I used to get them mixed up. But not as mixed up as another student in my economics class who came there direct from a physics laboratory. He was a tackle on the football team, named Bolen-ciecwcz. At that time Ohio State University had one of the best football teams in the country, and Bolenciecwcz was one of its outstanding stars. In order to be eligible to play it was necessary for him to keep up in his studies, a very difficult matter, for while he was not dumber than an ox he was not any smarter. Most of his professors were lenient and helped him along. None gave him more hints, in answering questions, or asked him simpler ones than the economics professor, a thin, timid man named Bassum. One day when we were on the subject of transportation and distribution, it came Bolenciecwcz's turn to answer a question. 'Name one means of transportation,' the professor said to him. No light came

He Was Beginning to Quiver All Over Like Lionel Barrymore

into the big tackle's eyes. 'Just any means of transportation,' said the professor. Bolenciecwcz sat staring at him. 'That is,' pursued the professor, 'any medium, agency or method of going from one place to another.' Bolenciecwcz had the look of a man who is being led into a trap. 'You may choose among steam, horse-drawn or electrically propelled vehicles,' said the instructor. 'I might suggest the one which we commonly take in making long journeys across land.' There was a profound silence in which everybody stirred uneasily, including Bolenciecwcz and Mr Bassum. Mr Bassum abruptly broke this silence in an amazing manner. 'Choo-choo-choo,' he said, in a low voice, and turned instantly scarlet. He glanced appealingly around the room. All of us, of course, shared Mr Bassum's desire that Bolenciecwcz should stay abreast of the class in economics, for the Illinois game, one of the hardest and most important of the season, was only a week off. 'Toot, toot, too-toooooooot!' some student with a deep voice moaned, and we all looked encouragingly at Bolenciecwcz. Somebody else gave a fine imitation of a locomotive letting off steam. Mr Bassum himself rounded off the little show. 'Ding, dong, ding, dong,' he said hopefully. Bolenciecwcz was staring at the floor now, trying to think, his great brow furrowed, his huge hands rubbing together, his face red.

'How did you come to college this year, Mr Bolenciecwcz?' asked the professor. '*Chuff*a chuffa, *chuff*a chuffa.'

'M'father sent me,' said the football player.

'What on?' asked Bassum.

'I git an 'lowance,' said the tackle, in a low, husky voice, obviously embarrassed.

'No, no,' said Bassum. 'Name a means of transportation. What did you *ride* here on?'

'Train,' said Bolenciecwcz.

'Quite right,' said the professor. 'Now, Mr Nugent, will you tell us –'

If I went through anguish in botany and economics – for different reasons – gymnasium work was even worse. I don't even like to think about it. They wouldn't let you play games or join in the exercises with your glasses on and I couldn't see with mine off. I bumped into professors, horizontal bars, agricultural students,

Bolenciecwcz Was Trying to Think

and swinging iron rings. Not being able to see, I could take it but I couldn't dish it out. Also, in order to pass gymnasium (and you had to pass it to graduate) you had to learn to swim if you didn't know how. I didn't like the swimming pool, I didn't like swimming, and I didn't like the swimming instructor, and after all these years I still don't. I never swam but I passed my gym work anyway, by having another student give my gymnasium number (978) and swim across the pool in my place. He was a quiet, amiable blond youth, number 473, and he would have seen through a microscope for me if we could have got away with it, but we couldn't get away with it. Another thing I didn't like about gymnasium work was that they made you strip the day you registered. It is impossible for me to be happy when I am stripped and being asked a lot of questions. Still, I did better than a lanky agricultural student who was cross-examined just before I was. They asked each student what college he was in – that is, whether Arts, Engineering, Commerce, or Agriculture. 'What college are you in?' the instructor snapped at the youth in front of me. 'Ohio State University,' he said promptly.

It wasn't that agricultural student but it was another a whole lot like him who decided to take up journalism, possibly on the ground that when farming went to hell he could fall back on newspaper work. He didn't realize, of course, that that would be very much like falling back full-length on a kit of carpenter's tools. Haskins didn't seem cut out for journalism, being too embarrassed to talk to anybody and unable to use a typewriter, but the editor of the college paper assigned him to the cow barns, the sheep house, the horse pavilion, and the animal husbandry department generally. This was a genuinely big 'beat', for it took up five times as much ground and got ten times as great a legislative appropriation as the College of Liberal Arts. The agricultural student knew animals, but nevertheless his stories were dull and colourlessly written. He took all afternoon on each of them, on account of having to hunt for each letter on the typewriter. Once in a while he had to ask somebody to help him hunt. 'C' and 'L', in particular, were hard letters for him to find. His editor finally got pretty much annoyed at the farmer-journalist because his pieces were so uninteresting. 'See here, Haskins,' he snapped at him one day, 'Why is it we never

261

have anything hot from you on the horse pavilion? Here we have two hundred head of horses on this campus – more than any other university in the Western Conference except Purdue – and yet you never get any real low down on them. Now shoot over to the horse barns and dig up something lively.' Haskins shambled out and came back in about an hour; he said he had something. 'Well, start it off snappily,' said the editor. 'Something people will read.' Haskins set to work and in a couple of hours brought a sheet of typewritten paper to the desk; it was a two-hundred word story about some disease that had broken out among the horses. Its opening sentence was simple but arresting. It read: 'Who has noticed the sores on the tops of the horses in the animal husbandry building?'

Ohio State was a land grant university and therefore two years of military drill was compulsory. We drilled with old Springfield rifles and studied the tactics of the Civil War even though the World War was going on at the time. At eleven o'clock each morning thousands of freshmen and sophomores used to deploy over the campus, moodily creeping up on the old chemistry building. It was good training for the kind of warfare that was waged at Shiloh but it had no connexion with what was going on in Europe. Some people used to think there was German money behind it, but they didn't dare say so or they would have been thrown in jail as German spies. It was a period of muddy thought and marked, I believe, the decline of higher education in the Middle West.

As a soldier I was never any good at all. Most of the cadets were glumly indifferent soldiers, but I was no good at all. Once General Littlefield, who was commandant of the cadet corps, popped up in front of me during regimental drill and snapped, 'You are the main trouble with this university!' I think he meant that my type was the main trouble with the university but he may have meant me individually. I was mediocre at drill, certainly – that is, until my senior year. By that time I had drilled longer than anybody else in the Western Conference, having failed at military at the end of each preceding year so that I had to do it all over again. I was the only senior still in uniform. The uniform which, when new, had made me look like an inter-urban railway conductor, now that it had become faded and too tight made me look like Bert Williams in his

262

bellboy act. This had a definitely bad effect on my morale. Even so, I had become by sheer practice little short of wonderful at squad manoeuvres.

One day General Littlefield picked our company out of the whole regiment and tried to get it mixed up by putting it through one movement after another as fast as we could execute them: squads right, squads left, squads on right into line, squads right about, squads left front into line etc. In about three minutes one hundred and nine men were marching in one direction and I was marching away from them at an angle of forty degrees, all alone. 'Company, halt!' shouted General Littlefield, 'That man is the only man who has it right!' I was made a corporal for my achievement.

The next day General Littlefield summoned me to his office. He was swatting flies when I went in. I was silent and he was silent too, for a long time. I don't think he remembered me or why he had sent for me, but he didn't want to admit it. He swatted some more flies, keeping his eyes on them narrowly before he let go with the swatter. 'Button up your coat!' he snapped. Looking back on it now I can see that he meant me although he was looking at a fly but I just stood there. Another fly came to rest on a paper in front of the general and began rubbing its hind legs together. The general lifted the swatter cautiously. I moved restlessly and the fly flew away. 'You startled him!' barked General Littlefield, looking at me severely. I said I was sorry. 'That won't help the situation!' snapped the General, with cold military logic. I didn't see what I could do except offer to chase some more flies toward his desk, but I didn't say anything. He stared out the window at the faraway figures of co-eds crossing the campus toward the library. Finally, he told me I could go. So I went. He either didn't know which cadet I was or else he forgot what he wanted to see me about. It may have been that he wished to apologize for having called me the main trouble with the university; or maybe he had decided to compliment me on my brilliant drilling of the day before and then at the last minute decided not to. I don't know. I don't think about it much any more.

I left the University in June, 1918, but I couldn't get into the army on account of my sight, just as grandfather couldn't get in on account of his age. He applied several times and each time he took off his coat and threatened to whip the men who said he was too old. The disappointment of not getting to Germany (he saw no sense in everybody going to France) and the strain of running around town seeing influential officials finally got him down in bed. He had wanted to lead a division and his chagrin at not even being able to enlist as a private was too much for him. His brother Jake

About Four O'Clock He Caught His Brother Asleep

some fifteen years younger than he was, sat up at night with him after he took to bed, because we were afraid he might leave the house without even putting on his clothes. Grandfather was against the idea of Jake watching over him – he thought it was a lot of tomfoolery – but Jake hadn't been able to sleep at night for twenty-eight years, so he was the perfect person for such a vigil.

On the third night, grandfather was wakeful. He would open his eyes, look at Jake, and close them again, frowning. He never

264

answered any question Jake asked him. About four o'clock that morning, he caught his brother sound asleep in the big leather chair beside the bed. When once Jake did fall asleep he slept deeply, so that grandfather was able to get up, dress himself, undress Jake, and put him in bed without waking him. When my Aunt Florence came into the room at seven o'clock, grandfather was sitting in the chair reading the *Memoirs of U.S. Grant* and Jake was sleeping in the bed. 'He watched while I slept,' said grandfather, 'so now I'm watchin' while he sleeps.' It seemed fair enough.

One reason we didn't want grandfather to roam around at night was that he had said something once or twice about going over to Lancaster, his old home town, and putting his problem up to 'Cump' – that is, General William Tecumseh Sherman, also an old Lancaster boy. We knew that his inability to find Sherman would be bad for him and we were afraid that he might try to get there in the little electric runabout that had been bought for my grandmother. She had become, surprisingly enough, quite skilful at getting around town in it. Grandfather was astonished and a little indignant when he saw her get into the contraption and drive off smoothly and easily. It was her first vehicular triumph over him in almost fifty years of married life and he determined to learn to drive the thing himself. A famous old horseman, he approached it as he might have approached a wild colt. His brow would darken and he would begin to curse. He always leaped into it quickly, as if it might pull out from under him if he didn't get into the seat fast enough. The first few times he tried to run the electric, he went swiftly around in a small circle, drove over the kerb, across the sidewalk, and up, on to the lawn. We all tried to persuade him to give up, but his spirit was aroused. 'Git that goddam buggy back in the road!' he would say, imperiously. So we would manoeuvre it back into the street and he would try again. Pulling too savagely on the guiding-bar – to teach the electric a lesson – was what took him around in a circle, and it was difficult to make him understand that it was best to relax and not get mad. He had the notion that if you didn't hold her, she would throw you. And a man who (or so he often told us) had driven a four-horse McCormick reaper when he was five years old did not intend to be thrown by an electric runabout.

Since there was no way of getting him to give up learning to operate the electric, we would take him out to Franklin Park, where the roadways were wide and unfrequented, and spend an hour or so trying to explain the differences between driving a horse and carriage and driving an electric. He would keep muttering all the time; he never got it out of his head that when he took the driver's seat the machine flattened its ears on him, so to speak. After a few weeks, nevertheless, he got so he could run the electric for a hundred yards or so along a fairly straight line. But whenever he took a curve, he invariably pulled or pushed the bar too quickly and too hard and headed for a tree or a flower bed. Someone was always with him and we would never let him take the car out of the park.

There Was a Tremendous To-Do

One morning when grandmother was all ready to go to market, she called the garage and told them to send the electric around. They said that grandfather had already been there and taken it out. There was a tremendous to-do. We telephoned Uncle Will and he got out his Lozier and we started off to hunt for grandfather. It

266

was not yet seven o'clock and there was fortunately little traffic. We headed for Franklin Park, figuring that he might have gone out there to try to break the car's spirit. One or two early pedestrians had seen a tall old gentleman with a white beard driving a little electric and cussing as he drove. We followed a tortuous trail and found them finally on Nelson Road, about four miles from the town of Shepard. Grandfather was standing in the road shouting, and the back wheels of the electric were deeply entangled in a barbed-wire fence. Two workmen and a farmhand were trying to get the thing loose. Grandfather was in a state of high wrath about the electric. 'The —— —— backed up on me!' he told us.

But to get back to the war. The Columbus draft board never called grandfather for service, which was a lucky thing for them because they would have had to take him. There were stories that several old men of eighty or ninety had been summoned in the confusion, but somehow or other grandfather was missed. He waited every day for the call, but it never came. My own experience was quite different. I was called almost every week, even though I had been exempted from service the first time I went before the medical examiners. Either they were never convinced that it was me or else there was some clerical error in the records which was never cleared up. Anyway, there was usually a letter for me on Monday ordering me to report for examination on the second floor of Memorial Hall the following Wednesday at 9 p.m. The second time I went up I tried to explain to one of the doctors that I had already been exempted. 'You're just a blur to me,' I said, taking off my glasses. 'You're absolutely nothing to me,' he snapped, sharply.

I had to take off all my clothes each time and jog around the hall with a lot of porters and bank presidents' sons and clerks and poets. Our hearts and lungs would be examined, and then our feet; and finally our eyes. That always came last. When the eye specialist got around to me, he would always say, 'Why, you couldn't get into the service with sight like that!' 'I know,' I would say. Then a week or two later I would be summoned again and go through the same rigmarole. The ninth or tenth time I was called, I happened to pick up one of several stethoscopes that were lying on a table and suddenly, instead of finding myself in the line of draft men, I found myself in the line of examiners. 'Hello, doctor,' said one of them, nodding. 'Hello,' I said. That, of course, was before I took my clothes off, I might have managed it naked, but I doubt it. I was assigned, or rather drifted, to the chest-and-lung section, where I began to examine every other man, thus cutting old Dr Ridgeway's work in two. 'I'm glad to have you here, doctor,' he said.

I passed most of the men that came to me, but now and then I would exempt one just to be on the safe side. I began by making each of them hold his breath and then say 'mi, mi, mi, mi,' until I noticed Ridgeway looking at me curiously. He, I discovered, simply made them say 'ah', and sometimes he didn't make them say anything. Once I got hold of a man who, it came out later, had swallowed a watch – to make the doctors believe there was something wrong with him inside (it was a common subterfuge: men swallowed nails, hairpins, ink, etc., in an effort to be let out). Since I didn't know what you were supposed to hear through a stethoscope, the ticking of the watch at first didn't surprise me, but I decided to call Dr Ridgeway into consultation, because nobody else had ticked. 'This man seems to tick,' I said to him. He looked at me in surprise but didn't say anything. Then he thumped the man, laid his ear to his chest, and finally tried the stethoscope. 'Sound as a dollar,' he said. 'Listen lower down,' I told him. The man indicated his stomach. Ridgeway gave him a haughty, indignant look. 'That is for the abdominal men to worry about,' he said, and moved off. A few minutes later, Dr Blythe Ballomy got around to the man and listened, but he didn't blink an eye; his grim expression never changed. 'You have swallowed a watch, my man,' he said, crisply. The draftee reddened in embarrassment and uncertainty. 'On *purpose*?' he asked. 'That I can't say,' the doctor told him, and went on.

I served with the draft board for about four months. Until the summonses ceased, I couldn't leave town and as long as I stayed and appeared promptly for examination, even though I did the examining, I felt that technically I could not be convicted of evasion. During the daytime, I worked as publicity agent for an amusement park, the manager of which was a tall, unexpected

young man named Byron Landis. Some years before, he had dynamited the men's lounge in the statehouse annex for a prank: he enjoyed pouring buckets of water on sleeping persons, and once he had barely escaped arrest for jumping off the top of the old Columbus Transfer Company building with a homemade parachute.

He asked me one morning if I would like to take a ride in the new Scarlet Tornado, a steep and wavy roller-coaster. I didn't want to but I was afraid he would think I was afraid, so I went along. It was about ten o'clock and there was nobody at the park except workmen and attendants and concessionaires in their shirt-sleeves. We climbed into one of the long gondolas of the roller-coaster and while I was looking around for the man who was going to run it, we began to move off. Landis, I discovered, was running it himself. But it was too late to get out; we had begun to climb, clickety-clockety, up the first steep incline, down the other side of which we careened at eighty miles an hour. 'I didn't know you could run this thing!' I bawled at my companion, as we catapulted up a sixty-degree arch and looped headlong into space. 'I didn't either!' he bawled back. The racket and the rush of air were terrific as we roared into the pitch-black Cave of Darkness and came out and down Monohan's Leap, so called because a workman named Monohan had been forced to jump from it when caught between two approaching experimental cars while it was being completed. That trip, although it ended safely, made a lasting impression on me. It is not too much to say that it has flavoured my life. It is the reason I shout in my sleep, refuse to ride on the elevator, keep jerking the emergency brake in cars other people are driving, have the sensation of flying like a bird when I first lie down, and in certain months can't keep anything in my stomach.

During my last few trips to the draft board, I went again as a draft prospect, having grown tired of being an examiner. None of the doctors who had been my colleagues for so long recognized me, not even Dr Ridgeway. When he examined my chest for the last time, I asked him if there hadn't been another doctor helping him. He said there had been. 'Did he look anything like me?' I asked. Dr Ridgeway looked at me. 'I don't think so,' he said, 'he was taller.' (I had my shoes off while he was examining me.) 'A good pulmonary man,' added Ridgeway. 'Relative of yours?' I said yes. He sent me on to Dr Quimby, the specialist who had examined my eyes twelve or fifteen times before. He gave me some simple reading tests. 'You could never get into the army with eyes like that,' he said. 'I know,' I told him.

Late one morning, shortly after my last examination, I was awakened by the sound of bells ringing and whistles blowing. It grew louder and more insistent and wilder. It was the Armistice.

A Note
at the End

A Note at the End

The hard times of my middle years I pass over, leaving the ringing bells of 1918, with all their false promise, to mark the end of a special sequence. The sharp edges of old reticences are softened in the autobiographer by the passing of time – a man does not pull the pillow over his head when he wakes in the morning because he suddenly remembers some awful thing that happened to him fifteen or twenty years ago, but the confusions and the panics of last year and the year before are too close for contentment. Until a man can quit talking loudly to himself in order to shout down the memories of blunderings and gropings, he is in no shape for the painstaking examination of distress and the careful ordering of events so necessary to a calm and balanced exposition of what, exactly, was the matter. The time I fell out of the gun-room in Mr James Stanley's house in Green Lake, New York, is for instance, much too near for me to go into with any peace of mind, although

A Hotel Room in Louisville

275

it happened in 1925, the ill-fated year of 'Horses, Horses, Horses' and 'Valencia'. There is now, I understand, a porch to walk out on to when you open the door I opened that night, but there wasn't then.

The mistaken exits and entrances of my thirties have moved me several times to some thought of spending the rest of my days wandering aimlessly around the South Seas, like a character out of Conrad, silent and inscrutable. But the necessity for frequent visits to my oculist and dentist has prevented this. You can't be running back from Singapore every few months to get your lenses changed and still retain the proper mood for wandering. Furthermore, my horn-rimmed glasses and my Ohio accent betray me, even when I sit on the terrasses of little tropical cafes, wearing a pith helmet, staring straight ahead, and twitching a muscle in my jaw. I found this out when I tried wandering around the West Indies one

They Tried to Sell Me Baskets

summer. Instead of being followed by the whispers of men and the glances of women, I was followed by bead salesmen and native women with postcards. Nor did any dark girl, looking at all like Tondelaya in *White Cargo*, come forward and offer to go to pieces with me. They tried to sell me baskets.

Under these circumstances it is impossible to be inscrutable and a wanderer who isn't inscrutable might just as well be back at Broad and High Streets in Columbus sitting in the Baltimore Dairy Lunch. Nobody from Columbus has ever made a first rate wanderer in the Conradean tradition. Some of them have been fairly good at disappearing for a few days to turn up in a hotel in Louisville with a bad headache and no recollection of how they got there, but they always scurry back to their wives with some cock-and-bull story of having lost their memory or having gone away to attend the annual convention of the Fraternal Order of Eagles.

There was, of course, even for Conrad's Lord Jim, no running away. The cloud of his special discomfiture followed him like a pup, no matter what ships he took or what wildernesses he entered. In the pathways between office and home and home and houses of settled people there are always, ready to snap at you, the little perils of routine living, but there is no escape in the unplanned tangent, the sudden turn. In Martinique, when the whistle blew for the tourists to get back on the ship, I had a quick, wild, and lovely moment when I decided I wouldn't get back on the ship. I did, though. And I found that somebody had stolen the pants to my dinner jacket.

From *Fables for Our Time* and *Illustrated Poems*

The Birds and the Foxes

Once upon a time there was a bird sanctuary in which hundreds of Baltimore orioles lived together happily. The refuge consisted of a forest entirely surrounded by a high wire fence. When it was put up, a pack of foxes who lived nearby protested that it was an arbitrary and unnatural boundary. However, they did nothing about it at the time because they were interested in civilizing the geese and ducks on the neighbouring farms. When all the geese and ducks had been civilized, and there was nothing else left to eat, the foxes once more turned their attention to the bird sanctuary. Their leader announced that there had once been foxes in the sanctuary but that they had been driven out. He proclaimed that Baltimore orioles belonged in Baltimore. He said, furthermore, that the orioles in the sanctuary were a continuous menace to the peace of the world. The other animals cautioned the foxes not to disturb the birds in their sanctuary.

So the foxes attacked the sanctuary one night and tore down the fence that surrounded it. The orioles rushed out and were instantly killed and eaten by the foxes.

The next day the leader of the foxes, a fox from whom God was receiving daily guidance, got upon the rostrum and addressed the other foxes. His message was simple and sublime. 'You see before you,' he said, 'another Lincoln. We have liberated all those birds!'

Moral: Government of the orioles, by the foxes, and for the foxes, must perish from the earth.

The Little Girl and the Wolf

One afternoon a big wolf waited in a dark forest for a little girl to come along carrying a basket of food to her grandmother. Finally a little girl did come along and she was carrying a basket of food. 'Are you carrying that basket to your grandmother?' asked the wolf. The little girl said yes, she was. So the wolf asked her where her grandmother lived and the little girl told him and he disappeared into the wood.

When the little girl opened the door of her grandmother's house she saw that there was somebody in bed with a nightcap and nightgown on. She had approached no nearer than twenty-five feet from the bed when she saw that it was not her grandmother but the wolf, for even in a nightcap a wolf does not look any more like your grandmother than the Metro-Goldwyn lion looks like Calvin Coolidge. So the little girl took an automatic out of her basket and shot the wolf dead.

Moral: It is not so easy to fool little girls nowadays as it used to be.

The Scotty Who Knew Too Much

Several summers ago there was a Scotty who went to the country for a visit. He decided that all the farm dogs were cowards, because they were afraid of a certain animal that had a white stripe down its back. 'You are a pussy-cat and I can lick you,' the Scotty said to the farm dog who lived in the house where the Scotty was visiting. 'I can lick the little animal with the white stripe, too. Show him to me.' 'Don't you want to ask any questions about him?' said the farm dog. 'Naw,' said the Scotty. '*You* ask the questions.'

So the farm dog took the Scotty into the woods and showed him the white-striped animal and the Scotty closed in on him, growling and slashing. It was all over in a moment and the Scotty lay on his back. When he came to, the farm dog said, 'What happened?' 'He threw vitriol,' said the Scotty, 'but he never laid a glove on me.'

A few days later the farm dog told the Scotty there was another animal all the farm dogs were afraid of. 'Lead me to him,' said the Scotty. 'I can lick anything that doesn't wear horseshoes.' 'Don't you want to ask any questions about him?' said the farm dog. 'Naw,' said the Scotty. 'Just show me where he hangs out.' So the farm dog led him to a place in the woods and pointed out the little animal when he came along. 'A clown,' said the Scotty, 'a pushover,' and he closed in, leading with his left and exhibiting some mighty fancy footwork. In less than a second the Scotty was flat on his back, and when he woke up the farm dog was pulling quills out of him. 'What happened?' said the farm dog. 'He pulled a knife on me,' said the Scotty, 'but at least I have learned how you fight out here in the country, and now I am going to beat *you* up.' So he closed in on the farm dog, holding his nose with one front paw to ward off the vitriol and covered his eyes with the other front paw to keep out the knives. The Scotty couldn't see his opponent and he couldn't smell his opponent and he was so badly beaten that he had to be taken back to the city and put in a nursing home.

Moral: It is better to ask some of the questions than to know all the answers.

The Very Proper Gander

Not so very long ago there was a very fine gander. He was strong and smooth and beautiful and he spent most of his time singing to his wife and children. One day somebody who saw him strutting up and down in his yard and singing remarked, 'There is a very proper gander.' An old hen overheard this and told her husband about it that night in the roost. 'They said something about propaganda,' she said. 'I have always suspected that,' said the rooster, and he went around the barnyard next day telling everybody that the very fine gander was a dangerous bird, more than likely a hawk in gander's clothing. A small brown hen remembered a time when at a great distance she had seen the gander talking with some hawks in the forest. 'They were up to no good,' she said. A duck remembered that the gander had once told him he did not believe in anything. 'He said to hell with the flag, too,' said the duck. A guinea hen recalled that she had once seen somebody who looked very much like the gander throw something that looked a great deal like a bomb. Finally everybody snatched up sticks and stones and descended on the gander's house. He was strutting in his front yard, singing to his children and his wife. 'There he is!' everybody cried. 'Hawk-lover! Unbeliever! Flag-hater! Bomb-thrower!' So they set upon him and drove him out of the country.

Moral: Anybody who you or your wife thinks is going to overthrow the government by violence must be driven out of the country.

The Bear Who Let It Alone

In the woods of the Far West there once lived a brown bear who could take it or let it alone. He would go into a bar where they sold mead, a fermented drink made of honey, and he would have just two drinks. Then he would put some money on the bar and say, 'See what the bears in the back room will have,' and he would go home. But finally he took to drinking by himself most of the day. He would reel home at night, kick over the umbrella stand, knock down the bridge lamps, and ram his elbows through the windows. Then he would collapse on the floor and lie there until he went to sleep. His wife was greatly distressed and his children were very frightened.

At length the bear saw the error of his ways and began to reform. In the end he became a famous teetotaller and a persistent temperance lecturer. He would tell everybody that came to his house about the awful effects of drink, and he would boast about how strong and well he had become since he gave up touching the stuff. To demonstrate this, he would stand on his head and on his hands and he would turn cartwheels in the house, kicking over the umbrella stand, knocking down the bridge lamps, and ramming his elbows through the windows. Then he would lie down on the floor, tired by his healthful exercise, and go to sleep. His wife was greatly distressed and his children were very frightened.

Moral: You might as well fall flat on your face as lean over too far backward.

The Shrike and the Chipmunks

Once upon a time there were two chipmunks, a male and a female. The male chipmunk thought that arranging nuts in artistic patterns was more fun than just piling them up to see how many you could pile up. The female was all for piling up as many as you could. She told her husband that if he gave up making designs with the nuts there would be room in their large cave for a great many more and he would soon become the wealthiest chipmunk in the woods. But he would not let her interfere with his designs, so she flew into a rage and left him. 'The shrike will get you,' she said, 'because you are helpless and cannot look after yourself.' To be sure, the female chipmunk had not been gone three nights before the male had to dress for a banquet and could not find his studs or shirt or suspenders. So he couldn't go to the banquet, but that was just as well, because all the chipmunks who did go were attacked and killed by a weasel.

The next day the shrike began hanging around outside the chipmunk's cave, waiting to catch him. The shrike couldn't get in because the doorway was clogged up with soiled laundry and dirty dishes. 'He will come out for a walk after breakfast and I will get him then,' thought the shrike. But the chipmunk slept all day and did not get up and have breakfast until after dark. Then he came out for a breath of air before beginning work on a new design. The shrike swooped down to snatch up the chipmunk, but could not see very well on account of the dark, so he batted his head against an alder branch and was killed.

A few days later the female chipmunk returned and saw the awful mess the house was in. She went to the bed and shook her husband. 'What would you do without me?' she demanded. 'Just go on living, I guess,' he said. 'You wouldn't last five days,' she told him. She swept the house and did the dishes and sent out the laundry, and then she made the chipmunk get up and wash and dress. 'You can't be healthy if you lie in bed all day and never get any exercise,' she told him. So she took him for a walk in the bright sunlight and they were both caught and killed by the shrike's brother, a shrike named Stoop.

Moral: Early to rise and early to bed makes a male healthy and wealthy and dead.

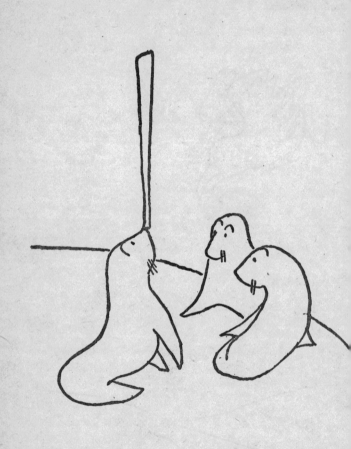

The Seal Who Became Famous

 seal who lay basking on a large, smooth rock said to himself: all ever do is swim. None of the other seals can swim any better than can, he reflected, but, on the other hand, they can all swim just as ell. The more he pondered the monotony and uniformity of his fe, the more depressed he became. That night he swam away and ined a circus.

Within two years the seal had become a great balancer. He could alance lamps, billiard cues, medicine balls, hassocks, taborets, ollar cigars, and anything else you gave him. When he read in a ook a reference to the Great Seal of the United States, he thought meant him. In the winter of his third year as a performer he went ack to the large, smooth rock to visit his friends and family. He ave them the Big Town stuff right away: the latest slang, liquor in golden flask, zippers, a gardenia in his lapel. He balanced for them verything there was on the rock to balance, which wasn't much. Vhen he had run through his repertory, he asked the other seals if ey could do what he had done and they all said no. 'O.K.,' he id. 'Let's see you do something I can't do.' Since the only thing ey could do was swim, they all plunged off the rock into the sea. he circus seal plunged right after them, but he was so hampered y his smart city clothes, including a pair of seventeen-dollar shoes, at he began to founder at once. Since he hadn't been in swimming r three years, he had forgot what to do with his flippers and tail, nd he went down for the third time before the other seals could ach him. They gave him a simple but dignified funeral.

Moral: Whom God has equipped with flippers should not monkey round with zippers.

The Crow and the Oriole

Once upon a time a crow fell in love with a Baltimore oriole. He had seen her flying past his nest every spring on her way North and every autumn on her way South, and he had decided that she was a tasty dish. He had observed that she came North every year with a different gentleman, but he paid no attention to the fact that all the gentlemen were Baltimore orioles. 'Anybody can have that mouse,' he said to himself. So he went to his wife and told her that he was in love with a Baltimore oriole who was as cute as a cuff link. He said he wanted a divorce, so his wife gave him one simply by opening the door and handing him his hat. 'Don't come crying to me when she throws you down,' she said. 'That fly-by-season hasn't got a brain in her head. She can't cook or sew. Her upper register sounds like a streetcar taking a curve. You can find out in any dictionary that the crow is the smartest and most capable of birds - or was till you became one.' 'Tush!' said the male crow. 'Pish! You are simply a jealous woman.' He tossed her a few dollars. 'Here,' he said, 'go buy yourself some finery. You look like the bottom of an old tea-kettle.' And off he went to look for the oriole.

This was in the springtime and he met her coming North with an oriole he had never seen before. The crow stopped the female oriole and pleaded his cause – or should we say cawed his pleas? At any rate, he courted her in a harsh, grating voice, which made her laugh merrily. 'You sound like an old window shutter,' she said, and she snapped her fingers at him. 'I am bigger and stronger than your gentleman friend,' said the crow. 'I have a vocabulary larger than his. All the orioles in the country couldn't even lift the corn I own. I am a fine sentinel and my voice can be heard for miles in case of danger.' 'I don't see how that could interest anybody but another crow,' said the female oriole, and she laughed at him and flew on toward the North. The male oriole tossed the crow some coins. 'Here,' he said, 'go buy yourself a blazer or something. You look like the bottom of an old coffeepot.'

The crow flew back sadly to his nest, but his wife was not there. He found a note pinned to the front door. 'I have gone away with Bert,' it read. 'You will find some arsenic in the medicine chest.'

Moral: Even the llama should stick to mamma.

The Moth and the Star

A young and impressionable moth once set his heart on a certain star. He told his mother about this and she counselled him to set his heart on a bridge lamp instead. 'Stars aren't the thing to hang around,' she said; 'lamps are the thing to hang around.' 'You get somewhere that way,' said the moth's father. 'You don't get anywhere chasing stars.' But the moth would not heed the words of either parent. Every evening at dusk when the star came out he would start flying toward it and every morning at dawn he would crawl back home worn out with his vain endeavour. One day his father said to him, 'You haven't burned a wing in months, boy, and it looks to me as if you were never going to. All your brothers have been badly burned flying around street lamps and all your sisters have been terribly singed flying around house lamps. Come on, now, get out of here and get yourself scorched! A big strapping moth like you without a mark on him!'

The moth left his father's house, but he would not fly around street lamps and he would not fly around house lamps. He went right on trying to reach the star, which was four and one-third light years, or twenty-five trillion miles, away. The moth thought it was just caught in the top branches of an elm. He never did reach the star, but he went right on trying, night after night, and when he was a very, very old moth he began to think that he really had reached the star and he went around saying so. This gave him a deep and lasting pleasure, and he lived to a great old age. His parents and his brothers and his sisters had all been burned to death when they were quite young.

Moral: Who flies afar from the sphere of our sorrow is here today and here tomorrow.

The Glass in the Field

A short time ago some builders, working on a studio in Connecticut, left a huge square of plate glass standing upright in a field one day. A goldfinch flying swiftly across the field struck the glass and was knocked cold. When he came to he hastened to his club, where an attendant bandaged his head and gave him a stiff drink. 'What the hell happened?' asked a sea-gull. 'I was flying across a meadow when all of a sudden the air crystallized on me,' said the goldfinch. The sea-gull and a hawk and an eagle all laughed heartily. A swallow listened gravely. 'For fifteen years, fledgling and bird, I've flown this country,' said the eagle, 'and I assure you there is no such thing as air crystallizing. Water, yes; air, no.' 'You were probably struck by a hailstone,' the hawk told the goldfinch. 'Or he may have had a stroke,' said the sea-gull. 'What do you think, swallow?' 'Why, I – I think maybe the air crystallized on him,' said the swallow. The large birds laughed so loudly that the goldfinch became annoyed and bet them each a dozen worms that they couldn't follow the course he had flown across the field without encountering the hardened atmosphere. They all took his bet; the swallow went along to watch. The sea-gull, the eagle, and the hawk decided to fly together over the route the goldfinch indicated. 'You come, too,' they said to the swallow. 'I – I – well, no,' said the swallow. 'I don't think I will.' So the three large birds took off together and they hit the glass together and they were all knocked cold.

Moral: He who hesitates is sometimes saved.

The Rabbits Who Caused All The Trouble

Within the memory of the youngest child there was a family of rabbits who lived near a pack of wolves. The wolves announced that they did not like the way the rabbits were living. (The wolves were crazy about the way they themselves were living, because it was the only way to live.) One night several wolves were killed in an earthquake and this was blamed on the rabbits, for it is well known that rabbits pound on the ground with their hind legs and cause earthquakes. On another night one of the wolves was killed by a bolt of lightning and this was also blamed on the rabbits, for it is well known that lettuce-eaters cause lightning. The wolves threatened to civilize the rabbits if they didn't behave, and the rabbits decided to run away to a desert island. But the other animals, who lived at a great distance, shamed them, saying, 'You must stay where you are and be brave. This is no world for escapists. If the wolves attack you, we will come to your aid, in all probability.' So the rabbits continued to live near the wolves and one day there was a terrible flood which drowned a great many wolves. This was blamed on the rabbits, for it is well known that carrot-nibblers with long ears cause floods. The wolves descended on the rabbits, for their own good, and imprisoned them in a dark cave, for their own protection.

When nothing was heard about the rabbits for some weeks, the other animals demanded to know what had happened to them. The wolves replied that the rabbits had been eaten and since they had been eaten the affair was a purely internal matter. But the other animals warned that they might possibly unite against the wolves unless some reason was given for the destruction of the rabbits. So the wolves gave them one. 'They were trying to escape,' said the wolves, 'and, as you know, this is no world for escapists.'

Moral: Run, don't walk, to the nearest desert island.

The Owl Who Was God

Once upon a starless midnight there was an owl who sat on the branch of an oak tree. Two ground moles tried to slip quietly by, unnoticed. 'You!' said the owl. 'Who?' they quavered, in fear and astonishment, for they could not believe it was possible for anyone to see them in that thick darkness. 'You two!' said the owl. The moles hurried away and told the other creatures of the field and forest that the owl was the greatest and wisest of all animals because he could see in the dark and because he could answer any question. 'I'll see about that,' said a secretary bird, and he called on the owl one night when it was again very dark. 'How many claws am I holding up?' said the secretary bird, 'Two,' said the owl, and that was right. 'Can you give me another expression for "that is to say" or "namely"?' asked the secretary bird. 'To wit,' said the owl. 'Why does a lover call on his love?' asked the secretary bird. 'To woo,' said the owl.

The secretary bird hastened back to the other creatures and reported that the owl was indeed the greatest and wisest animal in the world because he could see in the dark and because he could answer any question. 'Can he see in the daytime, too?' asked a red fox. 'Yes,' echoed a dormouse and a French poodle. 'Can he see in the daytime, too?' All the other creatures laughed loudly at this silly question, and they set upon the red fox and his friends and drove them out of the region. Then they sent a messenger to the owl and asked him to be their leader.

When the owl appeared among the animals it was high noon and the sun was shining brightly. He walked very slowly, which gave him an appearance of great dignity, and he peered about him with large, staring eyes, which gave him an air of tremendous importance. 'He's God!' screamed a Plymouth Rock hen. And the others took up the cry 'He's God!' So they followed him wherever he went and when he began to bump into things they began to bump into things, too. Finally he came to a concrete highway and he started up the middle of it and all the other creatures followed him. Presently a hawk, who was acting as outrider, observed a truck coming toward them at fifty miles an hour, and he reported to the secretary bird and the secretary bird reported to the owl. 'There's danger ahead,' said the secretary bird. 'To wit?' said the owl. The secretary bird told him. 'Aren't you afraid?' He asked. 'Who?' said the owl calmly, for he could not see the truck. 'He's God!' cried all the creatures again, and they were still crying 'He's God!' when the truck hit them and ran them down. Some of the animals were merely injured, but most of them, including the owl, were killed.

Moral: You can fool too many of the people too much of the time.

The Unicorn in the Garden

Once upon a sunny morning a man who sat in a breakfast nook looked up from his scrambled eggs to see a white unicorn with a gold horn quietly cropping the roses in the garden. The man went up to the bedroom where his wife was still asleep and woke her. 'There's a unicorn in the garden,' he said. 'Eating roses.' She opened one unfriendly eye and looked at him. 'The unicorn is a mythical beast,' she said, and turned her back on him. The man walked slowly downstairs and out into the garden. The unicorn was still there; he was now browsing among the tulips. 'Here, unicorn,' said the man, and he pulled up a lily and gave it to him. The unicorn ate it gravely. With a high heart, because there was a unicorn in his garden, the man went upstairs and roused his wife again. 'The unicorn,' he said, 'ate a lily.' His wife sat up in bed and looked at him, coldly. 'You are a booby,' she said, 'and I am going to have you put in the booby-hatch.' The man, who had never liked the words 'booby' and 'booby-hatch', and who liked them even less on a shining morning when there was a unicorn in the garden, thought for a moment. 'We'll see about that,' he said. He walked over to the door. 'He has a golden horn in the middle of his forehead,' he told her. Then he went back to the garden to watch the unicorn; but the unicorn had gone away. The man sat down among the roses and went to sleep.

As soon as the husband had gone out of the house, the wife got up and dressed as fast as she could. She was very excited and there was a gloat in her eye. She telephoned the police and she telephoned a psychiatrist; she told them to hurry to her house and bring a strait-jacket. When the police and the psychiatrist arrived they sat down in chairs and looked at her, with great interest. 'My husband,' she said, 'saw a unicorn this morning.' The police looked at the psychiatrist and the psychiatrist looked at the police. 'He told me it ate a lily,' she said. The psychiatrist looked at the police and the police looked at the psychiatrist. 'He told me it had a golden horn in the middle of its forehead,' she said. At a solemn signal from the psychiatrist, the police leaped from their chairs and seized the wife. They had a hard time subduing her, for she put up a terrific struggle, but they finally subdued her. Just as they got her into the strait-jacket, the husband came back into the house.

'Did you tell your wife you saw a unicorn?' asked the police. 'Of course not,' said the husband. 'The unicorn is a mythical beast.' 'That's all I wanted to know,' said the psychiatrist. 'Take her away. I'm sorry, sir, but your wife is as crazy as a jay bird.' So they took her away, cursing and screaming, and shut her up in an institution. The husband lived happily ever after.

Moral: Don't count your boobies until they are hatched.

Excelsior

By Henry Wadsworth Longfellow

The shades of night were falling fast,
As through an Alpine village passed
A youth, who bore, 'mid snow and ice,
A banner with the strange device –
        Excelsior!

'Try not the pass,' the old man said;
'Dark lowers the tempest overhead;
The roaring torrent is deep and wide!'
And loud that clarion voice replied,
                    Excelsior!

'O stay,' the maiden said, 'and rest
Thy weary head upon this breast!'
A tear stood in his bright blue eye,
But still he answered, with a sigh,
                        Excelsior!

'Beware the pine-tree's withered branch!
Beware the awful avalanche!'
This was the peasant's last good night:
A voice replied, far up the height,
               Excelsior!

At break of day, as heavenward
The pious monks of Saint Bernard
Uttered the oft-repeated prayer,
A voice cried through the startled air,
        Excelsior!

A traveller, by the faithful hound,
Half-buried in the snow was found,
Still grasping in his hand of ice
That banner with the strange device,
        Excelsior!

There in the twilight cold and grey,
Lifeless, but beautiful, he lay,
And from the sky, serene and far,
A voice fell, like a falling star –
        Excelsior!

O When I Was . . .*

By A. E. Housman

Oh when I was in love with you,
Then I was clean and brave,
And miles around the wonder grew
How well did I behave.

* From *A Shropshire Lad*, by A. E. Housman, by permission of Jonathan Cape, Ltd.

And now the fancy passes by,
And nothing will remain,
And miles around they'll say that I
Am quite myself again.

Barbara Frietchie

By John Greenleaf Whittier

On that pleasant morn of the early fall
When Lee marched over the mountain wall;

Over the mountains winding down,
Horse and foot, into Frederick town,

Forty flags with their silver stars,
Forty flags with their crimson bars,

Flapped in the morning wind . . .

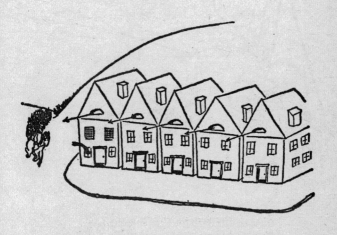

>   . . . the sun
> Of noon looked down, and saw not one.

Up rose old Barbara Frietchie then,
Bowed with her fourscore years and ten;

Bravest of all in Frederick town,
She took up the flag the men hauled down;

In her attic window the staff she set,
To show that one heart was loyal yet.

Up the street came the rebel tread,
Stonewall Jackson riding ahead.

Under his slouched hat left and right
He glanced; the old flag met his sight.

'Halt!' – the dust-brown ranks stood fast;
'Fire!' – out blazed the rifle-blast.

It shivered the window, pane and sash;
It rent the banner with seam and gash.

Quick, as it fell, from the broken staff
Dame Barbara snatched the silken scarf.

She leaned far out on the window-sill,
And shook it forth with a royal will.

'Shoot, if you must, this old grey head,
But spare your country's flag,' she said.

A shade of sadness, a blush of shame,
Over the face of the leader came;

The nobler nature within him stirred
To life at that woman's deed and word;

'Who touches a hair of yon grey head
Dies like a dog! March on!' he said.

All day long through Frederick street
Sounded the tread of marching feet

All day long that free flag tossed
Over the heads of the rebel host.

Ever its torn folds rose and fell
On the loyal winds that loved it well;

And through the hill-gaps sunset light
Shone over it with a warm good-night . . .

The Sands O' Dee

By Charles Kingsley

'O Mary, go and call the cattle home,
    And call the cattle home,
    And call the cattle home,
  Across the sands o' Dee!'
The western wind was wild and dank wi' foam,
    And all alone went she.

The creeping tide came up along the sand,
　　And o'er and o'er the sand,
　　And round and round the sand,
　　As far as eye could see;
The blinding mist came down and hid the land:
　　And never home came she.

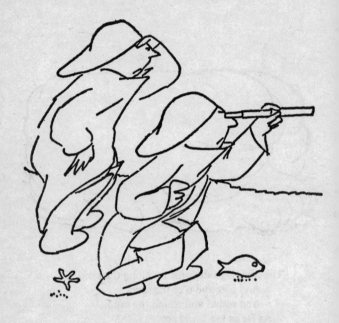

'Oh, is it weed, or fish, or floating hair –
  A tress o' golden hair,
    O' drownèd maiden's hair –
  Above the nets at sea?
Was never salmon yet that shone so fair
  Among the stakes on Dee.'

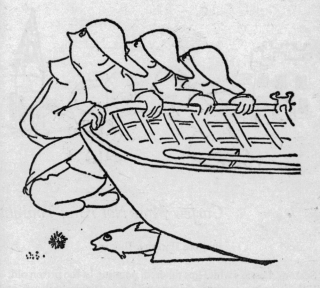

They rowed her in across the rolling foam,
    The cruel, crawling foam,
    The cruel, hungry foam,
  To her grave beside the sea;
But still the boatmen hear her call the cattle home
    Across the sands o' Dee.

Curfew Must Not Ring Tonight

By Rose Hartwick Thorpe

'Sexton,' Bessie's white lips faltered, pointing to the prison old,
With its turrets tall and gloomy, with its walls dark, damp, and
    cold,
'I've a lover in that prison, doomed this very night to die,
At the ringing of the Curfew, and no earthly help is nigh;
Cromwell will not come till sunset,' and her lips grew strangely
    white
As she breathed the husky whisper –
                    'Curfew must not ring tonight.'

'Bessie,' calmly spoke the sexton – every word pierced her young
    heart
Like the piercing of an arrow, like a deadly poisoned dart –
'Long, long years I've rung the Curfew from that gloomy,
    shadowed tower;
Every evening, just at sunset, it has told the twilight hour;
I have done my duty ever, tried to do it just and right,
Now I'm old I will not falter –

              Curfew, it must ring tonight.'

With quick step she bounded forward, sprang within the old
    church door,
Left the old man threading slowly paths so oft he'd trod before;
Not one moment paused the maiden, but with eye and cheek aglow
Mounted up the gloomy tower, where the bell swung to and fro:
As she climbed the dusty ladder, on which fell no ray of light,
Up and up – her white lips saying –

                'Curfew must not ring tonight.'

She has reached the topmost ladder; o'er her hangs the great dark bell;
Awful is the gloom beneath her, like the pathway down to hell.
Lo, the ponderous tongue is swinging – 'tis the hour of Curfew now,
And the sight has chilled her bosom, stopped her breath, and paled her brow.
Shall she let it ring? No, never! flash her eyes with sudden light,
As she springs and grasps it firmly –

                    'Curfew shall not ring tonight!'

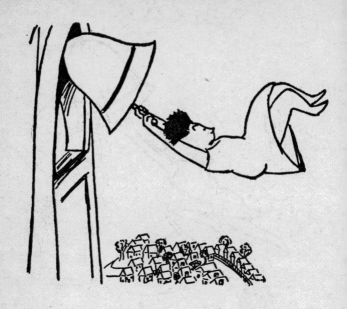

Out she swung – far out; the city seemed a speck of light below,
There 'twixt heaven and earth suspended as the bell swung to and
    fro,
And the sexton at the bell rope, old and deaf, heard not the bell,
Sadly thought, 'That twilight Curfew rang young Basil's funeral
    knell.'
Still the maiden clung more firmly and with trembling lips so
    white,
Said to hush her heart's wild throbbing –
                    'Curfew shall not ring tonight!'

O'er the distant hills came Cromwell; Bessie sees him, and her
   brow,
Lately white with fear and anguish, has no anxious traces now.
At his feet she tells her story, shows her hands all bruised and torn;
And her face so sweet and pleading, yet with sorrow pale and worn,
Touched his heart with sudden pity, lit his eyes with misty light:
'Go! your lover lives,' said Cromwell,
                              'Curfew shall not ring tonight.'

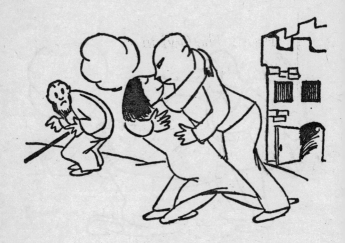

Wide they flung the massive portal; led the prisoner forth to die –
All his bright young life before him. 'Neath the darkening English
    sky
Bessie comes with flying footsteps, eyes aglow with love-light
    sweet;
Kneeling on the turf beside him, lays his pardon at his feet.
In his brave, strong arms he clasped her, kissed the face upturned
    and white,
Whispered, 'Darling, you have saved me –
                  Curfew will not ring tonight!'

7 | From *The Owl in the Attic*

The Pet Department

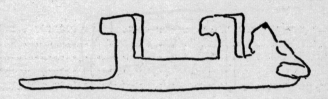

Q. I enclose a sketch of the way my dog, William, has been lying for two days now. I think there must be something wrong with him. Can you tell me how to get him out of this?

MRS L. L. G.

A. I should judge from the drawing that William is in a trance. Trance states, however, are rare with dogs. It may just be ecstasy. If at the end of another twenty-four hours he doesn't seem to be getting anywhere, I should give him up. The position of the ears leads me to believe that he may be enjoying himself in a quiet way, but the tail is somewhat alarming.

Q. Our cat, who is thirty-five, spends all of her time in bed. She follows every move I make, and this is beginning to get to me. She never seems sleepy nor particularly happy. Is there anything I could give her?

Miss L. Mc.

A. There are no medicines which can safely be given to induce felicity in a cat, but you might try lettuce, which is a soporific, for the wakefulness. I would have to see the cat watching you to tell whether anything could be done to divert her attention.

Q. My husband, who is an amateur hypnotizer, keeps trying to get our bloodhound under his control. I contend that this is not doing the dog any good. So far he has not yielded to my husband's influence, but I am afraid that if he once got under, we couldn't get him out of it.

A. A. T.

A. Dogs are usually left cold by all phases of psychology, mental telepathy, and the like. Attempts to hypnotize this particular breed, however, are likely to be fraught with a definite menace. A bloodhound, if stared at fixedly, is liable to gain the impression that it is under suspicion, being followed, and so on. This upsets a bloodhound's life, by completely reversing its whole scheme of behaviour.

Q. My wife found this owl in the attic among a lot of ormolu clocks and old crystal chandeliers. We can't tell whether it's stuffed or only dead. It is sitting on a strange and almost indescribable sort of iron dingbat.

MR MOLLEFF

A. What your wife found is a museum piece – a stuffed cockatoo. It looks to me like a rather botchy example of taxidermy. This is the first stuffed bird I have ever seen with its eyes shut, but whoever had it stuffed probably wanted it stuffed that way. I couldn't say what the thing it is sitting on is supposed to represent. It looks broken.

Q. Our gull cannot get his head down any farther than this, and bumps into things.

H. L. F.

A. You have no ordinary gull to begin with. He looks to me a great deal like a rabbit backing up. If he *is* a gull, it is impossible to keep him in the house. Naturally he will bump into things. Give him his freedom.

Q. My police dog has taken to acting very strange, on account of my father coming home from work every night for the past two years and saying to him, 'If you're a police dog, where's your badge?', after which he laughs (my father).

ELLA R.

A. The constant reiteration of any piece of badinage sometimes has the same effect on present-day neurotic dogs that it has on people. It is dangerous and thoughtless to twit a police dog on his powers, authority, and the like. From the way your dog seems to hide behind tables, large vases, and whatever that thing is that looks like a suitcase, I should imagine that your father has carried this thing far enough – perhaps even too far.

Q. My husband's seal will not juggle, although we have tried everything.

GRACE H.

A. Most seals will not juggle; I think I have never known one that juggled. Seals balance things, and sometimes toss objects (such as the large ball in your sketch) from one to another. This last will be difficult if your husband has but one seal. I'd try him in plain balancing, beginning with a billiard cue or something. It may be, of course, that he is a non-balancing seal.

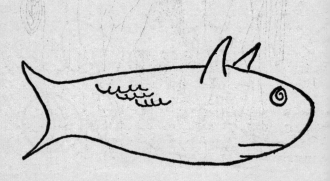

Q. We have a fish with ears and wonder if it is valuable.

JOE WRIGHT

A. I find no trace in the standard fish books of any fish with ears. Very likely the ears do not belong to the fish, but to some mammal. They look to me like a mammal's ears. It would be pretty hard to say what species of mammal, and almost impossible to determine what particular member of that species. They may merely be hysterical ears, in which case they will go away if you can get the fish's mind on something else.

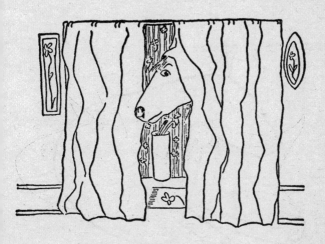

Q. How would you feel if every time you looked up from your work or anything, there was a horse peering at you from behind something? He prowls about the house at all hours of the day and night. Doesn't seem worried about anything, merely wakeful. What should I do to discourage him?

MRS GRACE VOYNTON

A. The horse is probably sad. Changing the flowered decorations of your home to something less like open meadows might discourage him, but then I doubt whether it is a good idea to discourage a sad horse. In any case speak to him quietly when he turns up from behind things. Leaping at a horse in a house and crying 'Roogie, roogie!' or 'Whoosh!' would only result in breakage and bedlam. Of course you might finally get used to having him around, if the house is big enough for both of you.

Q. The fact that my dog sits this way so often leads me to believe that something is preying on his mind. He seems always to be studying. Would there be any way of finding out what this is?

ARTHUR

A. Owing to the artificially complex life led by city dogs of the present day, they tend to lose the simpler systems of intuition which once guided all breeds, and frequently lapse into what comes very close to mental perplexity. I myself have known some very profoundly thoughtful dogs. Usually, however, their problems are not serious and I should judge that your dog has merely mislaid something and wonders where he put it.

Q. We have cats the way most people have mice.

MRS C. L. FOOTLOOSE

A. I see you have. I can't tell from your communication, however, whether you wish advice or are just boasting.

Q. No one has been able to tell us what kind of dog we have. I am enclosing a sketch of one of his two postures. He only has two. The other one is the same as this except he faces in the opposite direction.

MRS EUGENIA BLACK

A. I think that what you have is a cast-iron lawn dog. The expressionless eye and the rigid pose are characteristic of metal lawn animals. And that certainly is a cast-iron ear. You could, however, remove all doubt by means of a simple test with a hammer and a cold chisel, or an acetylene torch. If the animal chips, or melts, my diagnosis is correct.

Q. My oldest boy, Ford Maddox Ford Griswold, worked this wooden horse loose from a merry-go-round one night when he and some other young people were cutting up. Could you suggest any use for it in a family of five?

Mrs R. L. S. Griswold

A. I cannot try the patience of my public nor waste my own time dealing with the problems of insensate animals. Already I have gone perhaps too far afield in the case of stuffed birds and cast-iron lawn dogs. Pretty soon I should be giving advice on wire-haired fox terrier weather-vanes.

Q. Mr Jennings bought this beast when it was a pup in Montreal for a St Bernard, but I don't think it is. It's grown enormously and is stubborn about letting you have anything, like the bath towel it has its paws on, and the hat, both of which belong to Mr Jennings. He got it that bowling ball to play with but it doesn't seem to like it. Mr Jennings is greatly attached to the creature.

MRS FANNY EDWARDS JENNINGS

A. What you have is a bear. While it isn't my bear, I should recommend that you dispose of it. As these animals grow older they get more and more adamant about letting you have anything, until finally there might not be anything in the house you could call your own – except possibly the bowling ball. Zoos use bears. Mr Jennings could visit it.

Q. Sometimes my dog does not seem to know me. I think he must be crazy. He will draw away, or show his fangs, when I approach him.

H. M. MORGAN, JR

A. So would I, and I'm not crazy. If you creep up on your dog the way you indicate in the drawing, I can understand his viewpoint. Put your shirt in and straighten up; you look as if you had never seen a dog before, and that is undoubtedly what bothers the animal. These maladjustments can often be worked out by the use of a little common sense.

Q. After a severe storm we found this old male raven in the study of my father, the Hon. George Morton Bodwell, for many years head of the Latin Department at Tufts, sitting on a bust of Livy which was a gift to him from the class of '92. All that the old bird will say is 'Grawk'. Can ravens be taught to talk or was Poe merely 'romancing'?

MRS H. BODWELL COLWETHER

A. I am handicapped by an uncertainty as to who says 'Grawk', the raven or your father. It just happens that 'Arrk' is what ravens say. I have never known a raven that said anything but 'Arrk'.

Q. I have three Scotch terriers which take things out of closets and down from shelves, etc. My veterinarian advised me to gather together all the wreckage, set them down in the midst of it, and say 'ba-ad Scotties!' This, however, merely seems to give them a kind of pleasure. If I spank one, the other two jump me – playfully, but they jump me.

MRS O. S. PROCTOR

A. To begin with, I question the advisability of having three Scotch terriers. They are bound to get you down. However, it seems to me that you are needlessly complicating your own problem. The Scotties probably think that you are trying to enter into the spirit of their play. Their inability to comprehend what you are trying to get at will in the end make them melancholy, and you and the dogs will begin to drift farther and farther apart. I'd deal with each terrier, and each object, separately, beginning with the telephone, the disconnexion of which must inconvenience you sorely.

352

Q. My husband paid a hundred and seventy-five dollars for this moose to a man in Dorset, Ontario, who said he had trapped it in the woods. Something is wrong with his antlers, for we have to keep twisting them back into place all the time. They're loose.

MRS OLIPHANT BEATTY

A. You people are living in a fool's paradise. The animal is obviously a horse with a span of antlers strapped on to his head. If you really want a moose, dispose of the horse; if you want to keep the horse, take the antlers off. Their constant pressure on his ears isn't a good idea.

From *The Seal in the Bedroom*

'With You I Have Known Peace, Lida, and Now You Say You're
Going Crazy'

'Are You the Young Man That Bit My Daughter?'

'Here's a Study for You, Doctor – He Faints'

'Mamma Always Gets Sore and Spoils the Game for Everybody'

For the Last Time – You and Your Horsie Get Away from Me and
Stay Away!'

'Well, What's Come Over *You* Suddenly?'

'Have You People Got Any ·38 Cartridges?'

'The Father Belonged to Some People Who Were Driving Through in
a Packard'

'Stop Me!'

'I Don't Know. George Got It Somewhere'

'All Right, Have It Your Way – You Heard a Seal Bark'

The Bloodhound
and the Bug

1

2

3

4

5

6

7

11

11½

12

9

*From Men, Women
and Dogs*

'This Is Not the Real Me You're Seeing, Mrs Clisbie'

'What's Come Over You Since Friday, Miss Schemke?'

'Hello, Darling – Woolgathering?'

'It's a Naïve Domestic Burgundy Without Any Breeding. But I
Think You'll be Amused by its Presumption'

'Oh, Doctor *Conroy – Look*!'

'I'd Feel a Great Deal Easier if Her Husband Hadn't Gone to Bed'

375

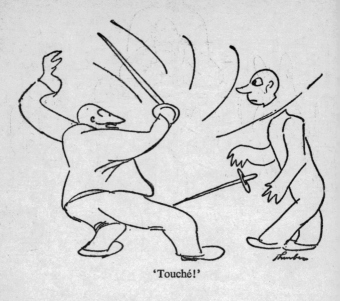

'Touché!'

'And This Is Tom Weatherby, an old Beau of Your Mother's. He Never Got to First Base!

'Perhaps *This* Will Refresh Your Memory'

' . . . And Keep Me a Normal, Healthy Girl'

'It's Parkins, Sir; We're 'Aving a Bit of a Time Below Stairs'

'Darling, I Seem to Have This Rabbit'

'That's My First Wife Up There, and This Is the *Present* Mrs Harris'

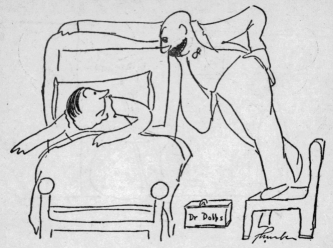

'You're Not My Patient, You're My Meat, Mrs Quist!'

'She Has the True Emily Dickinson Spirit Except That She Gets
Fed Up Occasionally'

'I Said the Hounds of Spring Are on Winter's Traces – But Let it
Pass, Let it Pass!'

'For Heaven's Sake, Why Don't You go Outdoors and Trace
Something?'

'I Don't Want Him to Be Comfortable if He's Going to Look Too Funny'

'Yoo-hoo, It's Me and the Ape Man'

'Look Out! Here They Come Again!'

'You Wait Here and I'll Bring the Etchings Down'

'Well, Who Made the Magic Go Out of Our Marriage – You or Me?'

House and Woman

'Well, if I Called the Wrong Number, Why Did You Answer the Phone?'

'This Gentleman Was Kind Enough to See Me Home, Darling'

'I Come From Haunts of Coot and Hern!'

'Well, I'm Disenchanted, Too. We're *All* Disenchanted'

'What Do You Want to Be Inscrutable *For*, Marcia?'

'You Said a Moment Ago That Everybody You Look at Seems to Be a Rabbit. Now Just What Do You Mean by That, Mrs Sprague?'

'Why, I Never Dreamed Your Union Had Been Blessed With Issue!'

'Have You Seen My Pistol, Honey-Bun?'

'It's Our *Own* Story *Exactly*! He Bold as a Hawk, She Soft as the Dawn'

'You and Your Premonitions!'

'All Right, All Right, Try it That Way! Go Ahead and Try it That Way!'

'Well, it Makes a Difference to *Me*!'

'There's no Use You Trying to Save *Me*, My Good Man'

Man in Tree

'What Have You Done with Dr Millmoss?'

The War Between Men and Women

I. The Overt Act

II. The Battle on the Stairs

397

III. The Fight in the Grocery

IV. Men's G.H.Q.

V. Women's G.H.Q.

VI. Capture of Three Physics Professors

VII. Surrender of Three Blondes

VIII. The Battle of Labrador

IX. The Spy

X. Mrs Pritchard's Leap

XI. Zero Hour – Connecticut

XII. The Sniper

XIII. Parley

XIV. Gettysburg

XV. Retreat

XVI. Rout

XVII. Surrender

More about Penguins
and Pelicans

Penguinews, which appears every month, contains details of all the new books issued by Penguins as they are published. From time to time it is supplemented by our stocklist, which is our complete list of almost 5,000 titles.

A specimen copy of *Penguinews* will be sent to you free on request. Please write to Dept EP, Penguin Books Ltd, Harmondsworth, Middlesex, for your copy.

In the U.S.A.: For a complete list of books available from Penguins in the United States write to Dept CS, Penguin Books, 625 Madison Avenue, New York, New York 10022.

In Canada: For a complete list of books available from Penguins in Canada write to Penguin Books Canada Ltd, 2801 John Street, Markham, Ontario L3R 1B4.

The Joys of Yiddish

Leo Rosten

Mordant Syntax 'smart he isn't'

Sarcasm Through Innocuous Diction
'He only tried to shoot himself'

Contempt via Affirmation
'My son-in-law he wants to be'

Leo Rosten, creator of the immortal H*Y*M*A*N
K*A*P*L*A*N, has crammed this book with the vernacular,
ritual, customs and jokes from the ghettos. If you want to get
the full weight of expressions like chutzpa, goy, kike, shmo,
nebbish, mish-mosh, shlimazl, shikker, in what *Stage &
Television Today* has called 'the ideal bedside book for the
international show-biz buff', try Rosten for size, and lighten
your life evermore!

Puckoon

Spike Milligan

'Spike Milligan's first novel bursts at the seams with superb comic characters involved in unbelievably likely troubles on the Irish border' – *Observer*

'Pops with the erratic brilliance of a careless match in a box of fireworks' – *Daily Mail*

The Land of Rising Yen

George Mikes

'The Japanese are human beings like the rest of us, but they will strongly resent this insinuation. They are determined to be puzzling, quaint, unfathomable and inscrutable.'

Everyone writes about the tea ceremony in Japan, but who, except George Mikes, notices the way rubbish is thrown out? Everyone reports his own reaction to the Japanese sense of tradition; but who else spots the reaction of the Japanese to their own sense of tradition?

Whether he is describing morals or manners, George Mikes looks at the Japanese as he looks at the rest of mankind: with his own inimitable blend of curiosity, respect, affection and irreverence.

There's Always Another Windmill

Ogden Nash

—'easily the best known – and possibly the best – American practitioner of a subtle art that is always more serious than it seems: the writing of light verse.'

There's Always Another Windmill is vintage Ogden Nash; it is an omnibus of a hundred and one verses which stops at all corners.

When Ogden Nash died, poet Morris Bishop offered this tribute in Nash's own language:

'Free from flashiness, free from trashiness
Is the essence of Ogdenashiness
Rich, original, rash and rational
Stands the monument Ogdenational'

How to be an Alien

George Mikes

George Mikes says 'the English have no soul; they have the understatement instead'.

But they *do* have a sense of humour – they proved it by buying some three hundred thousand copies of a book that took them quietly and completely apart, a book that really took the Mikes out of them.

Silly Verse For Kids

Spike Milligan

I'M NOT FRIGHTENED OF PUSSY CATS

I'm not frightened of Pussy Cats,
They only eat up mice and rats,
But a Hippopotamus
Could eat the Lotofus!

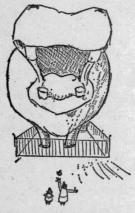

Once again Spike Milligan puts pen to paper and produces a
delightful collection of silly verse – for kids and adults.

A Puffin Book

A Book of Milliganimals

Spike Milligan

Do you know what a
Onecan is? Have you
met a Gofongo or the
Bald Twit Lion? Can
you guess what the
Wiggle-Woggle said?

Another collection of
goonish poems and zany
drawings by Spike Milligan.

A STRAWBERRY MOOSE

A Puffin Book

Small Dreams of a Scorpion

They chop down 100ft trees
To make chairs
I bought one
I am six-foot one inch
When I sit in the chair
I'm four foot two.
Did they really chop down a 100ft tree
To make me look shorter?

Here's a volume of Millipoems on pollution,
population and conservation – serious subjects,
overlaid by the inimitable Milligan humour.

Adolf Hitler – My Part in His Downfall

'*At Victoria Station the R.T.O. gave me a travel warrant, a white feather and a picture of Hitler marked "This is your enemy". I searched every compartment but he wasn't on the train . . .*'

Spike Milligan's on the march, blitzing friend and foe alike with his uproarious recollections of army life from enlistment to the landing at Algiers in 1943. Bathos, pathos, gales of drunken laughter, and insane military goonery explode in superlative Milliganese.

'It is the most irreverent, hilarious book about the war that I have ever read' – *Sunday Express*